manhattan's little secrets

secrets

Uncovering Mysteries
in Brick and Mortar,
Glass and Stone

JOHN TAURANAC

Globe
Pequot

GUILFORD, CONNECTICUT

photography by KATHRYN GERHARDT

In memory of my parents,
who imbued in me a special appreciation of this wonderful city

Globe
Pequot

An imprint of The Rowman & Littlefield Publishing Group, Inc.
4501 Forbes Blvd., Ste. 200
Lanham, MD 20706
www.rowman.com

Distributed by NATIONAL BOOK NETWORK

British Library Cataloguing in Publication Information available

Library of Congress Cataloging-in-Publication Data available

ISBN 978-1-4930-3047-7 (paperback)
ISBN 978-1-4930-3048-4 (e-book)

∞™ The paper used in this publication meets the minimum requirements
of American National Standard for Information Sciences—Permanence
of Paper for Printed Library Materials, ANSI/NISO Z39.48-1992

Printed in the United States of America

Contents

Introduction

I am not a philosopher by nature. I like things that are concrete, which is why I like New York City. Now here's the rub: While I like to think that New York is a concrete thing, it isn't. It is a living thing, and like any healthy organism, old cells die off, to be replaced by new ones. That fact, of course, is part of the city's mystery, its mystique, and a large part of my discomfort.

The city is here today, and although it won't necessarily be gone tomorrow, it will be different. It's called progress.

This progress makes it difficult to write a book on the contemporary city. In the relatively short time since I started working on this book, some subjects that I had hoped to include have already disappeared. Gone is the building at 29 West 57th Street that included the Cross of the Legion of Honor on its rooftop, there to honor the Chickering Piano Company. The Frank Lloyd Wright Jaguar showroom at 430 Park Avenue is gone. And as good as gone is a poster painted on a wall on Lexington Avenue and 135th Street that reminded us that all cars—meaning streetcars—transferred for Bloomingdale's. It was there until someone whitewashed it into oblivion. And the already-faded sign heralding the presence of Macy's on 14th Street just east of Sixth Avenue, like the old soldier it was, just faded away.

Another problem presented by the ever-changing cityscape was the ability to photograph all the subjects. In the summer of 2017, thousands of buildings in the city were covered in scaffolding. The result is that wonderful subjects such as the Tammany Hall on Union Square East, which was enshrouded, fell by the metaphorical wayside. The Breese town house on West 16th Street was covered, but its next-door twin was pristine, so our photographer, Kathy Gerhardt, shot the neighbor in the foreground.

The good news is that there is still plenty of stuff of interest to see and enjoy, and I hope that I lead you on a merry chase. Running the risk of the pathetic fallacy and ascribing feelings to inanimate objects, the stuff is sitting there just waiting to be discovered, like the aspiring actress at Schwab's Drug Store on Sunset Strip in Los Angeles.

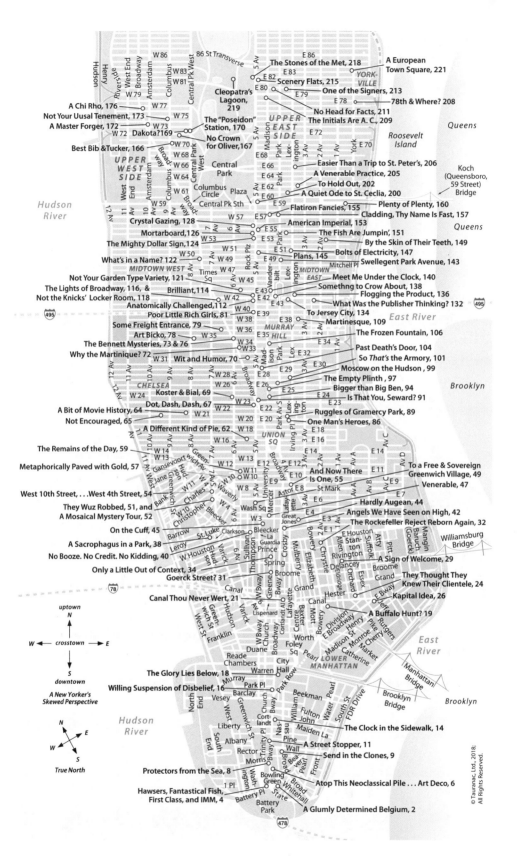

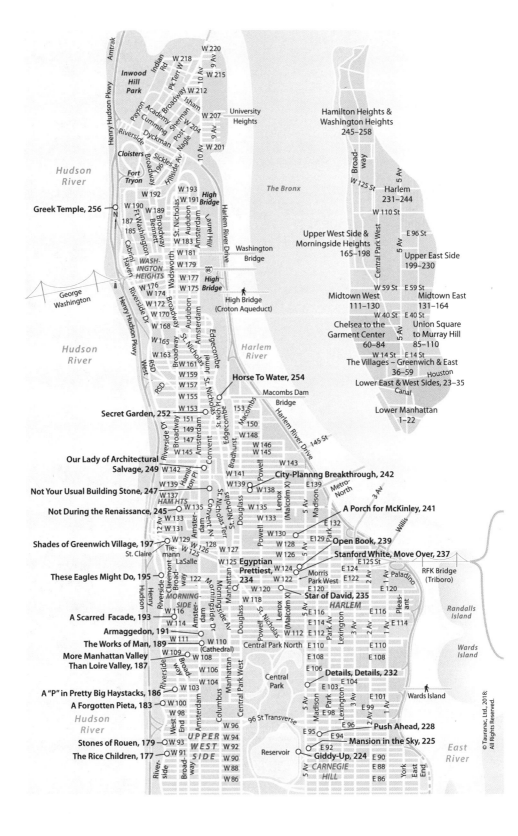

Amtrak

Indian Rd

W 220

W 218

Pk Terr W

W 215

10 Av

9 Av

Inwood
Hill
Park

Broadway

Isham

W 212

Payson

Academy

Sherman

Post

W 207

Cumming

Nagle

University
Heights

Hamilton Heights &
Washington Heights
245–258

Dyckman

Riverside

10 Av

9 Av

W 204

W 201

Broadway

Cloisters

Sickles

Hillside Av.

Broadway

Fort
Tryon

Hudson
River

Broad-
way

5 Av

W 125 St

Harlem
231–244

The Bronx

W 192

W 193

High
Bridge

W 191

Greek Temple, 256

W 190

W 189

St. Nicholas

Amsterdam

Laurel Hill

W 110 St

187

Bennett

Broadway

185

Audubon

W 183

Harlem River Drive

Upper West Side &
Morningside Heights
165–198

Central Park West

5 Av

E 96 St

Cabrini

Haven

Wadsworth

W 181

Washington
Bridge

WASH-
INGTON
HEIGHTS

W 179

Washington

Bridge

Upper East Side
199–230

95

W 177

High
Bridge

W 176

W 175

High Bridge
(Croton Aqueduct)

W 59 St

E 59 St

Riverside Dr

Broadway

W 174

Henry Hudson Pkwy

George
Washington

W 172

Audubon

Midtown West
111–130

Midtown East
131–164

W 170

St. Nicholas

Amsterdam

W 168

W 40 St

E 40 St

Hudson
River

W 165

Edgecombe

Harlem
River

Chelsea to the
Garment Center
60–84

5 Av

Union Square
to Murray Hill
85–110

W 163

RSD West

Broadway

W 161

W 14 St

E 14 St

The Villages – Greenwich & East
36–59

Houston

RSD

W 159

St. Nicholas Pl

Lower East & West Sides, 23–35

W 157

Horse To Water, 254

W 155

Macombs Dam
Bridge

Canal

W 153

Edgecombe

Macombs

153

Lower Manhattan
1–22

Secret Garden, 252

Riverside Dr

151

150

Amsterdam

149

St. Nich

Harlem River Drive

145 St

147

W 148

145

W 146
W 145

Our Lady of Architectural
Salvage, 249

W 142

Hamilton Pl

W 145

W 143

Not Your Usual Building Stone, 247

W 139

St. Nicholas Terr

Convent Nv.

W 139

Powell

E139

Metro-
North

City-Plannng Breakthrough, 242

HAM HTS

W 138

Lenox (Malcolm X)

Madison

5 Av

Not During the Renaissance, 245

W 135

Douglass

W 135

E 132

A Porch for McKinley, 241

12 Av

W 133

W 133

Willis

W 131

Amster-
dam

Powell

W 130

E129

Park

Open Book, 239

Shades of Greenwich Village, 197

W 129

Tie-
mann

128

W 126 W 127

W 128

E129

5 Av

Stanford White, Move Over, 237

St. Claire

LaSalle

W 125

E 125 St

RFK Bridge
(Triboro)

These Eagles Might Do, 195

Claremont

Broad-
way

122

Manhattan Av.

Morningside Av.

Egyptian
Prettiest,
234

W 124

W 122

Morris

Park West

E 124

E 122

2 Av

Paladino

1 Av

Randalls
Island

Henry Hudson

MORNING-
SIDE

W 116

Morningside Dr

W 120

Star of David, 235

E 120

E 120

A Scarred Facade, 193

Amster-
dam

W 114

W 118

Powell

Lenox (Malcolm X)

St. Nicholas

5 Av

E 116

HARLEM

E 116

Pleas-
ant

Wards
Island

Armaggedon, 191

W 111

E 114

3 Av

Lexington

2 Av

1 Av

E 114

The Works of Man, 189

Riverside

Broad-
way

W 110
(Cathedral)

Central Park North

E 112

E 112

E 110

E 110

More Manhattan Valley
Than Loire Valley, 187

W 109

W 108

E 108

E 108

A "P" in Pretty Big Haystacks, 186

W 106

Manhattan

Central Park West

E 106

E 104

Details, Details, 232

W 104

Central
Park

E 103

Wards Island

A Forgotten Pieta, 183

W 103

W 100

Amsterdam

Columbus

E 101

3 Av

Lexington

E 99

York

2 Av

E 98

Hudson
River

West End

W 98

5 Av

Madison

Park

Stones of Rouen, 179

W 93

W 96

96 St Transverse

E 96

2 Av

Push Ahead, 228

The Rice Children, 177

W 91

W 92

Reservoir

E 95

E 94

Mansion in the Sky, 225

UPPER
WEST
SIDE

W 94

Riverside

Broad-
way

W 90

E 92

Giddy-Up, 224

E 90

East
River

W 88

5 Av

CARNEGIE
HILL

E 88

York

East End

W 86

Madison

E 86

© Tauranac, Ltd, 2018;
All Rights Reserved.

1

Lower Manhattan

The Battery to Canal Street

A Glumly Determined Belgium

The Alexander Hamilton/U.S. Custom House, facing Bowling Green
between Broadway and State Street

The twelve statues atop the cornice of the 1907 Custom House represent great seafaring nations or major ports. This militaristic statue representing Belgium, which is hardly known as either a great seafaring- or a particularly bellicose nation, did not originally represent Belgium. It represented Germany, but all that changed in World War I, or soon after.

It wasn't surprising to find a lack of positive enthusiasm for things Teutonic during the war. The statue of Frederick the Great at the War College in Washington was moved to the basement, the Metropolitan Opera was refusing to perform Wagner's operas, the Architectural League launched a campaign to ban all "Hun materials" from the drafting room, and, in a fit of "Victory Cabbage-ism," the subject of this statue was changed from Albert Jaegers' *Germany* to Attilio Piccirilli's *Belgium.*

Germany had depicted a defiantly determined female figure in a chain coat of mail, with a leather doublet embossed with the imperial eagle of Germany. Even in those days of pomp and circumstance, her be-plumed and be-winged helmet was *ongepotchket*, too much of a gilded lily. Most critically, her left hand rested upon a shield bearing the monogram "W II," for Kaiser Wilhelm II, and "Kiel," the chief naval station of Germany.

The Customs Department was in the bailiwick of the Secretary of the Treasury, William McAdoo, and by the summer of 1918, after having been prodded by organizations such as the Sons of the American Revolution, this show of Teutonic pageantry had gotten to be too much. McAdoo ordered the subject of the statue changed from Germany to Belgium, the neutral nation that had been trampled by the German army on its march into France in 1914.

The sculptor Albert Jaegers was eight when he arrived in the United States from Germany, and he became a citizen at twenty-one. Although there was no hint of his being pro-German during the war, he was nevertheless described as a "hyphenated" German-American sculptor, and he was viewed with some suspicion. The architect of the Custom House, Cass Gilbert, asked Jaegers if he would remove the Kaiser's initials and the name "Kiel," and replace them with "Belgium." Gilbert's notes make no mention of other changes, but it seems that there were others. Jaegers said that he could not change the statue to the new standard and still make it an artistic success. He suggested having the statue placed in storage.

Gilbert found Attilio Piccirilli, the most prominent sculptor of the great family of sculptors and carvers. The six brothers and their father had carved or sculpted some of the city's major pieces of public sculpture, and they already knew the Custom House well. They had carved the building's "Four Continents" for Daniel Chester French.

Piccirilli did far more than Gilbert had apparently asked of Jaegers. The chain mail was stripped away, and as a consequence the statue developed mightier breasts; the imperial eagle of Germany was replaced by a Lion Rampant (a simplified version of the coat of arms of Belgium); and, despite the remaining Medieval accoutrements, the helmet was changed to an anachronistic Adrian helmet, the helmets worn by both the Belgian soldiers and the French poilus in World War

I. At the same time, the classically inspired face, with its Roman nose and fierce countenance, was given a face-lift, and, with it, a glum determination.

The work was to be done *in situ*, and the requisite scaffold was erected by October 7, 1918. By November 22, 1918, 11 days after the armistice and with talk of a Victory Arch already in the air, Piccirilli had not even begun.

Jaegers, of course, was right. Piccirilli did the best with what he had, but the revised statue was hardly a success. Instead of the record books identifying the sculptor as Albert Jaegers, it should be ascribed to Attilio Piccirilli with an asterisk. Don't blame it on Jaegers. Jaegers' work had panache.

Hawsers, Fantastical Fish, First Class, and IMM

An entrance to One Broadway on Battery Place, across from Battery Park

Bowling Green was known as Steamship Row between 1850 and 1950, so it should come as no surprise to find something nautical on this building. Hawsers and fantastical fish decorate this entrance and another on Battery Place, and nautical elements continue elsewhere. Crowning the Broadway entrance are panels depicting Poseidon, the god of the sea, and Mercury, the god of transportation, and ringing the second floor are the seals of great seaports. The building did not originally look like this. Behind today's neoclassical facade stands the Washington Building, an iron-framed building with masonry piers that dates from 1884, but that all changed in 1922 when the building was reconfigured and this facade was created.

Both of the Battery Place entrances still lead to a spacious hall with a compass rose in the floor and murals of shipping lanes decorating the walls. It is now a banking hall, but its original function, which explains "First Class" and "Cabin Class" at the doors, was a booking office for steamship companies. (True to the mores of the early 20th century, steerage passengers probably went to the Trinity Place corner and down a few steps. Whatever information had been above that door has faded into obscurity.)

The initials IMM stand for the International Mercantile Marine, the world's largest agglomeration of steamship lines in the early 20th century.

IMM was the brainchild of the banker J. Pierpont Morgan. By the early 1900s, Morgan essentially controlled railroad rates in the United States through what he euphemistically described as a "community of interest." It translated into his banking house holding so many seats on the boards of so many railroads that these interlocking directorates could work to his and his clients' advantages financially. But Morgan wanted to control the lucrative transatlantic shipping as well, whereupon the light bulb went on. Better than having a few key seats on various boards, he could own the ships, and not just a few ships, but whole fleets of ships. The combination would translate into favorable freight rates for Morgan's interests, and all at the expense of others.

Morgan succeeded in buying up just about every Anglo-American steamship line and every seaworthy ship he could find to ply the valuable North Atlantic, together with a working arrangement with the Hamburg-Amerika Line. IMM had as many as 120 ships under its direct control at one time, with Britain's Cunard Line the only major holdout. It was a monopoly, plain and simple.

One of the shipping lines that IMM owned was the terribly British-seeming White Star Line, which was in fierce competition with Cunard to build the biggest, fastest, and grandest ocean liners. The White Star Line was a special feather in Morgan's cap, and he prevailed upon J. Bruce Ismay, who chaired the steamship line, to assume IMM's presidency.

To win the race with Cunard, the White Star Line built and launched the *Titanic* in 1912, and it comes as a surprise to many people that the *Titanic*—British built and operated—was American owned.

Accounts differ on how much the *Titanic* was insured for. The worst case scenario was from the disgraced J. Bruce Iasmy, who had clambered into a lifeboat to save himself as the *Titanic* and over 1,500 lives were sinking into the depths. He testified at the Senate committee's inquiry that the insurance by Lloyd's of London only covered $5 million of the $7.5 million that the ship had cost to build.

Exacerbating Morgan's financial plight, his overall plan for monopolizing the North Atlantic wasn't working. The European sellers had recognized a hungry buyer when they saw one, complicated by the fact that the federal government had a thing about monopolies—these were trust-busting times—compounded by the fact that the British government wasn't overly keen on having so much of its shipping in American hands. In time of crisis, the Royal Navy could only requisition ships that sailed under the Union Jack.

IMM was described as a "half-baked plot" to begin with, and when things started going badly—by 1914 the wags were saying that IMM stock held more water than the *Titanic*—the company's finances were reorganized. The original sellers happily started buying back their old fleets at about half of what that they had sold them for.

When IMM moved into the first five floors of One Broadway in 1922, its holdings were essentially down to the United States Lines and the Panama-Pacific Lines—and by then Morgan was dead.

One of the crushing psychological blows for Morgan had been the sinking of the *Titanic*. He was devastated when he learned of the enormous loss of life, and he was even more devastated when he was personally excoriated for being involved in an undertaking that provided luxuries for the few at the expense of common safety for all. This entrance for first class passengers is a reminder, and it's just the tip of the iceberg.

And Atop This Neoclassical Pile . . . Art Deco

26 Broadway, northeast corner of Beaver Street

When the architect Thomas Hastings was given the plum commission of designing the 31-story office building for the Standard Oil Company, the first thing he did was sail off to Rome. He said that he wanted to study the architectural features that he would embody in his plans for the new skyscraper, an odd thing for Hastings to believe he needed. Hastings had worked for McKim, Mead & White, who had almost single-handedly been responsible for the classical revival in the United States in the late 19th century, and Hastings and his late partner, John Merven Carrère, had designed perhaps the grandest neoclassical building in the city, the main branch of the New York Public Library.

If Hastings had actually needed to brush up his Vitruvius, it worked. The Standard Oil Building is a huge neoclassical pile, incorporating just about every neoclassical chotchka known to man, from all three of the Greek orders to obelisks and urns, rustication and coining, rosettes and frets, eggs and darts, and on and on.

Hastings was no great fan of skyscrapers. He believed that the local zoning law should have mandated eight stories as the maximum building height, and he said that most of New York's skyscrapers were "elongated packing boxes, with the midriff sections better passed over in haste." If you translate the classical form into architecture talk—"beginning, middle, and end" translated into "horizontal, vertical, horizontal"—there is bound to be a certain repetition of the theme in the midriff section of a tall building, and not even Hastings could escape that reality.

Hastings also believed that "certainly no one can say that recessing back a skyscraper makes for beauty," yet topping off the Standard Oil Building is a series of setbacks, with a pyramid fashioned after the Tomb of Halicarnassus topping a freestanding setback tower, with a lamp at each of the four corners. The fuel for the lamps was kerosene, which had started Standard Oil in its world dominance in oil production. The capstone to this pile is another symbol of Rockefeller's beginnings, an oil lamp, which in reality is a cleverly designed chimney that sends up occasional puffs of smoke and steam to reinforce the image.

Hastings lost his partner in 1911, and by the time this building was finished in 1925, he had also lost his get-up-and-go. His associates on the project, Shreve, Lamb & Blake, were doing more and more of the actual design work, with Richmond H. Shreve directly in charge of construction. This is the same Shreve and Lamb who would later team up with Arthur Loomis Harmon and go on to design some modern masterpieces.

Art Deco architects enjoyed updating classical themes, and that's just what the architects did here. Zodiac signs worked into the bowl of the urn, ox sculls (or bucrane), the honeysuckle leaf, and the anthemion are all venerable symbols, but these iterations are less in the neoclassical genre, more abstract, more geometric, more in the style of Art Deco. And those kerosene lamps seem the stylistic forerunner of the illuminated glass ball atop the Paramount Building on Broadway (1930), or the lamps held by the statues flanking the entrance to the former Mark Hellinger Theater on West 51st Street (1930), today's Times Square Church.

As a child might say, "This building has secwets."

Protectors from the Sea

25 Broadway, southwest corner of Morris Street

When the Cunard Building opened in 1921, all eyes were on the great booking hall. The usually understated *Times* reported that it was "the most imposing hall ever created for the booking of transatlantic passengers, [with] a series of mural decorative effects probably unsurpassed in the annals of commercial building construction." Almost as an afterthought, the paper reported that "a striking feature of the exterior is a group of marine horses firmly entrenched on bases resting on the setback of the 19th floor."

These "marine horses" are sculpture groups with women riders. There are two groups on one side of the pavilion, and two on the other, with the combination being the entire point. In fact, you could hardly ask for a more symbolically ideal combination than these sculpture groups for the Cunard Line and its fleet of passenger liners.

The "marine horses" are sea horses whose webbed hooves paw the air as they rise from the sea, their fish-like tails curling up behind them. Sea horses were said to be blessed by the god Poseidon, and they pulled his chariot that was usually seen just skimming the water. And the women astride the sea horses aren't just ordinary women, they are sea nymphs, or Nereids in Greek mythology. Unlike the Sirens, whose enticing songs were said to lure sailors to their watery deaths, Nereids were said to speed to the aid of sailors, especially in storms. To adapt the Navy Hymn, they would "hear us when we cry to thee, for those in peril on the sea."

The problem with these limestone sculpture groups is that although they are big—they weigh in at about nine tons apiece—they are barely visible. The average skyscraper simply doesn't provide many comfortable sites for sculpture groups.

The critic John C. Van Dyke had anticipated this very problem in 1909. Public buildings such as the Custom House that are low lying were appropriate places for sculpture, he said, but he tellingly asked if sculpture in its modest scale could make itself seen amid enormous masses of steel and granite. The answer is "no," and it's more the pity, since these sculpture groups are wonderful. They were sculpted by Rochette & Parzini, although Eugene Rochette had already retired by 1921, leaving Michael Parzini to carry on alone under the partnership name.

Parzini had grown up in Turin, had studied at l'Ecole des Beaux Arts in Paris, and immigrated to the United States in 1893, which propitiously coincided with the World's Columbian Exposition in Chicago, where he found work. Sometimes he modeled sculptures for others to cut, sometimes he did both, and sometimes he carved the work that others had modeled. He was a journeyman sculptor.

Parzini did other work on the Cunard Building. He sculpted the low-relief Phoenician sailing ships in the roundels flanking the entrance to the booking hall, and the statues in the keystones such as the "Four Winds."

Rochette & Parzini also sculpted the eight eagles that originally stood atop an overpass for the Shore Road Parkway in Bay Ridge, Brooklyn. When the Shore Road was recreated as the Belt Parkway in 1941, the bridge came down, sculpture and all. Robert Moses was heading both the Highway Department and the Parks Departments at the time, which greased the way for the eight eagles to be moved to the Central Park Zoo, where they watch over sea lions frolicking in a pool much like the Nereids watch out for those in peril on the sea.

Send in the Clones

8 Broad Street, between Exchange Place and Wall Street

Despite the illusion of verisimilitude, the figures in the pediment of the New York Stock Exchange have not been staring down on us since the day the statuary was installed in 1904, nor are these figures literally carved in stone. They were not carved at all, and they are not even marble. They are made of copper and painted to simulate marble, and they have only been up there in the pediment since 1936. They are replicas of the originals.

The original statues were weathering so poorly in New York's polluted environment of the 1930s that the prudent management of the Stock Exchange was fearful that the statues might fall.

The stage for potential danger had been set early on. In 1903, before the statuary was installed, architect George B. Post had discovered "grave defects" in the marble for both the building and the sculpture. He was concerned that some of the stones might develop rotten spots and break off, and falling sculpture means

trouble. Post devised a steel support for the sculpture, and the building committee reported that Post said there was "no unusual danger," and he suggested an examination every five or six years.

By the 1930s, the decision was made to destroy the old and send in the clones. Casts were made of the originals, and photographs were taken from just about every angle from across Broad Street. Then came the bizarre decision to change the statues in secret. Behind a protective curtain, the originals were broken apart and carted off, and the replicas were installed, with everything very hush-hush.

The goal was to create the illusion that these statues were in fact the originals, as if nothing had happened. Since this group was cast from the existing statues of the 1930s, the statuary would naturally have the same weathered appearance, and the group was painted to duplicate the color of the stone as it had appeared in its 1936 state. For even greater verisimilitude, dabs of lampblack were applied. Lampblack is a fine soot that is collected from incompletely burned coal, and coal is the stuff the city was burning by the mega-ton in the 1930s, the same stuff that was creating much of the pollution that settled on the statuary group that led to its deterioration in the first place.

The commission to create the original statuary had been awarded to the veteran sculptor John Quincy Adams Ward, who was in his seventies and soon to retire. Ward's associate, Paul W. Bartlett, did the work of modeling the figures, with the actual carving of the finished product being completed by the 18-year-old Getulio Piccirilli, a member of the family of great sculptors and stone carvers.

The theme George B. Post had determined was, appropriately enough, "Commerce" and "Industry," with the central 22-foot-high figure representing "Integrity Protecting the Works of Man."

The figures to the right of *Integrity* represent man-made inventions or discoveries, such as electricity, and to her left, the products of the earth, hence the farmer. By definition, figures at the extremities of triangular pediments either have to be reclining or crouching, and many of the secondary figures appear in various stages of discomfort, with the male figure on *Integrity*'s far left perhaps appearing the most uncomfortable. He represents "Mining."

A criticism made in 1904 was that the male figures were too frank in their nudity, and no doubt there are still people running around just waiting to slap a fig leaf here and another there.

A Street Stopper

Trinity Churchyard, Broadway, on a line with Pine Street

The idea for the Martyrs' Memorial was ostensibly noble. It would be "sacred to the memory of those good and brave men who died whilst imprisoned in this city for their devotion to the cause of American Independence."

During the American Revolution, American prisoners of war were incarcerated in sugar houses that the British used as prisons. One of the sugar houses abutted the northwest corner of Trinity's graveyard, and the original idea for this memorial was to commemorate only those who had died in that sugar house and had been buried in the churchyard. As the project progressed, the idea developed to be more inclusive, to memorialize all those who had died as prisoners of war in the city.

The numbers of those dead are staggering. More than 11,600 American prisoners of war died on British prison ships anchored in Wallabout Bay, or today's Brooklyn Navy Yard. That is almost twice the number of American soldiers killed in battle. The POWs interned in the sugar houses were dying at about the same rate; there were just fewer of them. They too died from malnutrition exacerbated by a lack of medical attention in general and typhus in particular.

The suggestion to erect the monument in 1852 was made at a town meeting being held to discuss a totally irrelevant matter, a proposal to extend Albany Street eastward from Greenwich Street to Trinity Place and continue through Trinity Churchyard to Broadway, creating a link with Pine Street. This was hardly a new proposal. In 1813 a similar movement had started that, according to Trinity's own Rev. Dr. Morgan Dix, was brought about by "a few individuals desiring to add to the value of their property west" of the site. The project was endorsed by "a portion of the press," he added, but the more thoughtful stood with Trinity's position that it was "an indignity and a misuse of private property." The proposed

memorial to the Revolutionary War dead would stand in the way of the proposed extension of Albany Street, which only strengthened Trinity's position of defending the memory of "those good and brave men" who had been buried there. Anyone willing to have the memorial destroyed just to have a new street cut through could be labeled as unpatriotic, as un-American.

A state law did give power to municipalities to take possession of any lands or property that were imperatively required by public necessity, but there was no imperative in extending Albany Street, as Trinity argued, and there was hardship to consider. Who, for instance, would pay to have the dead dug up and reinterred? This was all complicated by an 1842 state law that declared that dead bodies could only be removed from a burial ground with the consent of three-fourths of the congregation to whom the cemetery belonged. That approval was obviously not in the works, and in common law, the violation or disturbance of a burial place was an indictable offense. It was as simple as that.

Despite all the legalisms against it, the case to extend Albany Street kept being pressed. The City Council would pass the bill, then repeal the ordinance. It passed again in 1854, prompting George Templeton Strong to write that "they say that the price of a councilman is from $10 to $25." Still, no street was cut through, and when the issue was transferred to the New York State Legislature, it was "summarily squelched by a huge majority," reported Strong.

In 1858, Dix reported that the monument was "completed and put in position . . . directly opposite to Pine Street, on the line on which the extension of Albany Street had been proposed to be carried out. This," added Dix with a hint of gleeful satisfaction, "stopped any further attempt to connect Albany and Pine Streets."

Richard Upjohn was the architect of Trinity Church, but the memorial's design was by two other acolytes of the Gothic Revival, Wills & Dudley. The firm is little known for its work in New York City, but, individually or together, Frank Wills and Henry Dudley designed dozens of noteworthy ecclesiastical buildings and were enormously influential in their field. Wills wrote *Ancient Ecclesiastical Architecture and Its Principles, Applied to the Wants of the Church at the Present Day*, and Dudley was one of the founders of the American Institute of Architects.

The memorial is quite a show. It is composed of four elegantly carved Gothic arches, supported by columns and strengthened by buttresses, with the arches supporting four pinnacles filled with elaborate carving and quatrefoils. Its brownstone facing was intentionally chosen to jell architecturally with Trinity, and the memorial dominates the terminal vista of Pine Street with the same sort of exclamation point that Trinity does for Wall Street, only in a reduced fashion.

Perhaps just the idea of being labeled as against the memorial was enough to have put the kibosh on any further plans to extend Albany Street. As a reminder, atop the spire is a gilded eagle with wings outstretched, ready to swoop down on anyone foolish enough to even think about having Albany Street cut through.

The Clock in the Sidewalk

Northeast corner of Broadway and Maiden Lane, at 174 Broadway

You're probably not surprised to find clocks standing *on* sidewalks—there's one on Fifth Avenue at 23rd Street, another at 44th, a third at 59th, and so on—but who would think of looking for a clock embedded *in* a sidewalk?

The average street clock is usually not a simple act of magnanimity. It is ordinarily advertising, and this one is no different. From the time the Cushman Building opened in 1898 until 2006, the jewelry firm of William Barthman had occupied the corner shop. The first clock was placed in the sidewalk to herald the fact, in an understated way, that the jeweler was there; the face is angled with the XII pointing directly to what had been the entrance to the store.

The date on the clock, 1884, is the year Barthman opened his business. When this clock was installed, and by whom, is a mystery. There was a series of clocks in the sidewalk in front of the shop in the early 20th century, and, in all likelihood, this one was installed in the early 1950s.

Barthman died in 1914, and William Jr., took over. The younger Barthman clearly believed in the old public relations adage, "I don't care what you say about me as long as you spell my name right," and he succeeded in getting his name right in one plug. Barthman liked to throw corked bottles overboard from ocean liners with a card inside spelling out the ship's position and offering a $10 reward to anyone finding the bottle and returning the card. To Barthman's delight, the *Times* ran a story in 1926 reporting that a fisherman had found a bottle off the coast of Devon that Barthman had thrown overboard from the White Star liner *Majestic*, 367 miles from Cherbourg. The *Times* spelled Barthman's name right several times, including the fact that he was "a jeweler in this city." The fisherman said $10 would be a "bit of alright" for Christmas." The younger Barthman sounds like just the man to have installed the clock, but if it was that Barthman, he would have been foiled in terms of having generated any immediate publicity. Researchers have not been able to pin down the date the clock was installed with any certainty—it did not make the news.

Although the clock has stayed put while the city has swirled around it—a remarkable achievement in this ephemeral city—the clock's movement, at least, has moved with the times. It was originally mechanical, then electric, and now quartz.

You might wonder how the clock is maintained, especially how it was wound when it was mechanical, and the answer is from below. The average sidewalk in Manhattan is not sitting atop solid stuff. It is ordinarily the roof to a vault that is an extension of the building's basement. When the clock was mechanical, an employee would go down to the basement, enter the vault, and dutifully wind the clock once a week. As a quartz timepiece, a timekeeper might have to tend to it once every few years to change a battery.

The clock is set into a brass compass rose, so in addition to telling the time, the Barthman clock provides your geographic bearings. Unlike the compass rose set into the sidewalk on the northeast corner of Wall and William Streets—and you should take those coordinates with a grain of salt—the Barthman clock actually shows true north.

To a true New Yorker, north is straight up the numbered avenues, but true north from that perspective is on a northwest angle of about 27 degrees. If you want to find a street that is almost truly "north-south," walk up Broadway. When you reach 10th Street, Broadway takes a bend, and it almost follows a true north-south angle for about as far as 77th Street. (Stuyvesant Street, which cuts an angle between Third and Second Avenues from 9th to 10th Street, is said to be the only true east-west street in the city.)

After Barthman Jewelers had moved out of the corner shop and into a mid-block shop just a few doors north on Broadway at 176, Barthman's management thought it would be appropriate to install a replica in the sidewalk in front of their new shop. When they went to install it, however, the Landmarks Preservation Commission said "Uh uh! Your shop is in an historic district, and that includes the sidewalk in front. That sidewalk does not have a clock in it today, ergo it cannot have one in it tomorrow." Barthman did the only reasonable thing. They mounted the clock over the entrance, where it provides not just the time, but at least a hint of geography as you look at it. With the "east" arrow at the top, east is facing you, south is to your right, west is behind you, and north is to your left. Sort of.

Willing Suspension of Disbelief

233 Broadway, between Barclay Street and Park Place

A piece of sculpture representing a Native American in full headdress is a pretty unlikely subject in the Gothic period; equally unlikely is a skyscraper dressed up in Gothic clothes, but in the Woolworth Building you find both. The building was designed by Cass Gilbert, who believed that as anachronistic as the Gothic style was for a 20th-century skyscraper, the style was nevertheless ideal for expressing the verticality of the tower form.

The technology for a skyscraper required fixed locations for the steel frame, which established certain conditions not found in true Gothic buildings. Nevertheless, the vertical lines of Gothic architecture, along with elaborate Gothicized trim, were readily adapted to Gilbert's masterful skills. As one guidebook said, the true Gothic lines and tracery of the exterior had been executed with "studious care and fidelity to detail."

This buttress terminal of a Native American in full headdress, however, shatters any illusions of the real Gothic McCoy. Probably the first European to see a Plains Indian was Francisco Vasquez de Coronado in the 1540s, which would have been too late for major Gothic undertakings.

The statue here represents the Americas. It is joined by statues representing Europe, Asia, and Africa on all three facades. Although there would not have been any statues representing the Americas or Native Americans in any true Gothic work or for many centuries later, the idea of the Americas being represented by Native Americans began to appear by the late 19th century. For example, the Palace of Industry at Paris's Universal Exposition of 1878 featured a female Native American wearing a necklace of claws and a feathered headdress to represent North America. At the Albert Memorial in London, *America* centers on an idealized image of a woman riding a bison in true ladylike fashion, sidesaddle, although without benefit of saddle. An Anglicized Native American, holding a scepter and wearing a costume more akin to the uniform of a Roman centurion than to Native American garb, sits to her left.

Native American males appear in statuary representing the continent in two early 20th-century sculpture groups in New York City. In front of the Custom House, Daniel Chester French had a male Native American in full headdress peaking over the right shoulder of *America*, represented by an image of a clear-eyed, White woman. And then, flanked by Gothicized flora and fauna, is this image of *America* on the Woolworth Building, a Native American male, also in full headdress.

These carvings on the Woolworth Building are not marble, they are terra-cotta, which the *Times* praised as "the only building material that combines practical economy with architectural beauty." The sculptors were John Donnelly and Elisio V. Ricci, who were also responsible for the witty corbels in the lobby.

John Donnelly, the son of a sculptor, arrived in the United States from Ireland at the age of thirteen, and by the time he was thirty, he was the crew chief for the sculpture work on the home of Cornelius Vanderbilt II on Fifth Avenue at 57th Street. According to Donnelly's reckoning, there were only 320 stone carvers in the country in 1890, and 140 of them were on the job. Donnelly created the idea of the Saturday half-holiday because he liked to attend boat races on Saturday afternoons in the summer. Since he would not be on the site to supervise, he relieved himself of "considerable worry" by giving the workers Saturday afternoons off, which proved "so successful that at the end of August they voted to continue it all year."

Elisio V. Ricci was born in Florence in 1870 and studied at the School of Design there. He too arrived in the United States as a youth, and he went to work for the Perth Amboy Terra Cotta Company, where he rose to be the supervisor of modeling.

When the Woolworth Building was ready for its sculptural embellishment—the building opened in 1913—likely candidates as models for this buttress terminal included Sitting Bull and Chief Hollow Horn Bear, whose image was on the 1899 $5 bill. And the publicity mill for *Buffalo Bill's Wild West Show* was busy generating images of the show's stars, including Joe Iron Tail, the model for the 1913 buffalo nickel and the "Last of the Great Chiefs," as a poster for the show proclaimed. Whoever the model was in actuality, or whether Donnelly & Ricci created a composite image, hail to the chief, and to the willing suspension of disbelief that happily accepts the image of a Native American on a "Gothic" building.

The Glory Lies Below

In City Hall Park, northwest of the fountain

The subway is regarded by many people as a pedestrian form of transportation, so imagine their surprise when they learn what is under three sets of vault lights in City Hall Park. Below is the original City Hall subway station, where, in addition to chandeliers providing electric lighting, natural light was filtered through sets of elegant leaded glass in the ceiling. The mysterious trapezoidal vault lights in City Hall Park protected, and still protect, the leaded glass.

When the subway opened in 1904, the stations were described as clean, well-lighted places. The average stations had walls of Roman brick, with white tiles that have become so emblematic of the subway that similar tiles for the home are called "subway tiles." Setting off the tiles were polychromatic mosaics and bas-relief plaques in neoclassical trim, with the station markers carefully situated on the walls to be visible to the on-board passengers. Electric lighting was provided in some stations in elegant tulip-shaped sconces.

The architects were Heins & LaFarge, who were designing the Cathedral of St. John the Divine, and all the stations were grand, but City Hall station was the grandest of them all. It was more a Romanesque catacomb than a subway station, the ceiling a series of self-supporting vaults by Rafael Guastavino. The walls were entirely Roman brick, with tiling used as trim and tile station markers. Chandeliers and the leaded-glass skylights provided added extra oomph.

The City Hall station is not to be confused with the later City Hall station on Broadway (the Yellow Line), nor with today's "City Hall–Brooklyn Bridge" (the Green Line). This station was the southern terminus for the subway, and the station was designed as part of a loop, an ingenious idea. The average terminal is the end of the line, obliging the motorman to get out and walk back to what had been the last car, which then becomes the first car. With a loop, the motorman only had to stop to let the passengers off and on, and then he could continue.

The creation of the subway was a joint undertaking between the city and the operator. The city leased the space to the operator, in this case the Interborough Rapid Transit Company (the IRT), which paid for the construction and operation. The operator, in turn, essentially paid rent to the city for the use of the space. The city did not invest one penny in the original subway, but one administration after another took pride in it. Officials wanted to be able to show off the system to visiting firemen, so a station convenient to City Hall was mandatory. Entrances to the station were at the front steps of City Hall.

By 1945, so few people were using this station that it was closed. The Brooklyn Bridge station, which was only a few hundred feet away, was renamed City Hall–Brooklyn Bridge. Since then the original City Hall station has only been used for the Number 6 Local to go from its downtown run to its uptown run.

The station is off bounds to the average rider, but a pretty good simulacrum of the station is depicted in the denouement of J. K. Rowling's movie *Fantastic Beasts and Where to Find Them*. Some aspects are a little off, but the treats include the arched exit from the platform, the City Hall station marker, the vaults, and the leaded-glass in the ceiling. Fantastic.

A Buffalo Hunt? On the Manhattan Bridge?

Southeast of the Bowery at Canal Street

The Manhattan entrance to the Manhattan Bridge, an amalgam of Bernini's arcade at the Vatican and a triumphal arch modeled on Porte St. Denis in Paris, is one of the city's grandest evocations of majesty.

The sculptural motifs in Paris—and it was the city that paid for the arch—celebrate the military victories of Louis XIV. Just as Paris saw the wisdom in glorifying royal patronage, a source of its financial well-being, so the City of New York paid homage to its financial well-being in the sculpture groups *The Spirit of Industry* and *The Spirit of Commerce*. The subjects seem perfectly fitting for a civic project in early-20th-century New York, when the city was on the cusp of imperial glory in the marketplace. A buffalo hunt as the subject matter of the frieze, however, hardly makes sense for the New York of 1916, or any time.

The sculptor was the Harvard-educated Charles Cary Rumsey, who, like the bridge's architects, John Merven Carrère and Thomas Hastings, had studied at Paris's l'Ecole des Beaux Arts, and one commission changed Rumsey's life. He was commissioned to do some sculpture at Arden House, the estate built by the railroad man Edward H. Harriman in the hills of Tuxedo Park. The commission brought Rumsey into contact with Hastings, who was the architect of the mansion, and a friendship developed. Then Rumsey had the even better fortune of meeting Harriman's daughter, Mary, a relationship that blossomed into marriage in 1910. Both Mary and Charles were accomplished equestrians. Mary was a regular entrant at the National Horse Show, and Charles played polo with the likes of the great Tommy Hitchcock.

Rumsey was particularly partial to subjects dealing with the great outdoors, so instead of choosing a likely subject such as Saint Cecelia for a relief panel for the Organ Room at the Harriman house, he chose a subject as equally out of place as the subject on the bridge—a Plains Indian hunting a buffalo. Rumsey no doubt recognized the symbiotic oneness of hunting a buffalo while riding a horse bareback at full gallop and hitting a small ball with a mallet while riding a charging polo pony.

Polo was fairly indigenous and might have been a subject closer to home than a buffalo hunt for the Manhattan Bridge commission. The game had been played in the original Polo Grounds just north of Central Park, a reduced version of polo was played at the Squadron A Armory on Madison Avenue at 94th Street, and Rumsey played polo at the Meadowbrook Polo Club on Long Island's North Shore. If you were driving to the North Shore from Manhattan and took the Manhattan Bridge, you would at least pass under the frieze.

The themes celebrated in *Industry* and *Commerce* might have been even more appropriate. Just imagine big-shouldered longshoremen unloading a freighter, or seamstresses at work in a sweatshop, or newsies peddling their wares on a Broadway corner, anything but a buffalo hunt.

Canal Thou Never Wert.

Between Mulberry Street and West Street

anal Street was not a canal like the Erie Canal or the Panama Canal. Ever. No ship ever sailed on it, nor was it ever an irrigation tool. In fact, its creation was to serve as a dis-irrigation tool and as a way to carry off some of the city's detritus. It originally housed a sewer.

As late as the 1790s, two streams flowed from a five-acre fresh-water pond called the Collect, from the Dutch word *kolch*, a small body of water. On today's street pattern, the Collect stretched north of Foley Square, bounded by Canal, Baxter, and Lafayette Streets.

One stream flowed east from the Collect across a marsh to the East River, another flowed west, essentially along the line of today's Canal Street. The west-ward-flowing stream fed the Lispenard Meadows, a marshland, and the stream continued, emptying into the Hudson River.

A plan was put forward in the 1790s to create an inland harbor, with the two streams leading from the Collect serving as actual canals for shipping. Nothing came of the plan, and in 1803 planners decided to drain the Collect, which was becoming less and less salubrious, and to fill it with "good, clean earth." The run-off would drain to the East River via Catherine Street, and to the Hudson River via today's Canal Street. The common council did not give the drainage system a highfalutin name—they called it a ditch. The ditch could additionally be used to siphon off water from the Lispenard Meadows and link up with more drainage points, as well as run-off from rain.

A 75-foot-wide street was built east from Mulberry Street; from west of that point in 1811, appeared a 100-foot-wide street that stretched as far as the Hudson River. Its width was explained by the unseemly eight-foot-wide, open ditch in the center. Only then did the common council realize the short-sightedness of the plan. They should have enclosed the run-off in a pipe, and, better yet, place it underground, where it would be a real sewer. By 1819, the open ditch was conveniently out of sight.

The city fathers no doubt determined that to call the street Sewer Street, although forthright, would be off-putting. Canal Street had been bandied about as a result of the aborted plan for a real canal. The name stuck.

2

The Lower East and West Sides

From Canal to Houston Streets

They Thought They Knew Their Clientele

14A–16B Orchard Street, north of Canal Street

This pair of tenements had originally borne the more usual addresses of 14 and 16 Orchard Street, but the building on the corner of Canal Street, "Canal Condo," appropriated those addresses when the three buildings were converted into one. The building on the corner, aka 53 Canal Street, is not part of this story. This story is about the pair of tenement houses with the peculiar addresses and with the Stars of David on their facades.

When these tenements were built in 1887, many of the more than 80,000 Jews living in New York City called the Lower East Side home. As the *Jewish Messenger* wrote that year, some of the newspaper's readers had "visited old Jewish cemeteries and Ghetto remains in Europe: They would find much to interest them in a walk through East Broadway and its intersecting streets." East Broadway is two short blocks away.

By the 1910s, there were about five times as many Jews in the city, and down the block and across Canal Street was the Jarmulosky Bank, and around the corner on Ludlow Street was an immigrant aid society—a *landsmanshaft*. Orchard Street itself was synonymous with shopping, not only from shops but from the pushcarts that became the very image of the neighborhood.

Tenement-house facades in the late 19th century were frequently grand, and 14–16 Orchard Street is one of the grandest. The buildings are capped not just by cornices, but by pediments that border on the neo-Grec, and the brickwork is carefully laid and comes with expensive rounded corners. Terra-cotta string courses with delicate quatrefoil variants run the length of the buildings.

What sets these buildings even farther apart are the terra-cotta plaques bearing the symbol of Judaism, the Star of David. Here the triangles are so graphically interlaced that they reveal the interconnectedness, and they are encircled by twelve orbs, which represent the twelve tribes of Israel (same as on the Eldridge Street Synagogue nearby), and all within neoclassical scrollwork. Whether Jewish immigrants were interested in living in a building that shouts "Jew" when they were in all likelihood fleeing Jewish persecution, or whether the Stars of David were incorporated by the architects as a distinguishing graphic device they believed set the product apart, is the question.

The average walk-up tenement is five stories high, which means climbing about 60 steps to reach the top floor. These tenements are six stories high, so add another 15 steps or so. Despite the facade, the apartments are the usual, mean-spirited, post-1879 "model" tenements—railroad flats whose interior bedrooms had windows opening on airshafts, with either a blank wall facing you two-and-a-half feet away or the window of your neighbor's bedroom five feet away.

This pair of tenement houses was designed by the Herter Brothers, who also designed the Eldridge Street Synagogue, and therein lies a confusing story. There were two firms named Herter Brothers in the second half of the 19th century, and both in the same field.

The more renowned Herter Brothers were Gustave and Christian Herter, German immigrants who were designing and manufacturing furniture of the highest quality by the 1860s. They made a rosewood library table decorated with brass and marble for William H. Vanderbilt that is now in the Metropolitan Museum of Art, for instance, as well as a cherry wardrobe that was ebonized and inlaid as part of a bedroom suite for Jay Gould.

By the 1870s the phrase "interior decorator" was appearing, and these brothers were already at it. In 1875 they expanded even more when they engaged Charles B. Atwood to take charge of the architectural aspects of their work as an extension of their interior decorating. Gustave and Christian thereupon landed the plummiest of jobs—designing the Fifth Avenue–51st Street mansion for William H. Vanderbilt. From furniture makers to interior decorators to architects in the time it takes to say, "Shazam." Unfortunately, by 1887 those Herter Brothers were out of the running. Gustave retired by 1880, and Christian died in 1883.

In 1887, when one spoke about the Herter Brothers who designed the Orchard Street tenements and, in the same year, the Eldridge Street Synagogue, it was Peter and Frank H. Herter.

Peter Herter arrived from Germany, as his lawyer described, a "penniless immigrant," and he had the good fortune to marry fairly well. His wife's money helped launch him as a developer and architect, and by the 1880s, Herter had built a number of tenement houses on the Lower East Side and he owned real estate worth about $500,000.

The property was in his name in 1883, but he transferred seven pieces to his wife for one dollar in one day. He owed $34,000 to contractors, and mechanics' liens were being filed against him. He believed that transferring the property to his wife would put the property beyond the reach of the claimants.

At the same time, his brother, Frank Herter, who was also building in his own name, had mechanics' liens placed against him as well, and he pulled the same stunt as his brother. He transferred property to his wife for one dollar. He owed $6,000.

After some legal legerdemain, both brothers agreed to take back what had been deeded to their wives—it *was* fraudulent—and agreed to start paying off their debts.

In 1896, Frank Herter was back in court—he had let apartments at 140 Allen Street to women of "disorderly character." It was a good business. When the average three-room apartment might have rented for $13.50 a month, madams were paying rents ranging from $75 to $110. Frank Herter soon sank out of sight.

Peter Herter reconstituted himself as Peter Herter & Son, and in 1901 his firm was building an eight-story hotel on the south side of 59th Street between Madison and Park Avenues, back to back with three eight-story apartment houses on the north side of 58th Street, plus an eight-story apartment house on Park Avenue. In 1910, Peter erected a nine-story commercial building on the southeast corner of Lafayette and Fourth Streets. Before the building was even finished—just from the plans alone—he had leased the entire building to a single tenant for 21 years.

The Lower East Side has changed over the years. Gone are the pushcarts, and instead of finding shops that might have been selling lace remnants or a pocket watch that was intentionally given a dull finish to discourage thieves, you might find a shop selling high-end leather goods, an art gallery, and—heaven forfend—a restaurant/bar with oysters a specialty. Feh! Trayf.

Kapital Idea

173–175 East Broadway, between Rutgers and Jefferson Streets

Yes, that's Karl Marx, and the image of Friedrich Engels is also on the facade of this building. This was the home of the *Jewish Daily Forward*, the *Forverts*, the Yiddish-language newspaper that was started in 1897, and which, with a circulation of about 275,000 by the 1920s, was the largest-selling Yiddish-language newspaper in the world.

Despite sporting the images of Marx and Engels on the headquarters, the philosophy of the paper was not communist, it was socialist. One of its goals was to educate the recently arrived immigrants and help them get on with the process of assimilation. Central to this policy was encouraging a knowledge of English so that the immigrant generation could be more readily integrated into the larger society, a goal that was synthesized in a two-sided neon sign on the roof. Facing the Jewish neighborhood, the paper's name was in Yiddish; facing the rest of the city, the name was in English.

Most of the editorial content in the early days was in Yiddish, such as a full page devoted to the movie *Ben Hur,* with only the title in English. Some of the advertising was placed in both Yiddish and English, so you might see a one-column ad for Phillips' Milk of Magnesia with the headline "When Upset Stomach Gets You Down" in English, and an ad with the same layout in Yiddish. Ads that ran strictly in Yiddish were sure to have critical information such as the brand names in English, so the product could be readily found on the shelves.

Some features, especially in the rotogravure section, had captions in both languages. In 1924, a page featured the Progressive presidential candidate Robert LaFollette, the composer Pietro Mascagni, and Baroness Holub of Austria, a former New York cabaret singer who was suing her millionaire husband for a separation and a settlement of $600,000.

One of the paper's most popular columns was *Bintel Brief,* "A Bundle of Letters," an advice column that allowed letter writers to get things off their chest. Parents might write that they were worried about leaving their children unchaperoned for much of the day because the adults were both off struggling to make ends meet, or that their meager finances had led to taking in boarders in the already-cramped apartments, leading to sexual tensions.

Many men couldn't find work, and for the married man the concomitant shame frequently had him pull a disappearing act. Before World War I, the *Forward* started running "The Gallery of Missing Husbands," with photos of the absent men and their descriptions.

Another goal of the paper was the improvement of working conditions, which would lead to improved living conditions. There was the garment industry, with the sweat shops and the piece work that was done at home. There was the fight for the abolition of child labor, and the creation of eight-hour workdays, and improved municipal services at a most basic level. The newspaper ran a telling photograph of the Triangle Shirtwaist Fire that showed a fire department ladder that could only reach the sixth floor, when the fire was raging on the eighth, ninth, and tenth floors of the "fireproof" building.

The editor, Abraham Cahan, wrote about the prostitution on Allen Street, the street where Frank Herter had let his apartment building to women of "disorderly conduct." Essex Street was the red-light district of the Lower East Side in the 1890s, and just as renting to a madam was a lucrative business for the Herters, business was equally good for the prostitutes, who might make $20 to $30 a week, compared with the $12 tops that was earned by garment workers. But if the working conditions for the garment workers were egregious, the conditions for the prostitutes were worse. One woman wrote a letter to *Bintel Brief* that told of her stepping ashore at the Battery after having passed through Ellis Island, only to be handed over to a brothel keeper and essentially being enslaved, finally to escape.

The *Forward*'s headquarters building was built in 1912, and designed by George A. Boehm, the son of an immigrant architect, Abraham Boehm (George's middle initial was for Abraham). A Columbia graduate who studied in Rome and Paris, Boehm used a neoclassical vocabulary for the design. He had a Palladian arch framing the entrance, and reclining figures in a pediment enframed by dentils, a torch held on high in an escutcheon, and terra-cotta torches running up the corners of the building. As a symbol of enlightenment and hope, the torch made sense—the Statue of Liberty holds a torch, a torch is the symbol of New York University, and so on.

Boehm took the progressive preachings of the *Forward* to heart. There had always been slums, he said in a 1941 speech, but industrialization had brought about a change in the working conditions of people, a separation of living spaces from working spaces, and a tendency for large masses to congregate in dwellings located as close as possible to work places. This in turn "increased the speculative value of land (and) ever greater congestion," the problem compounded by the "lack of proper planning." The responsibility lay at the feet of planners and architects, and he was trying to make up for it.

Boehm was a guest lecturer at New York University on housing and related problems. He chaired the committee on laws and administration for the Citizens' Housing Council, he was a member of the advisory committee on the city's building code, he served on the executive legislative committees of the Citizens Union, and on the laws and administration committees of the Citizens Housing and Planning council, and on the housing section of the Welfare Council.

The *Forward* had passed the torch.

A Sign of Welcome

Church of Grace to Fujianese, 133 Allen Street,
between Rivington and Delancey Streets

The scallop-shell motif adorning this Fujian church is not comparable to the scallop shells associated with Saint James of Compostela, but it is a symbol of hospitality, a sign of welcome, and the shells on this building were a welcoming portent indeed for the residents of the Lower East Side in 1905. This building originally housed free public baths that had been built and paid for by the city, and all were welcome. The bathers' only obligations were to provide their own soap and towel.

Over a million Manhattan residents lived in tenements at the turn of the 20th century, 96 percent of them with no bathing facilities short of a sink. The Industrial Congress, a group of unions and reform groups, was advocating the establishment of public baths by the turn of the 1850s, and in 1852 the New York Association for Improving the Conditions of the Poor (AICP) actually established a bathhouse on Rivington Street. A bathhouse was certainly one way to improve the conditions of the poor.

By the 1880s, the city had taken the first step by inaugurating something euphemistically called "outdoor baths," barges outfitted as swimming pools and docked at the riverbanks that were open during the summer months. The water that was used was pumped straight from the rivers and into the baths. In 1893, Manhattan's raw sewage was blithely described as being "rendered innocuous" after being dumped from about 140 sewer outlets into those very same rivers, where, by virtue of the tides and the natural flow of water, the sewage was described as being carried seaward and away from the city. The water was pumped into the "baths" before, of course, it had had a chance to become "innocuous."

By the early 1900s, after much prodding by reformers, the city finally got into the business of erecting bathhouses, and the architects York & Sawyer were given their first assignment. They were assisted in the general planning by the Columbia-trained lawyer, John Seeley Ward, Jr., who had reported on municipal bathing facilities in major U.S. and European cities for the AICP. Ward recommended that the city should construct 16 bathhouses if an adequate municipal bath system was to be created, and in 1902, $300,000 was appropriated. Three bathhouses would go up immediately, with more on the boards. The three bathhouses—one in Seward Park, one on West 41st Street, and the third on Allen Street—were scheduled to be open 16 hours a day, so even workers who were putting in 12-hour workdays could probably find a chance to bathe.

On the first floor of the Allen Street bathhouse were two bathtubs and 49 showers for men; on the second floor were three bathtubs and 31 showers for women. As later bathhouses developed, fewer bathtubs were incorporated. Less time is usually spent in showers, which were also easier to maintain, with all the interiors having easy "wash down" surfaces and with rounded corners where the floors met the walls, based on the example set by good hospital design.

The Rivington Street bathhouse, like this one, was in a primarily Jewish neighborhood, and it seemed that no matter how hot the water got, it never seemed hot enough. The Lower East Siders had turned it into a *shvitzbud*, a sweat bath, the kinds of bathhouses that were popular among the Jews in the old country, and the resulting clouds of steam were sometimes so dense that it was impossible to see. To resolve the steam problem in the Allen Street bathhouse, York & Sawyer introduced a system by which a current of dry, hot air circulated at a height of about eight feet that absorbed the rising vapor and carried it away, clearing the atmosphere while maintaining the heated comfort factor.

The bathhouses presented themselves with all the dignity of municipal structures, but there was a downside to the formality and grandeur of the facades, compounded by the marble interiors and the polished fittings and the overall air of luxury. It all combined to frighten away the very people whom the baths were intended to attract, but the timorousness was soon overcome.

By the 1930s, the city had fourteen public baths. Reformers still kept up the pressure, and the old-law tenements continued to be retrofitted to include bathing and toilet facilities, which, combined with new construction that adhered to a higher code of decency, caused the need for municipal baths to wane. The one on Allen Street closed down in 1975, was boarded up by the city in 1988, and purchased at auction by the church in 1992.

Goerck Street?

On the Cast-Iron Building on the corner of 465 Broome Street
and 54 Greene Street

ne of the wonders of the cast-iron manufacturing process was how easily intricate forms could be readily stamped from molds to create buildings from whole iron, but why stop there? Why not advertise yourself as the cast-iron manufacturer and stamp out plaques with your name and address on them that could then be slapped on the building?

The main office for the Aetna Iron Works was on a north-south street called Goerck, at 104, as this plaque proclaims, and the building ran east through the block to 81–95 Mangin Street, which paralleled Goerck Street, and therein lies a great mapping tale.

In 1797, Casimir Goerck, a surveyor and mapmaker, and Joseph Francois Mangin, an engineer and the architect who teamed up with John McComb, Jr., to design today's City Hall, were asked by the Common Council to draft a map of the city, which in those days was solely Manhattan Island. A year later, Goerck died in a yellow fever epidemic, and Mangin soldiered on without him.

Unfortunately, Mangin's fancy got the better of his pragmatism. Instead of depicting what was, his plan depicted "such as it is to be," and he proceeded to map land and streets that only existed in his mind's eye. One of the paper streets he named Goerck Street in memory of his former partner, and the neighboring street to the east he named after himself.

The Common Council was outraged. They had wanted a "state of the city map," and they pasted a notice on the maps saying that none of the streets between Division Street and today's Houston Street had been "approved and opened under their authority." The area had been the Delancey Farm, and the Delanceys had been Royalists. Their land came to the city as forfeiture after the Revolution, and some of it had already been sold, and the city was in the process of selling the balance. The corporation was not willing to get into boundary disputes with property owners, nor to carve up the land according to the caprice of some mapmaker.

The irony is that when the street commissioners promulgated their gridiron plan in 1811, the East River shoreline of the Lower East Side reflected Mangin's depiction of it in a straight line, and the commissioners' map included many of the streets Mangin had named, including the ones honoring his late partner and himself.

Goerck Street lasted until about 1940 as a name before it was changed to Baruch Place; Mangin Street still exists in a truncated form. *Vita brevis, viae nominatae longae.*

The Rockefeller Reject Reborn Again

The Public Hotel, 215 Chrystie Street, between Stanton and Houston Streets

There is no missing this tapestry when you walk into the Diego Room—it dominates the wall on your left. The tapestry is a near copy of the fresco that you would have seen adorning the wall behind the concierge desk upon entering the lobby of 30 Rockefeller Plaza, Rockefeller Center's flagship building, if only it hadn't been destroyed.

The Rockefeller family had asked the Mexican artist, Diego Rivera, to paint the fresco. The family were great advocates of modern art, with Mrs. John D. "Abby" Rockefeller II serving as the treasurer of the Museum of Modern Art in the early 1930s, and her son, Nelson, later serving in the same role from 1935 to 1939.

With the country already deep into the Depression, the Rockefellers should have been provided a hint of Rivera's mood by *Frozen Assets*, a fresco that Rivera painted specifically for a one-man show at MoMA in 1931. Lucienne Bloch, who assisted Rivera on the ill-fated Rockefeller Center fresco, described *Frozen Assets* as "three horizontal scenes, the lowest, a bank vault; the middle, a dreary hall filled with sleeping unemployed men; and above ground, the skyline of the city, gray and lifeless."

Rivera's sense of social injustice got the *much* better of him on his assignment in 1934 to paint the fresco in question. Over the protestations of his wife and fellow workers, he included a portrait of Lenin, and a banner reading "Workers of the World Unite," and police using cudgels against peaceful demonstrators whose sign read "We Are Hungry. We Want Bread," along with card-playing women, a scandalously dressed dancer, and men and women drinking martinis and smoking cigarettes, subjects that were antithetical to everything that the Rockefeller family represented. The dilemma put Nelson Rockefeller between the rock of his belief in an artist's freedom of expression and the hard place of preserving the family's probity. He chose the family's probity.

We can't know how Rivera would have responded to criticism of his work, because he was not given the chance to comment or to remedy the perceived defects. Rivera had not bothered to read the contract that stipulated that Rockefeller Center owned the artwork and retained discretion over whether the work would be displayed. He was paid the full amount promised and ordered to leave the premises. The unfinished fresco was covered, and after a year, Nelson Rockefeller put forward the notion that the fresco should be removed to the walls of the Museum of Modern Art because Rivera would "probably be a good drawing card." That idea did not pan out, and the wreckers moved in with sledgehammers and knocked the fresco to smithereens.

A year later, Rivera painted a variation of the original for the Museo del Palacio de Bellas Artes in Mexico City that is about the same size as the original, about 16 by 38 feet.

The original had been called *Man at the Crossroads,* and the variation was called *Man, Controller of the Universe,* and that iteration was the model for this tapestry. It is not precisely what you would have seen in 30 Rockefeller Plaza, but when you visit 30 Rock, keep this vision in your mind and envision the original in its rightful place.

It was the imaginative hotelier, Ian Schrager, who bought the rights to the image from the Diego Rivera Foundation. At seven by eighteen feet, the tapestry is about half the size of the original, but it will no doubt come to loom as large as the original looms in legend.

Only a Little Out of Context

110 Greene Street, between Spring and Prince Streets

At first it appears to be an abstract landscape, but upon second look it is a very familiar landscape to the average New Yorker. Even after you've figured it out, it still comes as a surprise to find an art installation, *A Subway Map Floating on A New York Sidewalk,* actually floating on a New York sidewalk.

Instead of ink on paper, you find stainless-steel tracks on terrazzo, and serving as station indicators, you find vault lights. Vault lights are thick, round pieces of glass set into cast-iron frames that light the vaults below, and they represent SoHo, New York's great neighborhood of cast-iron.

The artist who created this subway map is the Belgium-born Francoise Schein, who was only 27 and a recent graduate of Columbia's School of Architecture with her master's in Urban Design when she accomplished the task in 1985. Schein intentionally chose the vault lights to mark the stations because they were traditionally in the sidewalks of SoHo, as you might have seen in the bottom left-hand corner of the photo of 465 Broome Street. Schein included vault lights in the hope

of resuscitating the local building practice. The use of vault lights was practical, and it was not exclusively limited to semi-industrial SoHo—some subway stations such as Bleecker Street had originally had vault lights lighting the platforms, and the practice is beginning to return. Updated vault lights now light a passageway for the underground promenade at Rockefeller Center, for instance.

The use of vault lights was the architectural-preservationist side of Schein. Her intellectual side had her thinking of the city as a giant integrated circuit, with people the electrons moving on a giant map, and a map on the sidewalk synthesized the idea.

If you know anything about dealing with a large city's bureaucracy, you'll understand that Schein's accomplishment was literally much greater than the sum of the parts required for the design and installation of an imaginative work of art.

The first hurdle to clear was the quasi-governmental local community board. The project was being commissioned by Tony Goldman, who owned the property and was one of the leading preservationist-owners in the neighborhood. The board welcomed the idea.

Then, because the map would be in a sidewalk in an Historic District, came the Landmarks Preservation Commission, and a higher hurdle. One question a commissioner posed was why a major site in the center of SoHo should be given to a young, unknown artist when the likes of Richard Serra lived nearby. Another commissioner did not like the piece because it lacked a frame. A third considered it dangerous, a potential hazard. One by one, the objections fizzled.

Next came the Department of Transportation, and Schein had a race ahead of her that combined the high hurdles and a marathon. The department had no idea how to define this particularly strange object, and they asked Schein to put all the technical information in the form of an architect's plans. If she had been just a plain old artist, she would have been stopped cold, but the trained architect in her drew the plans to the department's specifications. A year later, permission was granted.

For Schein, the subway map is her homage to the city, her present to New York. And, after all the stumbling blocks that the bureaucracy had thrown in her way, one city department saw the light. In 1986, about six months after the opening, Schein received a letter from the office of Mayor Edward I. Koch revealing that The New York City Art Commission had presented the project with an "Award for Excellence in Design."

3

The Villages: Greenwich and East

From Houston Street to 14th Street

Strange, a Sarcophagus in a Park

James J. Walker Park, St. Luke's Place, east of Hudson Street

Stumbling upon a sarcophagus in a public park can be unsettling, but somewhat mitigating the circumstances is the knowledge that this stone coffin never actually contained a body, although it had been placed over an actual grave a stone's throw from where the memorial stands. Today's James J. Walker Park is yesterday's St. John's Cemetery, and there are thousands of bodies still there in the ground.

St. John's Cemetery was part of Trinity Parish (the namesake chapel stood on Varick Street, just south of Canal Street), and in 1890 a city assemblyman succeeded in getting a bill passed condemning the cemetery property, which had been going to the dogs. Monuments had toppled over, tombstones had fallen, shrubbery was running riot, and the place was littered and vandalized.

By 1894, the City of New York informed the Trinity Corporation that condemnation proceedings were moving forward, and the city would give Trinity $520,000 for the property. Trinity seemed to forget all the legalisms over the extension of Albany Street through its graveyard, and simply argued that the city had no right to condemn the cemetery. It was a sacred place, and upon the decision of the court hinged the fate of many larger cemeteries and other sacred places, which Trinity argued deserved to be preserved from the attacks of "progress." It was a disingenuous argument for Trinity to make. In about 1805, Trinity had purchased the former Lutheran burying ground at the southwest corner of Broadway and Rector Street, and built the first Grace Church on the site.

Trinity did offer a quid pro quo. It would give the city a comparable piece of property in the neighborhood in exchange for keeping the cemetery.

No dice.

The cemetery was going to be metamorphosed into a park. The ground lay five feet lower than the sidewalk, and it had to be made level. Everything would be covered over, buried. Notices went out from the park commission stating that if friends or relatives of the interred wanted any trace of them, the living were obliged to remove the dead from the cemetery at their own expense. After the deadline, there could be "no disturbances," as it was quaintly phrased.

The shameful aspect of what Trinity had done with the Lutheran dead in 1805 was to put the remains "in open box carts promiscuously," and then have the "fragments of bones and coffins . . . dumped into the North (Hudson) River." Here, at least, the city would let bodies remain in their original place. The bodies had already mingled with the earth, went the argument, and the decision was to let sleeping bodies lie, along with their tombstones.

The one remaining monument, which was moved from its original site nearer Clarkson Street, had been erected by the volunteer firemen of Eagle Engine No. 13 and placed over the graves of the bodies of two of their own, 20-year-old

Eugene Underhill and 22-year-old Frederick A. Ward, killed while battling a fire in 1834. They were buried side by side, the one monument covering their remains.

In 1848, a Fire Department Monument was erected in Green-Wood Cemetery in Brooklyn by the Firemen's Benevolent Fund, and some volunteer firemen thought it fitting to have the remains of Ward and Underhill, along with the monument, removed to a site near the new monument. The plan was refused by the fund's benevolent trustees, who said that any obstruction of the view from the new memorial, or "unsightliness," would not be tolerated.

Many former volunteer firemen were still alive in the1890s, and they petitioned the city to allow the memorial to remain, close by its original site. This time their wishes were granted, perhaps for reasons irrelevant to the justness of their cause.

The assemblyman who had started the movement to close the cemetery was William H. Walker, and the act could be considered as much an act of home improvement as civic advancement. He lived at No. 6 St. Luke's Place, which overlooked the cemetery. Assemblyman Walker was the father of Mayor Jimmy "Beau James" Walker, who lived in the house during his mayoralty. Mayor's lamps still stand in front of the house, and the park is named in honor of "His Honor."

If the senior Walker had had anything to do with the preservation of the monument, he would have been appealing to a natural constituency—the professional fire force had evolved from the volunteer force, plus he could see the memorial from his front parlor. It's a case of YIMFY (Yes, In My Front Yard).

No Booze. No Credit. No Kidding.

160 Bleecker Street, between Thompson and Sullivan Streets

Today's apartment house might be called The Atrium, but the escutcheon clearly spells out Mills House No. 1. It was a hotel, and despite the elegance of its trim, it was hardly the Waldorf. It was a hotel specifically designed for the working man whose wallet was slim but who was clean and decent.

The hotel opened in 1896 to designs by the eminent architect, Ernest Flagg, and there would be a Mills House Nos. 2 and 3, the latter still standing on the northeast corner of Seventh Avenue and 36th Street.

The hotels were started by Darius Ogden Mills, who grew up in Westchester. The 23-year-old was struck by gold fever in 1848, and he struck gold in California by starting a general store, taking the profits from the store and doing some intercoastal trading, making bigger profits from the trading and using them to start a bank. With his fortune secured, Mills decided to come back East to flaunt it and to "do some good." One of his philanthropies was the establishment of a school for male nurses at Bellevue. Another was this hotel for working men. Here was an antidote for the Bowery's lodging houses, where the artful lodger could get a bed in a dormitory in the "fanciest" of them for two bits a night. Those lodging houses, according to Inspector Thomas Byrnes, the chief of the New York detectives in the 1890s, were seldom more than incubators of crime.

At a Mills House a man could get a five-by-seven-foot room—not just a bed in a dormitory—for 20 cents a night. The room came with a spring bed and a horsehair mattress with "snow-white sheets," a chair, a closet, a strip of carpet, an electric light, and a window facing either the street or a court. The partitions did not quite extend to the ceiling, but privacy was provided.

With the cost of the room came the use of bathtubs and showers, parlors, a library, and a reading- and writing room with writing tables and inkwells. Wholesome meals cost an additional 30 cents a day and were served on tables dressed in tablecloths, and laundry was done on the premises at cost. The laundry facilities were a special boon. The man with a limited wardrobe could still look clean and fresh.

The two former Mills Houses are now called "Atrium Somethings" because unlike the average dumbbell tenement, if a room in the Mills House did not look out over the street, it looked out over a glass-covered and steam-heated court (today's atriums) with the closest window 50 feet away.

For the classic urban immigrant male with a few bucks in his pocket, the Mills House was manna from heaven. Unlike A. T. Stewart's Home for Working Women, there were few restrictions, but there were two that might have prompted a young man to wonder about the advantages of having his own digs—no alcohol or ladies were permitted on the premises, not even in the front parlor. It was designed to be a wholesome establishment, and management intended to keep it that way in every entendre.

Angels We Have Seen on High

65 Bleecker Street, at Crosby Street, between Broadway and Lafayette Street

This terra-cotta "faery" angel—there are five more just like her under the roof-line cornice of the Bayard-Condict Building—seldom has a name attached to it. In fact, the only name ordinarily associated with the design of the Bayard-Condict Building is its architect, Louis Sullivan.

Sullivan was a master of architectural decoration, but he was not a "sculptor" per se—neither a modeler nor a carver he. However, he drew so artfully and with such precision that he only had to hand off his drawing to a model maker who would then create the form Sullivan had had in his mind's eye.

Curiously, despite the obvious quality of this angel, the likelihood of finding her or any of her sisters cataloged in the books on public sculpture in New York is pretty slim, and the likelihood of finding the name Kristian Schneider, who actually sculpted her, even slimmer.

Schneider, who arrived in the United States as a 20-year-old from Norway, was acknowledged as one of the best architectural modelers in the United States in the 1890s, and he did a lot of work with Sullivan. Schneider designed the

enormous Golden Arch for Sullivan's Transportation Building at the Columbian Exposition, a neo-Romanesque arch enriched with carvings and bas-reliefs. Schneider also did the architectural decorations for Sullivan's Auditorium Building in Chicago, and the Wainwright Building in St. Louis, and the angels here on Bleecker Street.

There are some who say that the idea for the "faery" angels belongs to Emmeline Condict, who, with her husband Silas, took over the building after the original developers had backed out. Unlike caryatids, who are burdened by the weight of their work, these angels are exulting in their workplace, freed from the tyranny over women, and the idea of the angels would certainly jell with Emmeline Condict's natural proclivities. A graduate of Brooklyn's Packer Collegiate Institute, she was a suffragist and a member of Sorosis, the organization that argued for equality in the workplace. However, the timing is a little off. The Condicts did not take possession until six months before the building opened in December, 1899, and Sullivan liked angels—he had already used a similar motif on the Transportation Building at the Columbian Exposition.

Like the angels, the facade is terra-cotta, which made its first appearance as a complete facade in the city in 1877 when George B. Post used it on a row house at 15 East 37th Street. Terra-cotta is literally baked earth, and it has two specific advantages as a building facade—it can be stamped out of molds and essentially slapped up to cover common brick, which made it cost effective, and it is a fire retardant.

Proof of the building's precautions against fire came only a year after the building had opened, when a fire broke out in the offices of a garment manufacturer on the tenth floor, with material in stock that was highly combustible. The *Times* reported that although much of the stock had been destroyed, the building was so well constructed that the firemen were able to prevent the flames from spreading. That's almost the classic definition of a fireproof building.

Sullivan was known for his aphorisms such as "form follows function," and if he had responded to Ludwig Mies van der Rohe's famous aphorism on decoration, "less is more," Sullivan would no doubt have said "uh, uh, more is not enough." Some say that Sullivan was the first Modernist, but he liked decoration. His decoration was organic, never just slapped onto a building as an afterthought. He would never have said to a sculptor, "Can you put one of your little putti here and another there, and perhaps some heraldic device over there?"

Sullivan was a classicist. He believed in the sonata form, with a statement of the theme, the development and recapitulation of the theme, a beginning, middle, and end.

Decoration was always an integral part of the design, and the form of those angelic creatures is no different. Their function is to serve as the horizontal capstone of the building, and they are up there to draw the building to its logical conclusion. Their form is their function.

Hardly Augean

33 Great Jones Street, between Lafayette Street and the Bowery

Bernhard Beinecke was a wholesale butcher whose career began in New York in 1865 when he was a 19-year-old German emigrant. By the 1870s, his business included making deliveries directly to his clients. He needed horse-drawn wagons as delivery vans along with a place to house them, so he built this three-story stable.

By the 1890s, Beinecke was operating the largest stockyard in the city, at 59th Street and the Hudson River, and not only did Beinecke's client list include great shipping lines, it also included some of the city's grandest hotels. He soon realized that there was more profit to be made operating hotels than there was in simply supplying them, so in 1896, Beinecke built and operated the Manhattan Hotel on the northwest corner of Madison Avenue at 42nd Street. The hotel was designed by Henry J. Hardenbergh, whose Waldorf-Astoria had just opened to great huzzahs.

Beinecke consequently became associated with Harry S. Black, the president of the Fuller Construction Company, who had built the Flatiron Building. Together they created the United States Realty & Improvement Company, and they interested John "Bet-a-Million" Gates in a new Plaza Hotel, which Hardenbergh would also design and which Beinecke operated until the 1930s. United States Realty went on to build the Nacional in Havana, the Copley Plaza in Boston, and the Savoy Plaza in New York City, which was across from *the* Plaza.

By the time the Savoy Plaza opened in 1928, Beinecke was in his eighties. According to his grandson, Walter Beinecke, Jr., Beinecke had been opposed to the construction of the Savoy Plaza, which was "built in a wave of enthusiasm in the late 1920s." The Depression "set in, and my grandfather, who had moved to the Plaza . . . sat in the window in his last years and watched everything go. He ended up the way he started; he ended up broke."

"Broke," of course, is a relative term. The family retained an interest in Fuller, which was the largest building construction company in the United States, and one family member founded Sperry & Hutchinson, which distributed "Green Stamps," the trading stamps that grocery stores used to hand out instead of discounts.

The third generation of Beineckes created a memorial to the second generation of Beineckes, the children of Bernhard Beinecke. They built a library at Yale, which Walter Beinecke, Jr., modestly described as being "rather well known." It's the Beinecke Library, the largest rare book and manuscript archive in the world.

On the Cuff, Literally

On the east side of La Guardia Place, between Bleecker and West Third Streets

This statue of a spirited Fiorello La Guardia didn't leave much room for the sculptor Neil Estern to stick his name. When asked why he put it where he did, he said, "Well, I had to put it somewhere," and, there it is, on the cuff of the former mayor's trousers. It wasn't the first time a sculptor had found an interesting place to sign his work. The French Huguenot sculptor Hubert Le Sueur signed his equestrian statue of the English King Charles I on the horse's left forefoot, but you might not find a foundry mark on that statue. On the heel of La Guardia's shoe is an "M," for the Modern Art Foundry in Astoria, Queens.

With the coming of the urban renewal project that resulted in Washington Square Village in the late 1950s, this stretch along what was then still called West Broadway was a barren and deserted place. The big bad wolf in the form of Robert Moses, who was both the transportation and the parks commissioner at the same time, had huffed and puffed and blown the houses down to make way for a highway that would cut through Washington Square and continue south to

link up with his proposed elevated highways for Lower Manhattan. His proposal sank, thanks to community opposition, but the buildings that had lined the east side of West Broadway were felled before Moses' plan could be.

In 1967, West Broadway was named La Guardia Place between Houston Street and Washington Square, and a local activist thought that Estern's *La Guardia,* originally commissioned by the Port Authority for La Guardia Airport before the funds ran out, would be a marvelously appropriate addition. Estern's depiction shows a man of action, catching the mayor in mid-stride, bringing his hands together to make a point. "He was always railing against something, some injustice or corruption," said Estern. Before having the Art Commission give the sculpture its imprimatur, the owner of the property had to approve the statue, and the owner just happened to be the Department of Transportation, which had created the void in the first place. DOT approved it.

About six months after the installation in 1994, the sculptor just happened to be passing by and he noticed that the six-foot, seven-inch, one-and-a-half-ton statue was leaning. One of the supports between the statue and the base had given way. A week later, the statue was returned to its site, this time with the supports solidly embedded in epoxy. Estern's wry sense of humor had him wondering whether anyone noticed that the statue had gone missing.

Venerable

Founders Memorial, Schwartz Plaza, linking West 3rd and West 4th Streets, between Mercer Street and La Guardia Place

This Gothic Revival finial once crested a buttress on New York University's original 1837 building, which stood on Washington Square East between Washington Place and Waverly Place. The buttresses were engaged, a part of the wall, and they flanked the triple portal that served as the main entrance to the building. The combined buttresses and finials were about two-and-a-half stories high, and this finial provides a glimpse of the scale of the building. It was 180 feet long, and four very high-ceilinged stories high, five if you include the squared, freestanding towers at its corners.

The noble building was torn down in 1894 when NYU moved to The Bronx. This finial was salvaged and put to use as Founders Memorial at the new campus, where it stood at the main entrance. When NYU returned to Washington Square, the finial was again salvaged and installed here in 1973.

Gothic was not part of the nation's architectural heritage, but the Gothic Revival started in earnest in the United States in 1816 when Ithiel Town, the engineer and architect, designed Trinity Church in New Haven, Connecticut. Another architect in the vanguard of the style was Alexander Jackson Davis, who in 1832 designed a house near Baltimore called Glen Ellen, a crenellated mansion with turrets and towers and finials. Two years later, a proposal for John Jacob Astor's hotel, the Astor House, included an elaborate fan-faulted hall modeled on the ceiling in King's College Chapel, Cambridge, which only made it as far as the drawing board.

The original NYU building was designed by two partners who were in business together just long enough, from 1829 to 1835, to have designed it. They were the proto-Gothic Revivalists, Ithiel Town and A. J. Davis, and it was Town & Davis who had drawn up the unfulfilled plans for the Astor House.

Town & Davis's design for the original NYU building was the first important building in the English collegiate style of architecture in this country, and it was the first building in the Gothic Revival style in the city. St. Peter's Church on 20th Street in Chelsea, billed as the city's earliest Gothic Revival church, opened in 1838, one year after NYU. The Church of the Ascension opened in 1841, and Grace, Trinity, and First Presbyterian all opened in 1846. Those dates make this finial a vestige of the city's first manifestation of the style.

The facade's central feature was the chapel's 50-foot-wide Gothic-style window that was set in above a triple portal, with this finial one of the elements. The central portal and window were flanked by a pair of barbicans, towers that ran up the height of the building and terminated in battlements, the overall scheme also inspired by King's College Chapel, Cambridge.

When NYU opened for business in its new building, it was off to a rocky start financially. Town & Davis's design had included major buttresses for the side

streets, but the buttresses did a bit too much "butting" beyond the building line and onto the sidewalk. The Common Council did not deem it "expedient to authorize any encroachment upon the streets," and refused a permit. The buttresses had to be scaled back.

The contractor was Seth Geer, who was building the Greek Revival Colonnade Row on today's Lafayette Street. Geer was using prison labor from Sing Sing to cut the marble for that project. To cut corners on the NYU job, Geer decided to do the same. The General Trades Union protested, masons and stonecutters paraded, the protests led to rioting in the streets, and the Seventh Regiment was called up to quell the troubles. The military bivouacked on Washington Square for four days and nights.

The building wound up taking longer to build and costing more than antici-pated, and NYU's financial cupboard was bare. The number of students did not fill the classroom space, so NYU started renting out space on the upper floors as studios or apartments, and some interesting tenants moved in.

The architect A. J. Davis took quarters, and Samuel F. B Morse, NYU's first professor of painting and sculpture, established his studio in the northwest tower. Morse was perhaps the first artist to work on Washington Square, and he was certainly the first artist to depict the university's new building. His 1836 painting, "Allegorical Landscape of New York University," set the building in a dreamy neoclassical landscape that hinted at the nascent Hudson River School. The money from his painting and the few students he taught hardly paid the rent, but in 1838 Morse exhibited something in the building that would contribute to his upkeep and maintenance—his telegraph.

Another early resident was the multi-talented John W. Draper, a professor of botany and chemistry. Draper was one of the earliest to photograph the human face, and he took the photograph outdoors because the light was better. The result, his "sun picture," went missing for about 40 years, to be unearthed in 1893. The picture was forwarded to NYU's chancellor, Henry MacCracken, who placed the photograph along with Morse's first telegraph message in the universi-ty's exhibit at the Columbian Exhibition in Chicago.

The surviving finial moved to The Bronx the following year. As for the finial's anonymous stone cutters, the odds are they were law-abiding citizens.

Through This Door to a Free and Sovereign Republic of Greenwich Village

Washington Arch, in Washington Square, Fifth Avenue south of Eighth Street

Greenwich Village has had a long history of social activism, with Washington Square serving as the epicenter and Washington Arch itself serving as the stepping off point for protest marches ranging from better working condi-tions or votes for women to the policies of a newly elected president.

It only makes sense. Greenwich Village was home to more artists and writers per capita than anywhere else in the city in the first half of the 20th century, the city's very own Latin Quarter. A rebellious streak comes with the territory.

It was here, atop Washington Arch on the evening of January 23, 1917, that a Free and Sovereign Republic of Greenwich Village was declared by Gertrude Drick, who had left Texas to combine two ambitions—to learn the violin and to

study with the Ashcan artist John Sloan, coincidentally becoming part of the New York art scene.

The Independence movement took shape after Drick noticed that the small iron doorway in the west pier of Washington Arch was open one night. She walked the circular stairway's 101 steps that lead to the roof and then thought it would be a lark to sneak up to the roof one night to declare the secession of the Village from big business and small minds, and to declare a free and sovereign republic.

She invited John Sloan, and the French émigré artist Marcel Duchamp, and three actors from the Provincetown Playhouse to her revolutionary party. The rebellious six gathered, climbed the steps, and proceeded to the serious matter at hand.

Drick provided candles, balloons, and some sandwiches. A pot of beans was heated over a makeshift fire, cap guns were fired off to provide the rockets' red glare, and some reports have the revelers drinking tea in honor of the Boston Tea Party. John Sloan sketched the gathering, which shows one of the revelers drinking from what looks suspiciously like a wine bottle, with nary a teacup in sight.

Drick's hand-lettered declaration parodied official proclamations, with script that had great flourishes and long, undecipherable lines, much like the later "proclamations" by the *New Yorker* cartoonist Saul Steinberg. There was "The Great Seal of the Village," which represented the north face of Washington Arch, with a ribbon affixed to the document by an embossed seal, as if it carried the weight of true and legal authority. And her prose parodied official proclamations in its pomposity, with three uses of "whereas" and one "therefore" in large, bold-face type. Following "We the undersigned" were the signatures of the six. In the tradition of John Hancock, Gertrude Drick's signature was the first and the largest.

After the reading aloud of the document, its signing, and the other revolutionary revelries, the rebels made it safely home, leaving behind the balloons floating from the roofline to the befuddlement of passersby the next morning. Since their escapade, the small iron doorway on the west side of the west pier of Washington Arch has been carefully locked.

The Village is still a different state of mind, still a Free and Sovereign Republic, despite the fact that the average artist can no longer afford the rents there.

They Wuz Robbed

110 Seventh Avenue South, on the southwest corner of Christopher Street

I n the sidewalk in front of the one-story taxpayer that houses the Village Cigar Store is a strange message in mosaic. This is not your usual brass property-line marker set discreetly into a sidewalk. This message is defiant.

It's all explained by the "cut." Seventh Avenue South has nothing to do with the Street Commissioners' Plan of 1811, but with planning in the early 20th century. Before 1917, there was only Seventh Avenue, which began at West 11th Street and went north with true Cartesian regularity. Seventh Avenue South made its appearance when a major routing change for the subway was in the works. Seventh Avenue South takes a bend south of 11th Street and angles its way downtown to merge with Varick Street at the crossing of Carmine and Clarkson Streets. It, and Park Avenue South (aka, Fourth Avenue), are the only avenues in Manhattan that are "South" anything.

The original path of the first subway was a Z pattern. Its route went up the East Side from City Hall to Grand Central, where it zigged west on 42nd Street to Broadway, and zagged north on Broadway to 145th Street. Then came the H Plan, with an extension north from Grand Central on Lexington Avenue on the East Side (today's Green Line), and south from Times Square on the West Side (today's Red Line). The West Side Line continued south on Seventh Avenue to 11th Street, then on the newly created Seventh Avenue South to Varick Street and on to South Ferry or to Brooklyn.

The problem was that a solid mass of housing stood between 11th Street and Varick Street. The builders of the subway did not like to tunnel under already existing buildings because tunneling was an expensive process, requiring them to shore up everything above them. The cut-and-cover method was simpler. All they had to do was cut a trench in a street, negotiate pipes and wires, lay the tracks, and put a roof up. In a fit of Haussmanism, the city decided to *create* a street for the subway—Seventh Avenue South—as a link between Seventh Avenue and Varick Street.

The "cut" meant that a swath of Greenwich Village was condemned. Dozens of buildings disappeared, while many were only partially torn down, leaving the neighborhood with ugly scars.

In the early 1910s, the five-story Voorhis Apartments stood on the south side of Christopher Street, and stretched 60 feet east from this mosaic to overlook a corner of Sheridan Square. The Voorhis disappeared in the onslaught, leaving a sliver of its former plot remaining, some calling it "the world's smallest piece of real estate." As Terry Miller tells us, the city "tried to convince its owner, the estate of Philadelphian David Hess, that this plot—which was outside the limit of condemnation—was useless and should voluntarily be surrendered to become part of the sidewalk." The estate refused, and installed this mosaic. In 1938, Village Cigars bought the vestigial property, mosaic and all, and there it sits to remind the passing pedestrian of the injustice of it all.

A Mosaical Mystery Tour

The Christopher Street–Seventh Avenue South Subway Station

The mosaics and bas-reliefs on subway station walls usually depict local history, and many people believe that they were installed to aid the non-English-speaking immigrant or the illiterate. The problem is that some subjects, such as the beaver at Astor Place, are so arcane that even many a literate, English-speaking native is unlikely to make any connection between the subject and the station.

Perhaps the mother of all subway arcana is the mosaic of the State Prison at Greenwich. The prison stood about five blocks west of the station at the end of Christopher Street. It was built in 1797 and torn down in 1853, although some of its outer walls survived in different guises until the 20th century.

The prison was designed by Joseph Francois Mangin, the imaginative map-maker who would go on to design City Hall with John McComb, Jr.. The prison itself was a great sight, even a tourist attraction. Bigger and better prisons were being built at the turn of the 19th century, in large part because prison reformers had succeeded in having the number of capital crimes reduced to three—arson, murder, and treason. Instead of death sentences being given for crimes such as highway robbery, prison sentences for as long as 21 years were being meted out. More commodious prisons were required to house the growing prison population, and the State Prison at Greenwich was one of them.

The State Prison stretched between Christopher Street and Perry Street, from west of Washington Street to the bank of the Hudson River. There were 54 rooms, each measuring 12 by 18 feet, with eight male prisoners in each space; female prisoners had their own wing. The site was described as a "pleasant, airy, and salubrious spot," and real-estate ads today would say that some of the cells had "Riv Vu."

"This was one of the first prisons where the inmates were taught trades," said the historian Thomas Janvier, but there was a downside to this nobly progressive goal. Since the convicts were assembled in large workrooms, there were "abundant opportunities for concocting conspiracies," including mutinous outbreaks and escapes.

The prison was soon deemed too small, and it was clearly a failure as a lock-up. In 1828 the male prison population was sent up the Hudson River to a town called Sing Sing, and "up the river" is where long-term prisoners are still sent in New York parlance. (The town has changed its name to Ossining.)

After the state's female prisoners left in 1829, the building served various functions, and some of the outer walls were repurposed in 1853.

To commemorate the prison was a stretch, but in 1907 an architect, whose name conjures up images more reminiscent of the 18th-century English countryside than a 20th-century urban transportation system, took over the design of the subway. His name was Squire Vickers, and he continued the tradition of incorporating station markers that celebrated neighborhoods. The scene at the Christopher Street station is based on a print in the collection of the New-York Historical Society.

Vickers described the ceramic scenes as "plaques which nudge the memory to recall the past." A lot of nudging would have been required for anybody to recall this scene when the Christopher Street station opened in 1918.

West 10th Street, Let Me Introduce You to West 4th Street

The intersection of West 10th and West 4th Streets

Give the average New York cabby the address 184 West 10th Street, and he will do the address computation in his head that tells him that house numbers progress in hundreds between numbered avenues west of Fifth Avenue, so 184 West 10th Street must be between Sixth and Seventh Avenues. When you tell him, "It's where 10th Street meets 4th Street," he's just liable to drive you straight to Bellevue.

It makes no sense. Crosstown streets are straight and parallel to each other, at least according to the street plan of 1811, and if you believe the axiom about two parallel lines, they never meet. The only streets that east-west crosstown streets are supposed to intersect are north-south avenues.

When the subject is the West Village, however, one can abandon all hope of finding Cartesian regularity. The street commissioners did not enter the streets west of Sixth Avenue.

The 1811 plan had crosstown streets marching in lock-step regularity from First Street uptown to 155th, but the street numbering only began in earnest east of Sixth Avenue. The street commissioners realized that the city treasury could not afford to compensate the property owners on the already developed properties west of Sixth Avenue in Greenwich Village, so the streets between Houston and 14th Streets were shown in their already-existing every-which-way direction. The commissioners had West 10th Street ending at Sixth Avenue, west of which was numerically no man's land.

The West 10th Street that now angles southwesterly from Sixth Avenue to the river was called Amos Street in 1811, named for the property owner Richard Amos, who, with dreams of speculation dancing in his head, ceded some of his land for a public road in 1809. In 1857, property owners petitioned the Board of Aldermen to change the name to West 10th Street, perhaps because they wanted to appear part of the more orderly city. The idea was slow to catch on. The *Tribune* was still referring to Amos Street six months later.

And West 4th Street? Basically, the same story. The street commissioners ended West 4th Street at Sixth Avenue, and it too follows the path of another street, but it was northwesterly. If a pedestrian at Sixth Avenue had continued walking west before the name change, with a bit of a jag at Sixth Avenue he would have encountered Asylum Street, named for the orphan asylum that had been erected on that street in 1806. The name was changed to West 4th Street when the asylum moved uptown in 1836.

This is all complicated by whether to call either West 4th or West 10th a "crosstown" street west of Sixth Avenue. West 10th is essentially running downtown, and West 4th uptown. And they do meet.

And Now There Is One

In the gore on Fourth Avenue between Eighth and Ninth Streets

I n 1979, the Diamond Jubilee year celebrating the subway's 75th anniversary, a kiosk was used as the symbol of the subway for the MTA's logo. At the time, not a single kiosk was still standing, which begs the question of how this lone sentinel stands guard over the Astor Place subway station.

Cooper Union, the great school of art, architecture and engineering, is at Astor Place, and the architect Rolf Olhausen fondly remembered the original kiosk from his student days. When his firm, Prentice, Chan & Ohlhausen, was asked to refurbish the station, Ohlhausen suggested recreating the kiosk. He had taken a picture of it in 1958, and based on that photograph and the Heins & LaFarge drawings, as well as casts he made of the "calf's tongue" molding that he found, he had the kiosk recreated in 1986.

The contract for the subway had stipulated that the undertaking was a "great public work," designed with a view to aesthetics and efficiency, and the kiosks that originally served as subway entrances and exits lived up to those ideals. The kiosks "were once one of the finest pieces of street furniture in New York, tiny structures that . . . gave a sense of ceremony, even grandeur, to the act of ascending or descending," said the *Times* architecture critic, Paul Goldberger. And they were practical.

Board members, along with the subway's chief engineer, William Barclay Parsons, took a junket to inspect subway systems in Europe, and the kiosks for the Budapest subway, which had opened in 1896, inspired them. Unlike the entrances to the London Underground, the kiosks did not resemble mini-railroad stations, and unlike the Art Nouveau entrances to the Paris Metro, the kiosks protected passengers from inclement weather. The commissioners asked the subway's architects to do something similar for New York, and Heins & LaFarge obliged. The kiosks protected passengers from rain and snow, from gloom of night, from aromatic air, and they ensured the comfort of those entering and exiting.

At the average stations, separate sets of stairs were provided for passengers who were entering and exiting. The stairs closest to the track were used for exits, with gates swinging open directly from the platform for the exiting passengers to take. The stairs farthest from the tracks were entrances, which allowed room for purchasing tickets and fare collection. This eminently sensible arrangement meant that people weren't always dodging and weaving through the oncoming hordes.

To guide incoming passengers to the appropriate kiosk, the words "Exit" and "Entrance" announced the function a kiosk served, complemented by the shapes of the kiosks' roofs. Kiosks with flat, four-sided triangular roofs were specifically for exiting passengers. Kiosks with rounded, dome-like roofs were entrances. Double-wide kiosks, such as here at Astor Place, served both functions.

There was more to the design of kiosks than met the eye, and here's where the "aromatic air" comes in. The stations had men's and women's toilets, and the toilets had to be vented. The ventilation was through hollow columns in the kiosks.

Despite the commonsensicality of the kiosks, complaints started being lodged against them soon after their introduction. Merchants complained that their shop windows were obscured, and the few motorists complained that their views were blocked when turning corners.

And then there was the cost. Kiosks are little buildings unto themselves, and prudent management requires upkeep and maintenance. Although it's cheap enough to defer maintenance, it's cheaper still to maintain a hole in the ground, and by the 1960s all the kiosks had been cruelly destroyed. And since amenities such as toilets were being phased out, there was no need to ventilate anything when this kiosk was being designed, and there are no hollow columns serving as ventilators. The space on the uptown platform that had been for toilets was taken over by a newsstand, and you can still see the "Men" and "Women" signs flanking it.

The Streets Might Have Already Been Metaphorically Paved with Gold, But . . .

56 West 10th Street, between Fifth and Sixth Avenues

This red-brick, Greek Revival row house, with its newel posts graced by wrought-iron urns, was singled out by the architectural critic Ada Louise Huxtable as an example of "early 19th-century gentility." But how genteel was it on a day-to-day basis, and why is a boot scraper an integral part of the railing?

This house was built in 1832, and West 10th Street had been cut through only a few years before. Although the streets might have already been metaphorically paved with gold, as witnessed by this genteel house, the streets in this newly created neighborhood were not paved with anything. The streets were simply dirt, dusty in the dry and muddy in the wet, making the presence of boot scrapers eminently practical. Boots, not to forget milady's slippers, had to be scraped clean of the muck, and clearly the problem was not soon resolved. As late as 1846, when Grace Church was built down the block on Broadway, the front entrance was flanked by boot scrapers.

New York in the 1830s was essentially a Medieval city. There was no fresh water delivery system; the only sources of heat in the cold were fireplaces, pot belly stoves and kitchen ovens; candles and oil lamps were about the only sources of artificial light in the gloom; and the streets were literally pigpens, with pigs rooting around and eating whatever edible they could find. There was no department of sanitation.

In the 1830s to the 1850s, the city's grandest promenade, Broadway near City Hall, had a "wretched" pavement. Charles Dickens described the "narrow ways" of Five Points as "reeking everywhere with dirt and filth." The prominent Edinburgh publisher, William Chambers, said that downtown "the mire was ankle deep in Broadway, and the more narrow business streets were barely passable." After some nasty December weather in 1854, George Templeton Strong said that Broadway was "a long canal of mud syrup."

It wasn't as if residents hadn't complained. In the early 1650s, residents of New Amsterdam's Brouwer, or Brewer, Street didn't appreciate all the dust that was raised by the horse-drawn wagons hauling kegs of beer down their street. By 1656, the street was paved with cobblestones and, because of its singularity, Brouwer Street was renamed Stone Street.

Cobblestones, the street paving of choice until the early 19th century, had their drawbacks. Carriage rides were uncomfortably bouncy, teamsters suffered breakage, and walking was uncomfortable.

New techniques by the 1830s included the use of rock cut into large rectangular slabs and laid atop a bed of smaller stones for drainage, as well as Russ paving, which consisted of major slabs of stone. The smooth surfaces, however, had horses sliding all over the place, and the grooves that were consequently cut only created a bumpy ride.

Some streets were being macadamized, constructed by compacting layers of small broken stone into a solid mass with a binder such as concrete to hold it all together. The downside was that the concrete broke under the pounding of horses and their shoes.

In 1835, a macadamized stretch of Broadway by City Hall Park was being replaced by hexagonal wood blocks with tar filling the interstices, but wood blocks posed their own peculiar problem. Nineteenth-century cities averaged roughly one horse for every 20 people, so with a human population of about 200,000 in the 1830s, there were perhaps as many as 10,000 horses on the streets. The wood absorbed the urine, and leached the smell of ammonia on hot, dry days.

The 1850s witnessed the introduction of Belgian block, granite cut into rectangles that measured about eight inches by four by four, which is still found on stretches of the Village and SoHo.

By 1876, only 299 miles of streets had been paved (21st-century Manhattan has 508 miles of paved streets). In 1884, asphalt was introduced, providing a smoother, quieter surface, with the added virtue of being more easily swept by the newly created Department of Street Cleaning. By the 20th century, boot scrapers could be declared redundant.

The Remains of the Day

11th Street, east of Sixth Avenue and west of 70 West 11th Street

This little cemetery, the *Second* Cemetery of Congregation Shearith Israel, is now in the shape of a triangle that measures about 74 by 59 by 44 feet, and it comes with a story that in many ways parallels the history of the city, with one difference—instead of growing bigger, this cemetery has become smaller. It was originally 100 feet long on a northeasterly angle.

In 1654, Congregation Shearith Israel, the nation's first Jewish congregation, was established in New Amsterdam, and a year later the congregation petitioned Governor Peter Stuyvesant and the council "to be permitted to purchase a burying place for their nation." A year later, the request was granted.

The first cemetery was established south of Oliver Street on what is now St. James Place. Shearith Israel was the only synagogue in town, and the congregation's

cemetery came to serve as the only burial ground for the city's Jewish residents. Although it was named Beth Haim, or "House of Life," it came to be called the Jews' Burying Ground.

The increase in interments citywide kept pace with the rise in the population, and by the turn of the 19th century, yellow fever epidemics began to be associated with crowded burial grounds, a problem exacerbated by a casual approach to ensuring that the dead were, literally, interred. Anticipating a prohibition on burials within the populated area, in 1805 Shearith Israel established its second cemetery here in an open field that was well north of the developed city.

The cemetery was on the west side of the now-demapped Milligan Street, which, before today's street system, followed a northeasterly course from Greenwich Avenue until it ended at the junction with the Union Road, a similarly demapped street.

The new cemetery was created six years before the street commissioners promulgated their gridiron street plan, which caused Milligan Street to disappear from the map. Property boundary lines had followed the angle of Milligan Street, which explains, in the east, the angle of the cemetery along the west wall of the neighboring apartment house at 70 West 11th Street. Some of that property had originally been the roadbed of Milligan Street.

In 1829, West 11th Street was cut through, and the balance of the cemetery is now the street. Unlike some other cemeteries, Shearith Israel's was not simply paved over, nor were the bodies cavalierly disposed of. Shearith Israel opened a new cemetery, the Third Shearith Israel Cemetery, which is still on the south side of 21st Street, just west of Sixth Avenue, and the affected graves were re-interred there. By 1851, 21st Street was considered too central to the population for good health, and burials were banned south of 86th Street. Shearith Israel gave up on Manhattan, and joined forces with two other congregations to acquire land in Ridgewood, Queens, for a new Beth Haim. May their souls be bound up in the bond of life.

4

Chelsea to the Garment Center

From 14th to 40th Streets, West of Fifth Avenue

A Different Kind of Pie

Five West 16th Street was home to Frances and James L. Breese in the 1890s, and it was the scene of two news-making soirées in that decade. One of the soirées involved both of the Breeses, one and only one.

James Breese, a graduate of Rensselaer Polytechnic, did not follow engineering as a career path. He was a member of the Wall Street brokerage firm of Breese & Smith, which allowed him time to tinker with the newfangled automobile, and to develop the carbon process of photography, which made prints as permanent as ink. Breese established the Carbon Studio in this town house. The studio was spacious, with a double height ceiling, and parquet floors.

During the 1896 Christmas season, the Breeses hosted a fancy-dress soirée in the studio, which had been decorated to simulate a Parisian café. A light supper was being served at about 1:00 a.m., when suddenly the dress of Mrs. George B. De Forest was ablaze. The flames were quickly smothered, but water could not be immediately found to extinguish the embers, so several men did the next best thing—they broke the necks of champagne bottles and poured the bubbly over Mrs. De Forest. The story made the papers the very next news day.

James Breese and his friend Stanford White, who had remodeled both the Breese town house and Southampton house, were both club men, and their favorite was the "Boys Only Club." One soirée in the studio was held on May 20, 1895, and it was a sit-down, stag dinner for thirty at $110 a head. The dinner was hosted by the Wall Street banker Henry W. Poor for his friend John Elliott Cowdin. The occasion was not simply Mr. Cowdin's birthday; it was also his tenth wedding anniversary. (Mrs. Cowdin was conveniently off in Europe.) White had told the artist Charles Dana Gibson not to let on to anyone that one event at the dinner was expected to be titillating.

The dinner followed its natural course until dessert, whereupon six waiters entered the studio bearing a very large pie. They set their burden down, and banjo players struck up "Four and Twenty Blackbirds."

Out from the pie popped sixteen-year-old Susie Johnson bearing a cage with 24 canaries in it, which were easier to come by than blackbirds. Stories differ on what Johnson was wearing. It was either a wisp of chiffon, or a necklace and a smile, or she was "covered only by the ceiling."

The story did not make the newspapers as quickly as the story on Mrs. De Forest's dress. According to Evelyn Nesbit, White's most famous companion, "Stanny managed to keep the stories out of the newspapers for a while, but despite all his efforts, the *World* published the story. Somebody must have talked."

Susie Johnson had been living in a tenement with her parents and sister at 104 Eighth Avenue, between 15th and 16th Streets, and she had been earning her keep as an artists' model. She was paid well to be the girl in the pie—she earned $50—but it cost her dearly.

The building in the foreground is Seven West 16th Street, the twin of the scaffolded Breese house at Five West 16th Street.

In an "as-told-to" story that ran in the *Evening Journal* in 1903, after the dinner Johnson found herself "the queen of the revel." White plied her with glass after glass of champagne, until, in the wee hours and in her "stupefied condition," he took her to his apartment on West 24th Street. She had trusted him when he told her all the things he could do for her, but White reneged on his promises. She tried to "live an honest life," and she married, but her husband learned of the pie affair, and "cast" her off. She tried to make a living on stage in the chorus, but her health gave way. The moral of her story: Girls, if you are poor, stay in the safe factory or kitchen. Johnson died at age 23, perhaps a suicide. She was buried in a potters' field.

The Breese town house and the Eighth Avenue tenement remain standing and serve to remind us of poor Susie Johnson. Evelyn Nesbit's image is still with us. Breese teamed up with photographer Rudolf Eiskemeyer, Jr., who in 1902 took the famous photograph, "Tired Butterfly," showing Nesbit in a kimono while lying on a bear rug. By 1914, Breese was keeping a private office and studio at 38 East 23rd Street, where in the early 21st century a first-floor restaurant served a different kind of pie—pizza.

A Bit of Movie History

305 West 21st Street, just west of Eighth Avenue

In 1902, a movie called *Un Voyage dans la Lune (A Trip to the Moon)* was released in France. Its wondrous special effects included scenes such as a rocket landing in the eye of the unfortunate man in the moon, the scene depicted in high relief in this iron gate in Chelsea.

The movie was directed by Georges Méliès, who began his career as a magician. Méliès wrote and directed his own movies, and he brought his magic to the screen in movie after movie at the beginning of the 20th century, designing countless sets as backdrops for his fantasies. His sets might even have been the inspiration for the phantasmagorical facade of La Taverne des Truands on Boulevard de Clichy in Monmartre in 1910, if Méliès didn't actually design the facade himself.

Although the movie-going public had forgotten Méliès by the mid-20th century, he was well known to the medium's cognoscenti. Film historians Richard Griffith and Arthur Mayer said that Méliès "invented or stumbled upon double exposure, stop motion, fast and slow motion, animation, fades, dissolves, almost the entire repertory of the trick film."

By the 1920s, Méliès had lost his magic touch and was reduced to peddling newspapers in the Paris streets. Friends took pity on him and bought him a little toy- and candy store to operate in the railroad station, Gare Montparnasse.

It's the story told by Brian Selznick in *The Invention of Hugo Cabret* in 2007 and reinvented in 2011 as the Oscar-winning movie *Hugo,* which featured not just bits of *A Trip to the Moon,* but Méliès, as played by Ben Kingsley.

In 1997, 95 years after the release of *A Trip to the Moon* and 14 years before *Hugo,* came this gate, which was commissioned by a group of film-savvy documentary filmmakers whose offices were at the site.

The gate was designed and executed by Warren Holzman, a blacksmith headquartered in Philadelphia. It took Holzman the better part of a year of part-time work to fabricate the gate, but investing his time in this kind of project was right up his alley. Holzman, said the *Philadelphia Weekly*, was "determined to add character and flair to an ever-evolving cityscape that seems to grow increasingly homogenized and dull." Homogenized and dull this clearly ain't.

There is, however, something off about the image. It's flopped. In the movie, the rocket lands in the right eye of the man in the moon, whereas Holzman's version has the rocket landing in his left eye. The reason was not a form of graphic dyslexia suffered by Holzman, it was intentional. Holzman chose to flop the image, because, he said, "In my youth, I thought I needed to do that to make it more unique as an object referring to the film. I'm not sure if it ever really made a difference."

Not Encouraged

The Memorial Chapel of the Good Shepherd, The General Theological Seminary, 21st Street between Ninth and Tenth Avenues

Finding a rood screen—so called because *rood* meant a cross or crucifix in Old English, and one was always atop the screen at its midpoint—is a rare event these days. They started being taken down during the Reformation to open the service more to the congregation.

New York seems to have had only four churches that contained rood screens, and all Episcopalian. The only remaining two are in Holyrood Church on Fort Washington Avenue at 179th Street, and here, at the Memorial Chapel of The Good Shepherd.

The screen at Holyrood is so diaphanous that it is almost invisible; the screen at the seminary is not. This chapel was primarily designed for the benefit of the seminarians, who sit within the chancel stalls. A student's day in the early 20th century started with 8:00 a.m. communion in the chapel. For evensong, the students would be wearing academic robes and Oxford caps, or soft mortarboards. They would be on the chancel side of the rood screen, with guests on the other side.

The chapel was built in 1889 in a late Gothic Revival style designed by Charles C. Haight, who designed the majority of today's seminary's buildings, some of Columbia's buildings when it was in Midtown, and Trinity School on West 91st Street.

The full-block property was a gift from Clement Clark Moore, who taught Hebrew at the seminary, the same Moore responsible for St. Peter's Church on 20th Street. Keeping things in perspective, Benjamin I. Haight, the father of the architect Charles Haight, just happened to have been the church's first rector.

Charles Haight had the sculpture firm Ellin & Kitson execute the woodwork for the chapel. In 1902 the *Tribune* said that American wood carving as an art had begun in New York with the arrival of Robert Ellin from England in 1857, "just in time to help in the development of our best Gothic architecture." Ellin "gathered up a corps of workmen, each an artist, trained them, kept them together and made his shop a school of art and a center of art life. . . . He was able on one hand to divine the suggestions of the architect, and on the other to put his hand on the best man to carry them out."

The seminary was one of the richest ecclesiastical institutions at the turn of the 20th century, having attracted some major financial backers in the late 19th century, along with the fortuitous blessing of being in the right place at the right time. Before landfill, there was not much land west of Tenth Avenue, and the westernmost part of the property had been the bank of the Hudson River. Dr. R. H. Randolph Ray, Class of 1911 and the minister at the Little Church Around the Corner, said that the riparian rights allowed the seminary to "realize a sizable revenue from the rentals upon it."

There had been no tuition in the 19th century, nor charges for room and board, and the dormitories were hardly dormitory style—they were two-bedroom suites, with each bedroom occupied by a single student and only a living room to share. By 1901, a $225 fee was set for board, room, coal, and gas. There were about 100 students at the time, with 28 scholarships worth $150 apiece awarded every year, which left fees of $75 a year for 28 lucky students. They probably consumed $75 worth of food in a year. Breakfast alone was something. Three days a week beefsteak was served, with a choice of baked potato (sweet or white) or baked beans and pork with corn bread. On alternate days, the seminarians had their pick of mutton chops or veal cutlets, sausages, fried liver and bacon, fried fish, griddle cakes and syrup, or just plain ham and eggs. Tuition in the 2010s was still modest, on a par with out-of-state tuition for the City College of New York.

There was also the Rev. Eugene Augustus Hoffman, the dean of the seminary from 1876 to 1902, who was called "the richest clergyman in the United States." Hoffman had inherited $10 million in real-estate holdings from a New Amsterdam ancestor on his father's side, and his mother, Glorvina Rossell Hoffman, was no stranger to real estate. In 1827, her father purchased a piece of property from Trinity Church on the southwest corner of Broadway and Warren Street. In 1850, John B. Snook designed a five-story commercial "palace" for the 50-foot frontage. By 1900, Dean Hoffman had the site developed as an eight-story building for the clothier Rogers Peet.

Hoffman's father died in 1880, his mother in 1888. His mother had voiced a desire to have a chapel built in memory of her husband, and Hoffman saw to it a year later.

On the subject of rood screens, the Episcopal Church officially says that "such divisions of the congregation have not been encouraged in modern liturgical practice, and rood screens are seldom used today." Amen?

The Western Union Building, 186 Fifth Avenue,
on the southwest corner of 23rd Street

Samuel F. B. Morse's perfection of the telegraph in the early 1840s was a boon for three industries. The financial market loved the telegraph because stocks could be bought or sold at the sound of a few dashes or dots. Rail companies loved it because they only had to lay a single-track road and still have two-way traffic. A message by telegraph could have a train heading in one direction shunted off onto a side spur at the approach of a train traveling in the other direction. And newspapers could gather the information that allowed them to get out the news stories of the day. Using the telegraph was expensive, but it was such a potential boon to journalism that in 1846 some New York newspapers

banded together to pool information on the Mexican-American War, giving birth to the Associated Press.

By 1875, Western Union was the nation's major telegraph company, and it moved into its new headquarters on Broadway at Dey Street. At eleven stories high, and topped by a clock tower atop a mansard roof, it rose to 230 feet. One hundred telegraph operators tapped away on the eighth floor, and on the ground floor were the messengers.

In 1884, when this Western Union building was built on Fifth Avenue and before the city had banned above-ground telephone and telegraph wires, Western Union was already burying its wires. It had dug a four-foot-deep trench on Broadway from its Dey Street headquarters up to 23rd Street, and in the trench were laid two five-inch iron pipes for telegraph wires, along with four pneumatic tubes, each eight inches in diameter.

For most clients, Western Union's final product was in print form, and pneumatic tubes already ran to the city's major newspaper offices, to the Stock and Cotton Exchanges, the Equitable Building, and to its own offices for the delivery of printed matter. This building was built at 23rd Street because that was the end of the Broadway line, and messengers could take the telegrams from there.

A demonstration of the efficiency of forwarding a dispatch from the Dey Street building to the Tribune Building at Nassau Street was made for one of the newspaper's reporters in 1884. A cartridge was filled, and put into a pneumatic tube. Forced air sent the dispatch on its way, followed by a short puff of air, and the brass box was empty. "It's on its way over," said the operator, "moving underground like a mole—a pretty fast one." The operator had touched an annunciator informing the *Tribune* that a dispatch would be arriving, and he said "Just about now it has passed under the Franklin statue and reached the building. . . . There! That bell is the signal showing that it has arrived." It took just 30 seconds. The day the Fifth Avenue building opened, a pouch was sent on a test run on the pneumatic tube between the headquarters and the new office. Two minutes and ten seconds.

Henry J. Hardenbergh designed the building on Fifth Avenue, which opened in 1884, the same year as his more famous Dakota Apartments. This style is described as Queen Anne, which is not a true style but covers a multitude of picturesque sins. Some say that the style is based on Elizabethan country-house architecture, or it's a blending of Tudor Gothic, English Renaissance and, in the U.S., Colonial elements. Find them if you can.

The Adventures of Koster and Bial

729 Sixth Avenue, southwest corner of 24th Street

John Koster and Albert Bial started their professional lives in the 1870s as restaurateurs and brewers, and they were innovative brewers at that. They were the first to use the newly patented rubber-and-wire stoppers on bottles, for instance, doing away with old-fashioned corks. But they hankered after higher things than a nice lager with an easy-to-open bottle top. Koster and Bial wanted the bright lights.

In 1879 they rented a former minstrel theater at 115 West 23rd Street. They ripped out all the seats on the orchestra floor and put in tables and chairs, reserving the entire orchestra floor for table service, making it perhaps the first dinner-theater establishment in the city.

In the early 1890s, Koster and Bial realized that they needed a word to describe their new bill of fare—song-and-dance routines, juggling acts, slapstick comedy,

ribald humor, and so on. *Vaudeville* described comic operettas, and they took the word and metamorphosed it to define their lighter fare.

Business boomed with the likes of Mademoiselle Arman d'Ary from the Folies Bergère, and Maudi, the Lightning Calculator, but Koster and Bial's biggest draw was the Spanish dancer Carmencita, who is immortalized in portraits by John Singer Sargent and William H. Chase.

Soon champagne corks were popping in the Cork Room that had been built under the stage and where the stage-door johnnies could cavort with the hoofers in an atmosphere decorously described as "fast." Koster and Bial also added gardens at the rear of the theater that extended to 24th Street, and with the champagne set neatly ensconced in one quarter, beer was flowing in their German-style beer hall around the corner on Sixth Avenue, which the two named, originally enough, "The Corner." The building's nameplate is about all that stands to remind us of John Koster and Albert Bial on 23rd Street.

They moved to 34th Street in 1895 to go into business with Oscar Hammerstein, and all that's left to remind us of *that* venture—where the first moving picture was shown in New York—is a plaque on the wall of Macy's.

Wit and Humor

Today's Herald Square Hotel, 19 West 31st Street, between Fifth Avenue and Broadway

The dates 1883 and 1893 flank the main floor rustication, and escutcheons bear double L monograms, and the words *Wit* and *Humor* adorn scrolls above the Barococo pediment, and a winged cupid holds a book.

This is *Life*, the original headquarters of *Life* magazine, not the *Life* magazine of Henry Luce, who only bought the name in the 1930s, but the headquarters for the puckish humor magazine of John Ames Mitchell, who created the original *Life* magazine. With the motto, "While there's Life, there's hope," Mitchell launched the first issue in 1883.

Mitchell had attended both Harvard and l'Ecole des Beaux Arts, and he hired fellow Crimsonite Edward Sandford Martin, a founder of the *Harvard Lampoon,* as his first literary editor, and Martin did well. He attracted the likes of James Whitcomb Riley and Brander Matthews.

By 1893, Mitchell had made such a success of *Life* that he had his fellow Beaux Arts alumni John Merven Carrère and Thomas Hastings design the magazine's new building. Philip Martiny, the French ex pat, was the sculptor of *Winged Life,* the cupid above the door. Cupid is there because in Mitchell's eyes, Cupid personified a cheerful guide to truths about human nature and the creative spirit, and Mitchell adopted Cupid as the magazine's mascot.

Offices occupied the lower floors of the building, with apartments upstairs for staff. The most desirable apartment was the sky-lit studio apartment on the top floor that would be briefly occupied by *Life's* star artist, Charles Dana Gibson, the creator of the Gibson Girl. The Gibson Girl represented the new American woman. She rode a bicycle and played tennis, had a classic profile and an hourglass figure, attended the opera and the theater, and was the object of every man's attention.

But Gibson didn't just draw pretty faces. Some of his illustrations were social commentary, and they had an edge to them. He did a series called "When Our Betters Rule," which depicted women as professionals—as Madam President and Madam Secretary—and he frequently mirrored the Gibson Girl's unfortunate sister who had married for money, and who, while elegantly clad and sitting at one end of a baronial table with an old geezer at the other end, dreamed of her castle in the air, a modest house with children frolicking in front.

For the model of the Gibson Boy, Gibson used the writer, Richard Harding Davis. Gibson's boys were always well turned out in tweeds or dinner jacket, they fly fished or rode to the hounds, they dined well and drank heartily, and frequently looked imploringly into the eyes of a Gibson Girl.

Gibson denied that there ever had been a single model for the Gibson Girl. She was a composite, an ideal, but one woman, a "Gibson Girl come to life," began to appear so frequently in his artwork that friends thought that they sometimes recognized her twice in the same drawing. The model was his bride, Irene Langhorne, a southern belle. Among the ushers at their Richmond wedding in 1895 were Thomas Hastings and Richard Harding Davis; among the guests were Mr. and Mrs. Stanford White and James L. Breese.

The new Mr. and Mrs. Gibson moved into the Life Building's desirable top-floor apartment. This had Mitchell laughing to himself every time the competition paid a visit to his turf to make a pitch for Gibson to do a job, but Mitchell's schadenfreude was short lived. The Gibsons had a baby girl in 1897, and moved out.

Mitchell's stable of artists included James Montgomery Flagg, J. C. Leyendecker, and Norman Rockwell, and *Life* loomed large for all of them. On the title page of Fairfax Downey's biography of Gibson, for instance, is a Gibson Girl with a winged cupid sitting in front of her. She is smiling demurely into the eyes of the viewer. Copyright, Life Publishing Company.

Why the Martinique? Why Not the St. Jacques?

49 West 32nd Street, or 1260 Broadway, on the northeast corner

T he Martinique, designed by Henry J. Hardenbergh and opened in 1898, is emblazoned by scallop shells. Hotel developers in the late 19th and early 20th centuries frequently practiced niche marketing, and perhaps the scallop shells were a subtle form of niche marketing, carrying with them a hint of coquilles St. Jacques, accompanied by a dining room that specialized in Continental cuisine at a time when a more rarefied cuisine was gaining popularity with the haut bourgeoisie.

Niche marketing extended to developers giving hotels ethnic names in the hope of attracting certain nationalities. There were already the St. Denis, the Martin (as in Remy Martin) and Français, all designed to attract a French clientele; the Español appealed to a Spanish-speaking clientele; and the Brunswick, Clarendon, and Westminster were lures for English visitors. Niche marketing even extended to gender-specific names to attract certain sexes, such as the Martha Washington, a hotel for women.

Marketing, niche or otherwise, had nothing to do with naming this hotel for the French-speaking colony in the West Indies, however. The Martinique was built and operated by William R. H. Martin, who liked to work his name into his projects, perhaps the result of his *not* having his name on his primary source of income—Rogers Peet, the men's clothing shops that he had inherited. By the 1890s, Martin was amusing himself with the proceeds, investing in real estate and playing the role of philanthropist, all the while playing with variations on his name and his wife's, Elizabeth E. Trowbridge. One of his projects was the Trowmart Inn, at Hudson and West 12th Streets, which he established for low-waged working women, much like the Mills Houses. There was the Marbridge, an office building at 1328 Sixth Avenue, today's 2 Herald Square. And then there was the Hotel Martinique. Marbridge, Trowmart, Martinique, it all fits.

A Not Very Obvious Bennett Mystery

Minerva and the Bell Ringers, Herald Square, the juncture of Broadway and Sixth Avenue at 35th Street

This sculpture group, which now serves as a memorial to the newspaper publisher James Gordon Bennett, is the best known of the two Bennett mysteries, although it is hardly the most obvious. The bell ringers, who were dubbed Stuff and Guff, seriously swing away at the bell every hour on the hour, just as the statue of the pair of Moors swing away at the bell atop the clock tower on Piazza San Marco.

As James Morris wrote of the bell ringers in Venice, "after all their centuries of hammering, they have made only a modest indentation in the surface of the bell."

Here you see absolutely no evidence of wear, modest or otherwise, despite the fact that, with some time off, this bell has theoretically been wacked by one or the other of the bell ringers every hour on the hour since 1894.

The difference is that the bell ringers in Venice actually hit the bell. These bell ringers do not. Stuff and Guff pull their mallets short by about three inches. A cunningly designed box aligned to the edge of the bell accommodates the clapper that actually hits the bell.

The sculpture group originally stood just north of where it stands now, atop the two-story Herald Building. The building stood from 1894 until 1921, and the statuary group looked down on this very site from the 35th Street facade.

The building was commissioned by James Gordon Bennett, Jr., as the home for *The New York Herald*, the newspaper that his father had established and that Bennett the younger took over in 1867 at the age of twenty-six. Bennett well knew the work of McKim, Mead & White by the 1890s, and he hired Stanford White to design the newspaper's new headquarters.

The Herald Building's inspiration was the Palazzo del Consiglio in Verona, a two-story building that has statues on the roofline. The primary difference between the two was the choice of subjects for the statues. The Consiglio has people; the Herald Building had owls, lots of them.

On each of the four corners of the building was an owl whose wings were extended and whose eyes—which were electric lights—flashed the hours. (Two of those owls were salvaged and now stand atop the cenotaph.) There were also owls at rest. The narrow 35th Street facade had only two of them, but the Sixth Avenue facade sported eight of them, with a commensurate number on the other facades. It was as if the senior Bennett had decreed it.

Bennett the younger, the product of a broken home, had grown up living the life of a privileged child in France with his mother. His father wanted him to take over the newspaper, so when the 26-year-old returned to New York, Bennett Senior made him editor. Young Bennett, however, would leave the newspaper office before press time and go gallivanting, and his father did not approve. "Young man, your future career depends upon night work and eternal vigilance," said his father. "The owl—the bird of Minerva—should be your fetish.'"

The younger Bennett put in his time, but in his later years he stayed as far away from the daily grind as possible, communicating with the office by cable. Although he had several residences on the East Coast, his choice of residence in New York was the Union Club, and although he liked Newport and New York society well enough, he was most content in France, where he spent at least as much time as he did stateside. Bennett commissioned the French sculptor, Antonin Jean Paul Carles, to design this sculpture group. Carles had had won the grand prize for sculpture at the 1889 Paris Exposition, the exposition that featured the Eiffel Tower. The exposition attracted about 30 million visitors, among them, Bennett, who had established the Paris edition of the *Herald* in 1887.

Minerva might be the dominating figure in the ensemble, but it is best known for the mallet-bearing bell ringers, whose garb was certainly appropriate for statuary sponsored by a newspaperman. Workers in compositors' rooms in the 1890s usually wore aprons and frequently wore caps, so the bell ringers are in all likelihood moonlighting typesetters. One should never let an opportunity slip away to plug the product, even subliminally.

When the Herald Building gave up the ghost in 1921, the sculpture group was salvaged and presented to NYU, which in turn made a permanent loan of the group to the Department of Parks. The statuary group was placed here in 1940, with the Aymar Embury–designed cenotaph as its shelter. A greater mystery than how the bells are struck is on the rear of the memorial.

The Great Bennett Mystery

In the rear of the Bennett Memorial, Herald Square,
juncture of Broadway and Sixth Avenue at 35th Street

The best kept but most obvious secret of the Bennett Memorial is behind the memorial itself. Embedded in the door is a bronze plaque showing an owl seated on a sliver of a moon, with the phrase "La Nuit Porte Conseil." To the average student of French toting a French-English dictionary, the literal translation is "Night Bears, or Carries, Advice or Counsel." However, "La Nuit Porte Conseil" is an idiom, and if you are about to make a monumental decision, the smart thing to do before taking the plunge is to sleep on it, and that's what "La Nuit Porte Conseil" means—sleep on it.

Nobody seems sure how the plaque came to be, but one of James Gordon Bennett, Jr.'s more cockamamie plans was a memorial to himself that he planned at the turn of the 20th century. Unlike the existing Bennett Memorial, which was of fairly modest proportions, the memorial he was considering was more on a par with his outsized ego. You can forget little statues of owls. His memorial to himself was to have been a doozie. It would have been one giant—one gigantic—owl.

Bennett Junior had an estate in Washington Heights that stretched between 181st and 187th Streets from Broadway west a few blocks (think of Bennett Avenue and Bennett Park). The owl statue was to have been hollow and about 125 feet high (only about 26 feet shorter than the Statue of Liberty) and it would stand on a pedestal of about 75 feet, making the entire structure about 200 feet high. No less than the architect Stanford White was to have been in charge of the design.

The statue would have faced south, and it would have been open to the public. "A circular staircase was to ascend from the bottom of the pedestal" to a viewing area, reported the *Times,* where the owl's eyes would have been "windows looking out over New York City." No doubt the memorial would have been erected in or close to today's Bennett Park, which, at 265 feet above sea level, is Manhattan's highest natural point. From that spot, the view would have been over 450 feet above sea level, and the view of the city to the south in the early 1900s would have been unobstructed.

And here's the kicker. Upon his death, Bennett wanted his coffin suspended by two steel chains hanging from within the top of the owl's cranium so that the memorial would become his tomb. Visitors could still take the spiral staircase to the top for the view, since the staircase would have been designed to accommodate the coffin, with the stairs negotiating their way around it.

The combination memorial-tomb never was built, but the whole owl fetish that had been inculcated in Bennett Junior by his father seemed perfectly appropriate for a newspaperman.

Reporters and editors were notorious "night owls," and owls, the avian symbol of Minerva, symbolize wisdom, which newspaper publishers should have in abundance. Bennett did know how to sell newspapers, and he would frequently create stories to sell more newspapers by sending off reporters to faraway places like Africa in search of Livingstone, but wisdom is something that Bennett generally lacked.

Bennett was a party boy and roué. One of his predilections was to take night-time drives in his four-in-hand carriage around Newport or Manhattan or even the Champs Élysées in a state of *deshabillé*. Another of his amusements was to play puerile practical jokes on fellow diners in restaurants by pulling tablecloths off tables and having everything clatter to the floor, or worse, into the diners' laps. He paid for the mayhem he created, all the while having a good laugh at the expense of others.

Bennett was particularly fond of New Year's Eve, and one of his ways of celebrating was to have Stuff and Guff "hitting" the bell atop the Herald Building for five minutes beginning at midnight to announce the New Year. One celebratory New Year's Eve had him so drunk at his then-fiancée's house that he mistook the fireplace for a urinal and proceeded to use it as such. The engagement was short-lived.

For Bennett, night hardly bore or carried advice or counsel.

Art Bicko

488 Eighth Avenue, between 34th and 35th Streets

Bickford's is an almost totally forgotten chain of lunchrooms in New York that numbered about 25 outlets when this Bickford's was built in 1930, and the name of the architect, F. Russell Stuckert, is even less remembered, although he designed this building and the majority of the buildings that housed the Bickford restaurants.

When you do find mention of Stuckert, the words are less than glowing. There was a Bickford's on the northeast corner of Lexington Avenue and 45th Street that was built in 1932, and one architectural historian said it had been "designed by an architect named Stuckert" and it "represents the Art Deco at its most modest, both in stature and quality." The three-story building still stands, but it has been stripped of its "modest" Art Deco skin and given a glass facade that could be any Modern building, Anywhere, U.S.A.

This Bickford's on Eighth Avenue escaped the fate of its Lexington Avenue brother, and although it might be modest in stature, it is hardly modest in quality. True to Webster's second definition of "flamboyant," it is "marked by or given to strikingly elaborate or colorful display." The *Times* described the facade as "trim and tidy in white terra-cotta, [with Bickford's] distinctive script logo in a stepped entablature over a field of Art Deco chevrons."

We probably wouldn't be seeing this wonderful facade today if it hadn't been for the sexification of the neighborhood beginning in the 1960s, followed by the de-sexification of the neighborhood 30-or-so years later. By the 1960s, when the attraction of Bickford's had begun to fade, the strip along Eighth Avenue between 34th and 50th Streets began to be filled with "adult" bookstores and peep shows.

The Bickford's on this site went out of business, and an "adult" bookstore moved in, which represented a bit of good fortune in its own skewed fashion. The bookstore management was doing things on the cheap, and it was only willing to "improve" the lower part of the facade, so up went a huge sign advertising an "Adult Entertainment Center" that covered the upper part of the glorious Art Deco facade, which maintained its purity behind the sign.

By the 1990s there was a municipal initiative to clean up the area through revised zoning laws, and in the summer of 2000 the bookstore went out of business. Down came the sign to reveal this long-forgotten gem.

Some Freight Entrance

The Fashion Tower, 135 West 36th Street, between Broadway and Seventh Avenue

You wouldn't expect to find a polychromatic terra-cotta panel with a peacock motif—the very symbol of elegance and allure—atop something as mundane as a freight entrance, but the Fashion Tower was designed to house showrooms for the wholesale garment trade. If Clara Bow was the "It Girl," the Fashion Tower was the "It Building."

The front entrance, through which buyers would stream, originally had a panel just like the one above the freight entrance when the building opened in 1925, and in all likelihood the original intent was to create just one panel to decorate the main entrance and it alone. The thing is, once you have gone to all the trouble and expense of creating a mold for a terra-cotta panel, you might as well use it again. With the addition of the word *Freight,* this panel appeared.

Many of the commercial loft buildings in the Garment Center are elegant—elegance, after all, was the stock in trade of the tenants—and some of the best architects designed the buildings. The Fashion Tower's architect was Emery Roth, who already had some splendid buildings to his credit such as the Belleclaire on Broadway at 77th Street and Bancroft Hall on West 121st Street, and his attention to detail in the 1925 building is indicative of the quality of his work.

The building was "improved" in the post-war period in a style more Emery Roth & Sons than Emery Roth Senior, and all the elegance of the entrance was stripped away, replaced by a bland, "modern" entrance. Blessedly, the "improvement" has been improved again, this time with a recreation of the original.

It's odd that a delivery entrance would be sharing the same street front with the main entrance and not be sequestered and out of sight in the rear, but this is Manhattan, and the street plan has no true service facilities for loading and unloading—no back alleys—and the opportunities to buy property through the block to create a true service area are few. The average freight entrance was incorporated in the building's frontage, and the trucks had to be loaded and unloaded curbside.

The Garment District, today's Fashion District, did not spring up naturally. With Seventh Avenue its main north-south artery, most of the side streets flanking it between 35th and 40th Streets were designed specifically for the trade. There was nothing evolutionary about it.

The garment industry was primarily operated by Eastern European Jews, and the fact that loft buildings housing the needle trade were moving north on Fifth Avenue by the 1910s was anathema to the retailers who wanted to keep Fifth Avenue retail. They complained that thousands of garment workers streamed into and out of the loft buildings, that they clogged the sidewalks at the beginning and end of every working day and swarmed the avenue during lunch hours. The merchants began a public relations blitz aimed at putting a stop to the northward march. A story fabricated for the press claimed that out-of-town buyers were finding it increasingly inconvenient to cover the territory as it was, and concentration was the key. They told the garment manufacturers that concentrating in a definite locality would reduce overhead charges, and the threat was more than psychological extortion. The merchants had convinced major lending institutions not to issue loans to loft-building developers in the Fifth Avenue district north of 23rd Street. The manufacture and sale of the products of the garment industry could be somewhere else, anywhere else, but not on Fifth Avenue, and so, through some diabolical maneuvering, the Garment Center was born.

The special Garment Center zone was created in the early 1920s, which allowed for taller buildings than the norm. The Fashion Tower is seventeen stories high, and it faces the average 60-foot-wide side street. Assuming ten feet per floor, the height adds up to 170 feet. Even in the rare zone in which a 1916 zoning law allowed a building to rise two and a half times the width of the street it faced, the building could only have been fifteen stories, or 150 feet on this site.

With the establishment of the Garment Center, one would have found a whole spread in the *Times* devoted to the industry, with lists of buyers seeking coats and dresses, silks and woolens, and with offerings including blouses, skirts, rayons, and sportswear. And the addresses all seemed to be on or off Seventh Avenue between 35th and 40th Streets.

You would have seen ads for dealers specifically in the Fashion Tower. "Wholesale Only! Short Sleeve Dresses are the rage! Pagoda Crepe the fabric produced in the best-known mill in America! Gorgeously Styled! Superbly Made! The swiftest seller you've seen this season! Regent Waist and Dress Co., Inc."

Or this ad for the Parismaid (yes, Parismaid) Dress Company for "Dresses of Flock Dots on Heavy Silk. Genuine Velveray Process. Not a printed dot, but a genuine Flock Dot made by prominent Silk Mill."

And along with the address, "The Fashion Tower."

Poor Little Rich Girls

In a niche in the HSBC Tower, 452 Fifth Avenue, between 39th and 40th Streets

This plaque, dating from 1935, tells us that two Wendel sisters presented the property on the site to Drew University. What the tablet does not reveal are the circumstances under which the sisters had lived.

The Wendels were Astors by marriage, and the family had lots of money tied up in New York real estate. There were six sisters and one brother in the third generation of Wendels, but they insulated themselves. They summered together in Irvington or Quogue, and if trips were taken abroad, they were taken in family groups, and if they attended an occasional opera, they sat huddled together. The sisters seldom ventured into society individually, although their brother would.

The brother, John Gottlieb Wendel, had several phobias. He believed that dyed wool was a skin irritant, so his tailor could only order Scottish wool that came naturally in his favorite colors. He also believed that disease would pass through the soles of his shoes from the pavement, so he had his cobbler custom make shoes with one-inch-thick soles to ward off the evils.

By the early 20th century, the Wendels were a dying breed, in part because of another of the brother's phobias. Sharing the philosophy of Dr. Sloper in Henry James' *Washington Square*, Wendel feared that any suitor of one of his sisters would have been interested only in her money, and he convinced his sisters to reject any amorous overture that might be made. All the sisters but one abided

by his wishes. In 1903, at age 61, Rebecca Wendel married Luther Swope and moved out, but she remained faithful to the family in her way. She managed the Wendel landholdings for her generation, holding firm to Astor rules: Never sell any property, never mortgage anything, remember that Broadway moves north ten blocks every decade, and tenants make their own repairs.

Another sister, Georgianna, rebelled enough to leave home and go to live in a hotel, whereupon brother Wendel arranged to have her committed. Rather than spend the rest of her life in an asylum, she returned to the bosom of the family.

John Wendel died in 1914, and one by one the remaining sisters died, their virtues unsullied. By 1930, the Wendels' four-story house, which had been built in 1856 with a stable and a fenced-in yard, was the last major residential building on Fifth Avenue between 34th and 42nd Streets. Ella Wendel was the last of the Wendels living in the house, and the last of the Astors in the neighborhood. The rest of the Astor clan had moved uptown decades before. There was no mystery why the house had been dubbed the "mystery house."

Only once since 1915 had the front door been unbolted, and then only because an ambulance had been summoned for an employee. The wash was still done by hand in the basement, and hung out to dry in the backyard. The house had never been wired for electricity and was lighted by candles and sputtering gas jets. No telephone had ever been installed, and certainly no 78 had ever played on a phonograph.

For more than 20 years, Ella Wendel lived alone in the house with her staff. The house was clean and well maintained, but the drapes were always pulled. A dog was Ella's only true companion. In her later years, she never appeared in public, and anyone who called upon the house was informed by a servant that nobody was at home. As the Astor biographer Harvey O'Connor said, she and her sisters had been "cheated of life, paralyzed by Midas."

Ella Wendel died in 1931, and estimates of the family's wealth varied wildly, some as high as $100 million plus.

Ella is given equal billing as the donor of the property to Drew University, but it hadn't been her idea. It was Rebecca who in her will had wished to make the gift to Drew, but the family way was for individual wishes to be subordinated to members of the family in order to keep the estate intact. If there was one Wendel still standing, everything was passed to that one. Ella came into the entire family fortune, and it was Ella who honored her sister's wish by having the bequest to Drew become a reality.

The property had been long sought by real-estate interests as a site for high-end retailing. Fifth Avenue neighbors already included Lord & Taylor, Tiffany, Gorham, and Arnold Constable. Drew leased the site to S. H. Kress, and Kress put up a nine-story building, the "finest unit in the Kress chain."

Kress was the first merchant to recognize that the Fifth Avenue double-decker buses had created a new audience for their windows, and Kress inaugurated show windows on the second floor. It is that Kress that is depicted in the panels flanking the tablet.

The Kress building was designed by Edward F. Sibbert, the in-house architect responsible for the design of about 50 of the chain's stores nationwide. Many of Sibbert's designs were in the chic style of the 1930s, frequently with Mayan touches and geometric patterning, which makes you wonder whether Sibbert might also have designed this tablet. It had originally adorned the store's northern door on Fifth Avenue.

The lease, which was deemed modest, allowed Drew to draw at least $50,000 a year from the property. A professor in 1935 might have been making $3,500 a year, so that's a few faculty posts.

By the late 1970s, the Kress store on the site had closed. In 1983, the Republic National Bank, whose offices were next door in the landmark Knox Building on 40th Street, decided to expand southward, and the tablet was installed in a niche close to where it had originally been.

This tablet is a sad reminder of the poor little rich girls and their controlling brother who had once lived on the site.

5

Union Square to Murray Hill

From 14th to 40th Streets, East of Fifth Avenue

One Man's Heroes

15 Gramercy Park South, 20th Street between Irving Place
and Park Avenue South, today's National Arts Club

This is not your average late-19th-century New York home. This was the home of Samuel J. Tilden, a lawyer (Yale and NYU), politician, and bibliophile, aspects of Tilden's personality that explain the portrait busts of Shakespeare, Milton, Dante, Goethe, and Benjamin Franklin on the facade.

By the time this house was being remodeled in the mid-1870s, Tilden was one of the nation's most famous personages. He had taken on the Tweed Ring, the entrenched political gang that was looting the city treasury of millions, and won. He ran for the governorship of New York State in 1874, and won. Two years later he was the Democratic Party's standard bearer in the presidential election. He lost. If you say that politics in the early 21st century had a sense of *déjà vu* you'd be onto something vis-à-vis the 1876 election. Tilden won the popular vote but lost the electoral college, and the state that Tilden needed in his win column was Florida. One political party simpy outspent the other. Tilden graciously retired to private life, spending time at his estate on the Hudson, and remodeling this house.

Tilden's house is really two houses, and the originals were brownstone with the drip moldings associated with Gothic Revival houses, much like upper floors of the neighboring house east of it.

Tilden bought the first house in the 1860s, and he had the interiors redone. About ten years later, after the purchase of the adjoining house, he had the fronts of both houses removed and rebuilt—the two most prominent features are the semi-hexagonal and semi-rectangular bays that run from the ground to the third story—and he had the interiors reconfigured to make one sprawling spread.

The style of the remodeling job is sort of a mélange of Gothic and Renaissance, or, if you choose, Victorian Gothic or Eastlake. The architect was Calvert Vaux, the same Vaux who, with Frederick Clarke Withers, designed the idiosyncratic Jefferson Market Courthouse on Sixth Avenue at 10th Street, the same Vaux who partnered with Frederick Law Olmsted to design Central Park. The idea for the statuary—a synthesis of Tilden's interests—was said to be his.

As reported in the 1883 edition of *Artistic Houses*, Vaux "seems to have said to himself, 'Persons who walk in front of the Governor's house will naturally turn their eyes toward it, and, in order that they may not feel that they are impertinently staring into the windows, I will put before them some pieces of statuary which will invite consideration, and will justify it.'" Forty artisans were employed in the carving of the facade for several months, and the five heads were carved by the English-émigré sculptor Samuel J. Kitson, the brother of John William Kitson, of Ellin & Kitson.

The interiors were sumptuous. Tilden's dining room was "lined with carved satin wood and blue tiles, and lighted by a massive chandelier designed by Calvert

Vaux, in harmony with the general spirit of the decorations," reported *Harper's Weekly.* The great stained-glass artist John LaFarge did some back-lit windows, and Kitson did some of the interior woodwork.

The library consisted of three large rooms, and Tilden had practically every work of importance on political, social, and historical subjects, including the most beautiful illustrated books. For the design of the head of Milton, for instance, Kitson had access to Tilden's collection of thousands of plates of Milton and his works.

A back-lit, stained-glass dome was installed in the ceiling of the room overlooking the park. This "reading light" was the product of Donald MacDonald of Boston, and a light shaft provided natural light by day, with gas jets illuminating it at night. (The light shaft has since been closed, and the stained glass backlit by electricity.) Estimates on the cost of the house and furnishings ranged from $400,000 to $600,000. To put things in perspective, in 1884 the average brownstone row house was selling in the range of $12,000 to $15,000.

Tilden died in 1886, soon after his Gramercy Park house had been finished, and true to his lawyerly nature, his will was explicit and filled with details, yet wide discretion was left to his executors and trustees, John Bigelow, Andrew Haswell Green, and G. W. Smith. Bigelow and Green had been friends of long standing, and Smith had been his private secretary for 20 years.

The feature that made the will so remarkable was that about four-fifths of Tilden's $5 million fortune was to be applied to public purposes, and the first thing the executors were to do was to establish the Tilden Trust. Three public libraries were to be established, with the largest of them in New York City. The Gramercy Park house could be used to house the library, but the major drawback was that it was not fireproof. The property could be sold, with the proceeds of the sale deposited with the trust. Tilden's books, art treasures, and other articles would be used to supply any or all of the libraries, at the discretion of the trustees.

The will set aside money for relatives, who were to receive the income from about $1 million for life. It was clearly stipulated that upon the pensioner's death, the annuity was to be passed to the Tilden Trust, and that the relatives were to have no say regarding any part of the property. It was all up to the trustees.

It took all of 24 hours after the reading of the will before rumors started circulating that the legatees would see the estate in court. By 1892 there were only $2 million left for the library, not enough for a comprehensive library. The trustees began to consider merging the Tilden Trust with other libraries to create a great public library supported by private contributions. The Lenox and Astor Libraries agreed, and trustee Andrew Haswell Green paved the way by arranging for a bill that allowed the consolidation. Trustee John Bigelow then struck a deal with the city that if the city provided a building, the private institutions would provide the books. The result was the Main Branch of the New York Public Library on Fifth Avenue between 40th and 42nd Streets. There, emblazoned in the cornice and along with the names Astor and Lenox, is "The Tilden Trust," and you can still read books stamped "Tilden Trust" within.

Ruggles of Gramercy Park

Gramercy Park West, between 20th and 21st Streets

This plaque, dating from 1875, is probably the most venerable of all the plaques in Manhattan's sidewalks. It commemorates Samuel B. Ruggles, whose brainchild was Gramercy Park.

Ruggles was born in 1800, and at 12, when later generations of 12-year-olds might have been regarding *I Love Lucy* as high intellectual fare, Ruggles was already at Yale. He graduated at 14 with distinguished honors, and set out to study the law. At 21, he was admitted to the New York City Bar.

A year later, Ruggles married well. Mary Rathbone was well educated—she had attended the Moravian Seminary in Bethlehem, Pennsylvania—and she was a daughter of John Rathbone, a merchant who in 1799 was wise enough to invest in Aaron Burr's Manhattan Company, later to become the Chase Manhattan Bank.

Over the coming years, Ruggles had his fingers in many pies. He was a commissioner and later president of the Erie Canal Board; he served in the state assembly; he was a delegate to various conferences, such as the International Monetary Conference in Paris and the International Statistical Conference at The Hague; he was a prominent member of the New York Chamber of Commerce, and; he was a trustee of the Astor Library, where he served with the likes of Washington Irving. With all the encomiums at Ruggles's death in 1881, "the obituaries said a great deal about his genius for statistics, but nothing concerning his love for, and knowledge of, general literature," said one literary journal.

What Ruggles should probably be most remembered for is that he was a city planner before city planning was.

In the early 1830s, Ruggles bought the Gramercy Farm, which roughly stretched from today's Second Avenue to Broadway, from 19th to 23rd Streets, and he set about improving not just his property, but the urban fabric.

Inspired by St. John's Park, which the Trinity Corporation had developed, he established a small square and sold off plots around it. Like St. John's Park, his little park would be private, open only to the lucky few who owned the property on the periphery of the park. They would have the keys to the gates and the kingdom within.

In an early manifestation of zoning and similar to later developments such as Murray Hill, there was a covenant. With the exception of houses of worship, the area was to be strictly residential. There could be no commerce, no stables, only "dwelling houses" of brick or stone, and a minimum of three stories high. Property owners would be dunned an annual charge for the upkeep and maintenance of the private park, but Ruggles had finagled a deal with the city that made the private park tax exempt. He had argued that the park was an amenity that raised the value of the surrounding lots, hence property taxes were increased, all to the benefit of the city treasury. Then there was the fact that the vernal oasis was a benefit to all, if only from a distance.

Ruggles understood the benefits of small open spaces, and he didn't appreciate that the street commissioners of 1811 had pooh-poohed "supposed improvements" such as circles and ovals, especially since the commissioners acknowledged that so few vacant spaces had been "left, and those so small, for the benefit of fresh air, and consequent preservation of health."

Ruggles wrote about how the commissioners' straight streets would meet up with the old city's crooked streets, often making "curious work with the old lines," leaving "here and there some most oddly shaped fragments, which the commissioners, by an allowable figure of speech, spoke of as the 'Children of Necessity.'" Union Square, for instance, had been created by the "union" of the Albany Post Road (Broadway) and the Boston Post Road (the Bowery, in its original configuration), and it was one of those "Children of Necessity."

In 1830, Ruggles petitioned the Common Council to enlarge the space that would become Union Square, and, more than 15 years later, he was advocating the creation of Madison Square from the rump end of the commissioners' largest planned parkland, the Parade.

Another failing of the 1811 gridiron plan in Ruggles's eyes was that some east-west blocks were 920 feet long. If you were midblock on one of those streets and you wanted to find yourself midblock one street away, you had to walk 460 feet to reach the corner of the avenue, walk 200 feet to the next crosstown street, then another 460 feet to reach your destination. That's 1,120 feet, to travel 200. His idea combined altruism with pragmatism. By cutting through a new north-south avenue and sacrificing that much property, in addition to the benefit of the mobility that comes with it, with a new avenue came four new corner lots per old block, as well as four new mid-block lots. The most valuable lots are corner lots, the second most valuable are mid-block.

Ruggles wound up advocating the creation of two new north-south avenues: one between Third and Fourth Avenues beginning at 14th Street, the second between Fourth and Fifth Avenues beginning at 23rd Street. For the six-block stretch between Third and Fourth Avenues from 14th to 20th Streets, he honored his friend, Washington Irving. The avenue north of Gramercy Park he dubbed Lexington Avenue in honor of the first major skirmish of the Revolution. Madison Square and Madison Avenue were named for the recently deceased President James Madison. The two new avenues were not the standard 100-foot width (they were 75 feet wide as far north as 42nd Street) and neither of the new avenues perfectly straddled their flanking avenues.

Sales on his Gramercy Park lots lagged because of financial uncertainties until the 1840s, but by the 1850s the periphery of Gramercy Park was almost completely developed, and Gramercy Park quickly developed into an epicenter of intellectual, political, and technological leadership.

Living on the park were the likes of James Harper, the Harper of Harper & Row and a former mayor; Cyrus Field of Atlantic Cable fame; the great tragedian Edwin Booth, whose statue adorns the center of the park; the architect Stanford White and his wife, Bessie; Mary and James W. Pinchot, the parents of Gifford Pinchot, the chief of the U.S. Forest Service under Teddy Roosevelt, and she, the daughter of Amos R. Eno, who built the Fifth Avenue Hotel, and; Samuel J. Tilden.

One of the early residents was the Columbia-trained lawyer George Templeton Strong, who is most remembered for having written one of the city's greatest diaries. Strong's father presented the house on Gramercy Park to his son and daughter-in-law after their wedding at Grace Church in 1848. Young Strong had early thought about settling on Gramercy Park, and the fact of his marriage might have had something to do with his predilection. The future Mrs. Strong was Ellen Ruggles, the only daughter of Mr. and Mrs. Charles Ruggles.

Curiously missing from the list of notables living on Gramercy Park were the senior Ruggles themselves. They lived on Union Square.

Is That You, Seward?

Southwest corner of Madison Square, Fifth Avenue and 23rd Street

William H. Seward, an upstate New Yorker who served as both governor and U.S. senator, is perhaps best known for having served as Abraham Lincoln's Secretary of State and for his purchase of Alaska in 1867. He was not known for his height.

Seward died in 1872, and by 1876 a statue in his likeness had been created and installed in Madison Square. In accepting the statue on behalf of the city, Mayor William H. Wickham graciously said that Seward's "face and figure are

in this monument so perfectly reproduced," and therein lies an unresolved tale. Seward as depicted in this statue is a fairly tall, lean man. He was not pudgy, but at five feet six inches, he was hardly tall.

From the outset, there had been comments about the height of Seward as portrayed by the sculptor Randolph Rogers. D. Appleton & Co. published a commemorative brochure on the statue, and the text tried to explain away the discrepancy by saying that "in a figure of colossal proportions it is difficult to indicate stature." The reality was that "future generations, judging only from this monument, may suppose that Mr. Seward was a tall, imposing-looking gentleman; the legs and arms are certainly too long for the body."

The *Times* had not been very kind about the statue even in Rogers's obituary in 1892. The *Times* said that Rogers's "Columbus" doors in the Capitol in

Washington, D.C., had been his best performance. "New York does not remember him with so much gratitude. His seated statue of William H. Seward . . . has not even the merit of a good likeness."

By 1904, a letter writer to the *Times*, whose *nom de plume* was "Artist," fired an early salvo. "Possibly few persons who see the combination statue of Seward in Madison Square know what or whom it represents. . . . The body is that of the Lincoln statue in Fairmount Park, Philadelphia, with Seward's head upon it. The statues were both by the same sculptor, the late Randolph Rogers. The Fairmount statue was made first. Then when the Seward statue was called for, it was a great saving of time and labor to decapitate the Lincoln model and place the head of Seward on it. I know whereof I speak."

Perhaps "Artist" did not completely know whereof he or she spoke—the Seward statue is not a clone of the Lincoln statue—but something was amiss.

Variations on the theme of self-plagiarism continued. Josiah C. Pumpelly claimed that the Seward monument committee had asked Rogers to lower his price, which Rogers declined, although he did "offer to make a patchwork of the statue at a lower figure by attaching the head of Seward to a statue of Lincoln." The statue was not the one in Philadelphia, but one that had been left on Randolph's hands "by a defaulting Western city." Pumpelly's version has some credibility, although the "defaulting Western city" goes unnamed.

Then came a letter from Hopper Striker Mott, who said that he had tracked down Frederick W. Seward, the statesman's son. The Lincoln story was "unfounded and absurd," said the young Seward, who cited as proof the commemorative volume published by D. Appleton & Co., which provided "a detailed description and history of the statue." In general, the Appleton publication reads like a public relations puff piece.

The argument would be settled, in part, if the "paper" on Seward's lap had words on it, but it is a *tabula rasa*.

The motivating force behind the creation of the statue was Richard Schell, a Wall Street swashbuckler who made and lost fortunes with equal ease and aplomb. He had become a friend and adviser of Seward, even serving as an unofficial lobbyist, raising $6,000 for the defense fund of President Andrew Johnson during the president's impeachment hearings.

Schell held the first meeting of the Seward committee at his home at 22 West 21st Street in 1873, a year after Seward's death. On the committee were the landscape architect Frederick Law Olmsted, future-President Chester A. Arthur, future-Mayor Abram S. Hewitt, and the publisher William H. Appleton, the same Appleton whose publication the younger Seward cited as proof against the allegations leveled against the statue.

Randolph Rogers himself was also, surprisingly, at this preliminary meeting, and he already had several designs and drawings with him. Seward had believed in Rogers' talent, and had sponsored a study trip to Rome for Rogers from 1848 to 1850. Rogers then opened a studio in New York City, only to return to Rome in 1855 to become a permanent member of the American colony. It seems that the New York art-buying public was not particularly partial to local artists locally, but

American artists living abroad had panache. Schell had unilaterally determined that Rogers was to be the sculptor.

Contributions for the statue came in from the likes of President Ulysses S. Grant, General William Tecumseh Sherman, the restaurateurs Charles and Lorenzo Delmonico (Seward was a "devotee" of their establishment), and five Appletons, Daniel, George, John, William H. and William W.

Price had no doubt been an issue in private. The cost of the Lincoln statue is estimated to have been as high as $33,000, but Rogers was paid only $25,000 for the Seward statue. Although the Lincoln statue itself is smaller, it cost more, and the likelihood that the difference was made up by its larger pedestal is slim.

If Rogers did plop the head of Seward atop the Lincoln statue that he had prepared for the "defaulting Western city," Rogers was not above a similar kind of sleight of hand. The lunette panel on the bronze doors at the U.S. Capitol that the *Times* liked is blandly described as portraying Columbus's landing. If the scene is familiar, it is because the panel is based on John Vanderlyn's painting, *Landing of Columbus*, which hangs in the Capitol's rotunda. Maybe Josiah C. Pumpelly was on to something.

Bigger than Big Ben

The clock faces on Metropolitan Life Tower, the southeast corner of Madison Avenue and 24th Street

Sometimes some very large things in Manhattan seem small and don't receive the attention that would be paid to a comparable object in another city.

Think of Big Ben in London. Granted, Big Ben itself is not a clock, it is a bell, and at 13-plus tons it is a very big bell indeed. However when people visualize Big Ben they don't visualize a big bell, they see a big clock face, or a big clock face on each of the four sides of a bell tower. Those clock faces, officially called the Great Westminster Clock, are a symbol not just of London, but of England itself.

Cast your mind back across the pond to another island kingdom in 1909. Here is the Metropolitan Life Tower, and unlike the understated British who simply describe their bell tower as a bell tower, the Met Life bell tower was called a *campanile,* in part because the design of the tower was unabashedly modeled on Venice's Campanile of St. Mark.

John R. Hegeman, the president of the insurance company, was a great fan of the campanile at St. Mark's Square, and he might have initiated the idea of using it as a model. Met Life's version is an astigmatic vision of the original at best, and the tower was in reality neither a bell tower nor a campanile, it was an office building, and it was not just the city's tallest building when it was erected, at 700 feet it was the world's tallest building that just happened to come with four clock faces.

No other clock face is in the same league of fame as Big Ben, but Met Life had its own bragging rights. For starters, the whole shebang was described as the "largest four-dial tower clock in the world," and one statistic after another shored up the contention that Met Life beat Big Ben in scale, plus Big Ben's faces are only 180 feet up versus 350. Met Life's biggest bell, at a mere 7,000 pounds, however, is puny by comparison with the real Big Ben.

The faces on Met Life appear as if they are a continuation of the Tuckahoe marble facade, but they are very small pieces of mosaic set in about 30 concentric rings. Like other clocks with round faces in square frames, there is decoration in each of the four corners, with Rococo-like floral garlands capped by scallop shells. Twelve sets of neoclassical curlicues point to the hours from the center, and two concentric rings encircle the dots marking the minutes, with the outer ring semi-encircling the circles in a wave-like pattern. The arrow-tipped copper hands, weathered to almost the same turquoise as the curlicues and rings, repeat the curlicue theme. And the numbers are Arabic at a time when Roman numerals ruled, and the typeface is sans serif, hardly the usual typeface for its time.

At night, light might shine through individual panes of glass on Big Ben, and although Met Life's backdrop is solid, Met Life had a feature unlike any other clock in the world. Light shines from the hands as well as the numerals and circles that mark the minutes. Wire glass is set within "frames," and behind the glass are electric lights.

Big Ben was essentially powered by gravity and could be regulated by adding or taking a penny from the pendulum, a "Victorian wonder," said Blake Ehrlich, "keeping virtually perfect time since 1859," although the clock has been victimized by acts of nature. The Ministry of Works, for instance, "reported that it was once halted by roosting birds, in the Ministry's words, 'a murmuration of starlings.'" (In James Lipton's *An Exaltation of Larks*, "A Murmuration of Starlings" was wittily placed on the page opposite "A Parliament of Owls" without a word of explanation.)

According to the *Washington Post*, the Met Life clock was the "most elaborate public timepiece ever constructed." Electrical impulses were transmitted to the clock mechanism from a master clock in the Directors' Room, and at each quarter hour, the impulses activated the hammers to sound the chimes; on the hour, the impulses activated the big bell with an impact of about 200 pounds. The *Post* said that its sound could be "heard over in the Jersey villages."

The chimes at Metropolitan Life sounded every quarter hour from seven in the morning until ten at night, and if the sound could be heard as far away as New Jersey, what was music to some was noise to others. Soon after the building opened, some of Met Life's neighbors claimed that however musical the chimes might have been, they were doing little more than "attracting attention to the Metropolitan Life Insurance Building, and incidentally to its business." The tower, of course, was a palpable advertising tool, a chest-thumping "Look at me." And the advertising quality continued even at night, when a beacon light took over the watch, flashing red for the quarter hours and white for the hours.

A few weeks after the building opened, Metropolitan Life hosted a dinner at the Hotel Astor to honor the tower's architects, Pierre L. Le Brun and Michel Le Brun, the sons of the architect Napoleon Le Brun. The architects made a presentation of a three-foot-high silver clock to John R. Hegeman, the president of Met Life and the man who had guided the project. The clock was a model of the Met Life tower. Whether it came with the Westminster chimes went unreported.

The British know what a treasure they have in the Houses of Parliament. Unfortunately, Met Life tower has been treated cavalierly. In the 1960s, the building was stripped of its decorative details, and just about all that remains to remind us of the glory that was Met Life are the clocks themselves and the enframing garlands on the rims. After the insurance company moved out of its Madison Square headquarters and into the building that swallowed Park Avenue, the bells were turned off during a renovation. Since then, the bells have not been ringing for me, or anyone else.

The Empty Plinth

35 East 25th Street, the northeast corner, Madison Avenue

Eight eight-foot-high sculptural figures once stood upon the 25th Street parapet wall atop the Appellate Division Courthouse, four on one side of the central grouping of Justice, and four on the other. They were historical figures, there to represent the great legal systems, some civil, some religious. All the statues bore distinguishing attributes, such as a book, a scroll, a scepter, or a sword, reinforcing the roles of the subjects as makers or defenders of the law.

From left to right, the original eight were Islamic law (depicted by a sword-bearing Muhammad), Persian law (Zoroaster), Anglo-Saxon law (Alfred the Great), Spartan law (Lycurgus), Athenian law (Solon), French law (Louis IX), Indian law (Manu), and Byzantine law (Justinian). And now there are seven.

Muhammad is gone.

The explanation for the missing statue is that "graven images" of human figures have been frowned upon since Muhammad founded Islam in the seventh century. More to the point, figure paintings and sculpture are specifically prohibited on public, religious, and political edifices.

The statues had been standing on 25th Street since 1902, two years after the courthouse had opened, and although an occasional guidebook described the

statues, they were little recognized until 1953, when their identities were given wide exposure. Erosion and chemical corrosives in the atmosphere had destroyed some features of the marble effigies and had dangerously weakened their footings, much as the statuary on the stock exchange had been corroded. In this case, however, the original plan was not to restore the statuary, but to take down the statues and sell them. Offers came in—the city of St. Louis, for instance, wanted the statue of the French king, Louis IX, aka, Saint Louis—but the few requests to buy were overwhelmed by an "avalanche of letters" protesting the plan, demanding that the statues stay. The president of the National Academy of Design told the Municipal Art Commission that removal of the sculptures would establish "an unfortunate precedent [that] . . . might well lead to the removal of sculptural work on other buildings of the city later on, the result of a lack of adequate maintenance on the part of the city of monuments entrusted to the care of its elected officials."

What ensued was a cost analysis, a simple issue of money spent and value on hand, and it prevailed. The decision was to take down the Tuckahoe marble statuary, clean it and repair it, then set it up again on strengthened pedestals, otherwise the initial investment would be money down the drain.

This time letters came flooding in from individual Muslims, as well as official requests from the ambassadors of Indonesia, Egypt, and Pakistan, requesting that the statue of Muhammad not be repaired and restored to its original place but that it be taken down and destroyed.

The seven Appellate Court justices and the State Department all agreed to the request, and down came Muhammad. To fill the gap at the Madison Avenue corner, all the statues were shifted west by one bay after they had been restored, leaving the empty plinth at the east end, where it is about as far out of sight as possible.

Moscow on the Hudson

The New York Life Insurance Building, on the northwest corner
of Park Avenue South at 26th Street

I f Moscow has it over New York in one area, it is the design of its Metro, with its spacious halls, its artwork, its crystal chandeliers, its overall magnificence. The exception is the entrance to the subway in the New York Life Insurance Building. Here is Moscow on the Hudson.

The building opened in 1928, and its architectural style was described as "American Perpendicular" with "modified Gothic" lines, a style accepted as perfectly appropriate for the facade of a skyscraper. The design is ascribed to the master of the form, Cass Gilbert.

What we are looking at here, however, is hardly Gothic anything. It is a stylistic extension of the lobby and it is neo-very-High-Renaissance, almost neo-Baroque, with painted and gilded coffered ceilings, intricately worked brass railings, and a chandelier that could light your way to heaven, unless, of course, you are standing there thinking that you have already died and gone to heaven.

Gilbert usually contracted out the design of lobbies to architectural decorators, and one of his favorites was Paris & Wiley—William Francklyn Paris and Frederick J. Wiley. They were a team, the perfect yin and yang. Paris was an architectural decorator and Wiley a muralist, and, either individually or together, they collaborated on at least seven commissions with Gilbert, including the Woolworth Building, the Supreme Court in Washington, D.C., and the Minnesota State Capitol.

Paris & Wiley happily worked in the neo-Anything style, but at heart they were neoclassicists, ordinarily framing their artwork with neoclassical motifs, whether the artwork was for the Children's Room in the Detroit Public Library or a fleet of steamships plying the Great Lakes.

William Francklyn Paris came from money. He did not attend the average prep school or Ivy League college—he had private tutors. He did study at the Art Students League and he went gallivanting around Europe to study the past firsthand, and when he wasn't practicing the art of architectural decoration, he was writing on the subject. In 1907, Paris purchased a four-story row house at 53 West 39th Street which he used as a studio and a sometime gallery. He lived in the Plaza Hotel, and his name regularly appeared under "Social Notes," dining with the likes of the Duke and Duchess de Richelieu or the Duke and Duchess de Talleyrand. And he managed to find time to do good works. For his actions raising funds for the relief of families of French and Belgian artists during World War I, the French Cross of Chevalier of the Legion of Honor and the Belgian Knight of the Order of the Crown were conferred upon him.

Frederick J. Wiley was an Ivy Leaguer, whose first career was lawyering, which he chucked for painting and interior decoration. He lived the Bohemian life in

the Benedick on Washington Square and worked for the Herter Brothers as a draftsman and general decorator before linking up with Paris. He did not travel in the same social stratosphere as Paris, but he was a member of the Century Association and the Lotos Club. To keep himself busy while convalescing from a broken hip, Wiley translated Browning into modern Greek.

The architect Gilbert was ordinarily described as *le maître de l'oeuvre*, and although the design of the building is officially ascribed to him, the truth is a little different. Gilbert and his firm ended up having little to do with the actual overall layout and massing. The building committee started making suggestions on improving Gilbert's plans before construction had even begun. Then the committee asked Paul Starrett, whose firm was charged with the construction, what he thought of the design, and Starrett didn't pull any punches. He said that Gilbert had subordinated "all the important practical considerations to the artistic one." Since the insurance company was only going to occupy a portion of the building and rent out the bulk of it, the building couldn't just be a pretty thing. It had to combine beauty with utility. The committee asked Starrett to present some plans.

Yasuo Matsui, who was on Starrett's staff and would go on to work on 40 Wall Street and the Starrett-Lehigh Building, revised the massing and drew up revised floor plans. In a huff, Gilbert left for an extended stay in France, leaving the day-to-day operations to his in-house staff, returning later to deal with the interiors.

The building opened in 1928, and the subway entrance manifested the laudable service to the riding public that was prevalent among real-estate developers in the first third of the 20th century, when developers included entrances to subway stations in their plans almost as a matter of course. The lobby of the Equitable Life Building at 120 Broadway has a marble staircase leading down to the Wall Street station, the Royal Insurance Building incorporated an entrance in their building at 95 Fulton Street, and 30 Rockefeller Plaza opened onto the Sixth Avenue station at 50th Street. (Both the Woolworth Building and 570 Lexington had entrances that are now closed.)

The tradition of including subway entrances faded after Rockefeller Center. To encourage its return in the 1980s, the City of New York started giving developers building bonuses of as much as 20 percent above the ordinarily prescribed Floor Area Ratio (the envelope of space that the proposed building could fill) if the developer agreed to provide access to a nearby subway station.

You can readily find this glorious subway entrance on Park Avenue South by an elegant bronze sign over the sidewalk. Within the neoclassical frame are the words "Interborough Subway," which translates into the Downtown Number Six. Not as colorful, perhaps, but efficient.

So *That's* the Armory!

The Sixty-ninth Regiment Armory, Lexington Avenue between 26th and 27th Streets

The famous "Armory Show" of 1913 had to be held in some armory somewhere, and it might come as a surprise to many people that this otherwise anonymous building that housed the 69th Regiment was it.

There was not much talk of "modern art" in the United States in the early 20th century, and if you had wanted to see any in New York City you would not have visited the Metropolitan Museum of Art, which, as the repository of the Old Masters and Classical art, was not in the habit of dealing with much else. Nor would you

have gone to the Museum of Modern Art or to the Whitney for the simple reason that they had not been invented yet. You might have visited the gallery at 291 Fifth Avenue that had been established in 1908 by the photographer Alfred Stieglitz, who was the first to show the likes of Rodin, Cezanne, Matisse, and Picasso, but only a few among the cognoscenti knew about "291."

In 1910, some members of the "Eight," headed by Robert Henri, held a show of "Independents" who, like the secessionists in Europe, were in opposition to the academicians, in this case the National Academy of Design. The Independents' show resulted in plans to hold a big invitational show, the International Exhibition of Modern Art. Their choice of venue was Madison Square Garden.

Despite the fact that the wealthy Mabel Dodge and the lawyer and art collector John Quinn were among the patrons, the Garden's asking price was too high. The group settled on the 69th Regiment Armory.

The original plans for the armory had been drawn up by Tammany's pet architects, Horgan & Slattery, but Mayor Seth Low, the former president of Columbia University, a reformer, and a man who knew architecture, came into office. Horgan & Slattery were booted out, and with them, their elaborate scheme. The plans by Richard Howland Hunt and Joseph Howland Hunt, the sons of the architect Richard Morris Hunt, were accepted in 1903.

Hunt & Hunt's design for the armory was sort of French neoclassical, vaguely French Mansart, and what you see today is almost identical to what you would have seen in 1906 when the armory was finished. The brickwork framing the arched, recessed entrance is still glorious, the eagle's talons are still clutching the keystone above the entrance, and "SIXTY NINTH REGIMENT" is still in the facade above the oriel window. There have been minor changes to the facade. The "165th INF. N.Y.N.G." in the limestone arch was added because the unit was designated the 165th Infantry Regiment, New York National Guard, upon mustering for service during World War I. Missing are the howitzer-like torches that stood on the pylons to light the entrance

The drill hall's ceiling was over 100 feet high, and an 80-foot-wide skylight ran the length of the hall, with the ribbed ceiling supported by enormous steel trusses with spans of 189 feet (a peak at the roof will reveal the ribs).

The ceiling of this enormous interior was cleverly masked for the Independents' exhibition by a gossamer tent-like decoration, with the floor divided by screens into eighteen spaces, but the arrangement was at best higgledy-piggledy. Paintings were stacked one atop another on walls, sculpture was scattered about, and the notion of "modern" included Goya, who had died in 1828; Delacroix, who had died in 1863; and Ingres, who had died in 1867. The work of the older artists was still new to many eyes, and the newer European stuff set off a firestorm. The European art included Van Gogh, Gaugin, Cezanne, Picasso, Braque, and Duchamp, whose *Nude Descending a Staircase* attracted the most comment, and consequently the most interest and visitors. On the one hundredth anniversary of the Armory Show, the New-York Historical Society brought together some of the artwork, and the Duchamp was probably just as puzzling to the average viewer in 2013 as it had been in 1913.

Dozens of American artists were represented at the original show, including some members of the Ashcan School. John Sloan exhibited a small oil on canvas that depicts a subject near and dear to the hearts of many a New Yorker, McSorley's Old Ale House (the painting is now in the collection of the Detroit Art Institute; McSorley's is still on East 7th Street).

If the phrase *blockbuster* had been around in 1913, it would have been applied to this show. In the one month that the exhibition ran, February 17 to March 15, 87,000 visitors packed into the 69th Regiment Armory to see nearly 1,400 works of modern art by more than 300 artists.

Nothing quite as exciting has happened there since. The writer Roger Rosenblatt said that the drill hall was "where neighborhood kids watched the New York Knicks in the early 1950s, before pro basketball got big," and this writer remembers seeing the Harlem Globetrotters play there. As much as the Globetrotters shook up the competition, they were still no earthquake like the Armory Show.

Past Death's Door

One East 29th Street, between Fifth and Madison Avenues

The Church of the Transfiguration sits back from the street behind a garden, and it exudes the look of ye olde English church. Adding to the illusion is a lich gate, which seems a beguiling touch until you realize its function. Lich is Middle English for "corpse" or "body," and a lich gate was the traditional resting place for pallbearers to wait with the coffin until the funeral service was ready to begin. Lich gates were ordinarily outfitted with a resting place for the dead and benches for the living, and the benches were frequently put to long service. In the days when the average death took place at home, bodies were frequently removed from the house and taken to the lich gate, where mourners stayed with the body, day and night, until the funeral service was to begin.

With the coming of the Gothic Revival style, the Victorian period saw a revival of lich gates. Transfiguration's rector in the 1890s, the Rev. Dr. George H. Houghton, had been impressed by one at a church in Canterbury, and he thought that a lich gate was just the thing to add to the 29th Street scene, and Frederick Clarke Withers was just the architect to design it. Houghton knew Withers' work. Withers had designed St. John the Evangelist in Newport, Rhode Island, and Houghton had given the church's dedicatory sermon in 1894.

Withers had begun his professional career in England when the Gothic Revival was becoming all the rage, and his work was imbued by one form or another of the Gothic style for the rest of his career. He worked in partnership with Calvert Vaux, another practitioner of the Gothic Revival and all its permutations. As a solo practitioner, Withers designed the Chapel of the Good Shepherd on Roosevelt

Island, the reredos at Trinity Chapel on West 26th Street, the William Backhouse Astor altar and reredos at Trinity Church, and the reredos here at Transfiguration. The lich gate is filled with Gothic-style flourishes, from the lancet openings flanked by tracery to the foliated panels.

The Rev. Houghton seems to have made only one request for a donation to cover the cost of the gate. The request was to a woman who frequently attended service when she was in town, which was seldom enough in the 1890s, preferring the Hudson Valley or the French Riviera. She was Mrs. Franklin Delano, née Laura Astor, the daughter of William Backhouse Astor, and the last of the living granddaughters of John Jacob Astor.

Laura Astor's husband, Franklin Delano, was hardly a pauper when they were married in 1844. Franklin's father, Warren Delano, was accumulating a fortune in whale oil while captaining ships for the firm of Minturn, Grinnell. Franklin Delano entered the firm, and was a junior partner at the time of their marriage.

As a bride, Laura Astor was presented with $200,000 in trust, an estate up the Hudson near Hyde Park, and one of the elegant row houses in Colonnade Row on Lafayette Place. Part of her dowry was a piece of New York real estate that was bounded by Eighth Avenue and the Hudson River, between 54th and 57th Streets. Delano was no fool. He resigned from Minturn, Grinnell.

The Delanos died with no offspring, but Franklin Delano's name lived on. A niece, Sara Delano, married James Roosevelt, and she named her son in honor of her childless uncle.

The lich gate was finished in 1897, but Dr. Houghton died before its consecration. His funeral was held at the church, and although his body did not lie in the lich gate, it was carried through the gate on its way to a hearse and the cemetery. His might have been the gate's first funeral.

The Frozen Fountain

181 Madison Avenue, the southeast corner of 34th Street

The Cheney Brothers Silk Company and the French ironworker Edgar Brandt, both stars in their respective orbits, had an interestingly symbiotic relationship in the mid-1920s. Cheney Brothers liked the work of Brandt so much that in the fall of 1924 they introduced a line of silk fabric based on thirty of Brandt's geometric designs. To introduce the new line in their New York showroom, they draped their products atop some of the screens and a door that Brandt had designed and fabricated. The following February and March, 1925, a show in the Decorative Arts Section of the Louvre repeated a variation on the display, which made history. Cheney Brothers' silk was the first example of American decorative art to be exhibited in the Louvre.

Perhaps the most famous decorative arts show of the 20th century opened in Paris later that same spring. Called *l'Exposition Internationale des Arts Décoratifs et Industriels Modernes,* that tongue twister of a name gave birth to the phrase *Art Deco.* Although the work of the Frenchman Edgar Brandt was well represented at the exposition, there was no official participation from the U.S.— no Cheney Brothers silk, no book-jacket designs by Francis Cugat, no Pierce Arrow Runabout. Herbert Hoover, the Secretary of Commerce, believed that the country had nothing worthy enough to contribute in the field of the industrial arts, nothing that lived up to the exposition's standard for "strict originality—no adherence to past models."

One of Brandt's earliest manifestations of forward thinking was a five-panel screen that he had designed and manufactured in 1924, and it was on display at the exposition. Brandt was known as a *ferronnier*, an "artistic ironworker," and the central panel, which was the center of attention, depicted jets of water shooting up from a fountain and cascading down. It was a fountain frozen in time.

Brandt started getting so many commissions in the U.S. that he started a studio in New York called Ferrobrandt, which would create grilles, lighting fixtures, and hardware.

By October 1925, the Cheney Brothers were ensconced in a new showroom in the just-opened Madison Belmont Building, and the architectural trim was all by Brandt. The patinated and gilded bronze "frozen fountain" above the door to the Cheney Showroom crested in perfectly formed concentric arcs at their breaking points, and an openwork grille allowed the transom to be lit from behind to illuminate the tracery.

The building was designed by Warren & Wetmore, and the Cheney Brothers, as prime tenants with a 21-year lease, obviously had some say in the architecture. Most of the trim on the first-floor facade is Brandt's work, and it was a palpable hit. The *Christian Science Monitor* reported that the Cheney showroom was "one of the sights of the town."

With that kind of publicity, variations on the theme seemed inevitable. The sculptor Rene Chambellan incorporated the motif in the panels flanking the entrance to the 1928 Panhellenic Tower, today's Beekman Tower at 3 Mitchell Place, and he might have contributed another example. Chambellan was sort of a jack-of-all trades for Rockefeller Center, and up on the roofline of 30 Rockefeller Plaza and not readily visible to the passing pedestrian are spandrels that are a variation on the frozen fountain motif, and we might have Chambellan to thank for them.

Another unheralded example was a tower atop the Schaefer Center at the 1939 World's Fair. The restaurant, sponsored by the Brooklyn beer maker and designed by Eggers & Higgins, was a circular structure that was topped by a streamlined tower in the form of a three-dimensional frozen fountain, with eight sets of cascades emanating from the center and descending in perfectly formed concentric arcs. Adding to the night scene, vertical strips of neon played up the frozen fountain.

For the record, Herbert Hoover, who did not want to bother with the Paris Exposition, did send a congratulatory telegram to the Cheney Brothers Silk Company upon the opening of the showroom. It was a bit of too little, too late.

Martinesque

Today, the Carriage House Center for the Arts, 149 East 38th Street,
between Lexington and Third Avenues

This neo-Dutch Renaissance extravaganza of a stable with its stepped gable roof has few peers in this city. Good examples are some row houses by Clarence True, and the West End Collegiate Church by Robert W. Gibson, and the control houses that Heins & LaFarge designed for the IRT, but this stable transcends them all.

Even in the Gilded Age, lavishing the kind of money required to erect and maintain a private stable was beyond not just the means, but the ken of the average New Yorker. The estimated construction cost of this 25 by 85-foot stable was $15,000 in 1902, and that doesn't include the cost of the lot.

A good horse easily cost thousands, and a horse might consume about three tons of hay and 60 bushels of oats a year. Coachman's wages averaged $2,700 a year, and a hostler's a little less. The "stable requisites" included pitchforks and shovels, brooms, horse brushes and combs, And then there were the outfits. A 1904 catalogue for a New York clothing store that included a livery department "featured eleven pages of coats for coachmen and ten pages of coats for grooms," as Clay McShane and Joel A. Tarr described. For dress livery, the outfits included "breeches, boots, cuffs, gloves, scarves, trousers, waistcoats, and crepe bands," all paid for by the employer.

The man who built this stable could well afford it. The New York store with the livery department was none other than Rogers Peet, the clothing stores that William R. H. Martin had inherited, the same Martin who liked to work variations on his and his wife's names into his projects. The Martins lived at 114 East 36th Street, in the heart of Murray Hill, which explains why they built this stable where they did.

The Murray Hill Covenant condoned carriage houses, but did not encourage them. This was all complicated by the fact that Murray Hill land values were high enough to convince sensible residents to build their stables elsewhere. Murray Hill was strictly defined as bordered by 35th and 40th Streets, between Lexington and Madison Avenues. The block west would have meant Fifth Avenue prices, so the block east between Lexington and Third Avenues beckoned. Prices were lower, and it was conveniently close to Murray Hill.

Stables were usually built individually, like the Martins' stable, with some side streets lined with them, such as the south side of 73rd Street between Lexington and Third Avenues. Individual stables were also sometimes part of a mews, as exemplified by today's Sniffen Court on East 36th Street.

The Martin stable was designed by Ralph S. Townsend, and there are *volutes* (an easy pneumonic—they are convoluted, turning in upon themselves) and *voussoirs* (from the French, wedge-shaped stones that form an arch), coins or *quoins* (from the French, for corner), an over-the-top oval bull's-eye window (the French simply described small oval or round windows as *oeils de boeuf*), and the date "1902" worked into one escutcheon and the address "128" worked into another (an escutcheon is simply a plate in the form of a shield, from the Latin *scutum*).

The facade also includes the charming touch of a pair of high-relief statues of horses' heads, and a bulldog. The horses make eminently good sense as decoration on a stable, but why a bulldog, except that traits associated with bulldogs are doggedness, determination, and getting the job done, and Martin would never have been able to operate a chain of clothing stores and become a successful real-estate developer in New York without those traits. American Express had adopted the bulldog as its emblem by the turn of the twentieth century, and the American Express warehouse on the southeast corner of Laight and Collister Streets has a bulldog worked into its facade, just as this stable has.

By 1902, when this stable was built, Ralph Townsend was on his way to becoming the court architect for Martin. His other projects, which included the Trowbridge Building on Herald Square and the Rogers, Peet Building on the northeast corner of Fifth Avenue and 41st Street, were considerably less exuberant. The plot for the Rogers, Peet store was L-shaped, reaching 42nd Street mid-block between Madison and Fifth Avenues, where a large ad for Rogers, Peet had been painted on the east wall. The building is still there, but someone has come along and "beige"-washed away this last tangible memory of Rogers, Peet.

For the record, this stable is referred to by the Landmarks Preservation Commission as the "George S. Bowdoin Stable." Bowdoin, who lived at 39 Park Avenue and was a partner at J. P. Morgan, did nothing substantive regarding this stable. He simply bought it in 1907. He doesn't deserve naming rights.

6

Midtown West

40th to 59th Streets, from Fifth Avenue West

Anatomically Challenged

The sculpture group *History* in the north pediment of the
Main Branch of the New York Public Library (Schwarzman Building),
Fifth Avenue, south of 42nd Street

The architects of the Main Branch of the New York Public Library, John Merven Carrère and Thomas Hastings, met each other while students at l'Ecole des Beaux Arts in Paris, and their predilection was to work with others with like backgrounds.

The sculptor George Grey Barnard had studied at the Beaux Arts, which made him a natural fit for this project, and he was accomplished at creating large sculpture groups. Barnard had created a sculpture group for the 1894 Salon du Champ de Mars called *Struggle in The Two Natures of Man*, which was donated to the Metropolitan Museum of Art. In 1897 it was sitting in one of the museum's outbuildings. At about eight feet around, it was too great a struggle to get through the museum's doors.

Carrère and Hastings commissioned Barnard to do both the south and north pedimental statuary on the library, and when Hastings saw a model of one of the sculpture groups, he was said to have described it as "the finest thing that had ever been done in this country."

When the scaffolding came down at the end of 1913, Barnard's sculpture was no doubt viewed as straight out of the lesson books at l'Ecole. The *Times* described *History* as including a "reclining figure of a knight in armor, resting upon the book of life, as he dreams of war and victory . . . While the knight represents life itself, its ups and downs, strife and peace," an allegorical female figure is writing the "records of life."

But there is something wrong with this statuary group. Art students, especially sculpture students, are expected to study anatomy if they are to be successful figurative artists—Leonardo Da Vinci went so far as to dissect more than ten cadavers—and schools such as the Art Students League, where Barnard taught, and the National Academy of Design, where he was an associate member, offer anatomy courses as an integral part of the curriculum. Barnard was ordinarily a master of the human form, but where this knight's right arm is coming from and what it is attached to is the $64,000 question.

At least one observer noticed the anatomically questionable shoulder. L.V. Levengood, an architect, pointed out that "unless abnormally formed, [no knight] could keep the pose that this one does without having his right shoulder dislocated and an extension added, or else by using a dummy hand and forearm."

Perhaps, for argument's sake, it can't all be blamed on Barnard. The sculptors who worked on the library did not do the actual carving. They delivered full-size models of their work to stone carvers, in this case Donnelly & Ricci. Judging by the quality of Donnelly & Ricci's work at the Woolworth Building, they were up to the job.

Barnard had been hospitalized and could not check in with the stone carvers to make sure everything was proceeding to his satisfaction, and when he saw the sculpture group installed, he was appalled. He considered it a "disgrace to the library and a stain on [his] reputation."

Because of bureaucratic entanglements, although Hastings had contracted with Donnelly & Ricci, it was Barnard who was responsible for their $4,000 bill, and he refused to pay it. Donnelly & Ricci sued, so Barnard countersued. He said that their work was defective, that it was botched, that it was an insult to nature. He said that the work on the library as it appeared was in no respect what he had delivered as models.

Barnard claimed that Donnelly & Ricci had "made the vital error of working without a third dimension. They calculated on the length and height, but absolutely omitted to figure in the depth." He said that the figure of the knight lacked about 9 inches of marble on his chest, so there was no play of light and shadow. And where he had made the knight lean forward to attain the desired effect, Donnelly & Ricci had him leaning backward, "completely sacrificing the sense and beauty of the thing."

Donnelly & Ricci had taken photographs of Barnard's models, and they submitted them in court. The photographs showed that Donnelly & Ricci had followed Barnard's model to a T. And with all this litigiousness, there was not a word from Barnard on the misshapen shoulder.

The subject matter of a crusading knight might have clouded Barnard's judgment. Barnard was an aficionado of the art of the Middle Ages, and he had pedaled around the French countryside acquiring bits and pieces of Romanesque and Gothic art and whole swaths of architecture when, in his words, "it was worth nothing." When all this brouhaha was going on, Barnard was in the process of designing a gallery on Fort Washington Avenue in which he would install his Medieval treasures—the Barnard Cloisters. Barnard's collection would be purchased by John D. Rockefeller, Jr., who would present it to the Metropolitan Museum of Art, and we have Barnard and Rockefeller to thank for *The* Cloisters.

As for the lawsuits, the library's board of trustees remained above the fray. The sculpture group never was redone, and we still have the original, anatomically questionable shoulder and all. No record can be found regarding whether Donnelly & Ricci ever were paid.

Brilliant

500 Fifth Avenue, on the northwest corner of 42nd Street

A bove the entrance to 500 Fifth Avenue is a gilded bas-relief female figure who bears an ancient symbol in one hand while supporting the very symbol of 20th-century architecture with the other. She represents the *Genius of the Modern Skyscraper*.

With her right hand she holds a staff topped by a winged sun disk, which in ancient Egypt was a symbol frequently carved above temple gates to represent power, doubling as a symbol of protection for those who entered beneath it. The same symbol was used by other cultures, and just as the symbol was multicultural, so is the figure. She is no flapper. She is classically garbed in a highly stylized Art Deco style, and she seems of a vague ethnicity, although the Landmarks Preservation Commission unconditionally describes her as "Grecian."

What she supports with her left hand is a representation of the building itself, a classic 1931 skyscraper with the distinctive shape that adhered to the Zoning Law of 1916, which had freestanding towers springing from bases that maintained the street wall. What we see is the 42nd Street facade, and, curiously, the image is flopped.

The sculptor's name was Edmond, or Edward, Amateis. His immigrant parents were Italian, and he had been born in Rome. He was educated in both Paris and at New York's Beaux-Arts Institute of Design, which had been established as the American answer to the school in Paris, and he won the prestigious Prix de Rome in 1921. The art critic Royal Cortissoz described his high-relief sculpture as "majestic simplicity," a phrase equally appropriate for the low relief *Genius*.

The architects of 500 Fifth, Shreve, Lamb and Harmon, are best known as the architects of the Empire State Building, and both buildings were going up simultaneously. Five-Hundred Fifth opened on March 2, 1931, the Empire State, two months later. Both undertakings came in on time (500 Fifth was even early), and both came in on budget.

Five-Hundred Fifth was the brainchild of Walter F. Salmon, who had seen 42nd Street and Fifth Avenue as having potential for profit as early as 1899. Following his propensity for long-term leases instead of outright purchases, Salmon leased lot after lot on the northwest corner, and then he spread out. By 1915 he controlled three of the four corners—the fourth was, by then, the site of the public library. He wound up with 858 feet of property on 42nd Street, including the northeast corner of Sixth Avenue, and he hadn't been dealing with your average Joe Schmo. Salmon was negotiating with the savvy attorneys of some of the city's aristocracy, including former Vice President Levi P. Morton, Elbridge T. Gerry, Russell Sage, and General John Watts de Peyster, a direct descendant of Abraham de Peyster, the mayor from 1691 to 1694.

The site at 500 Fifth provided an interesting problem to solve for architects, and the solution is reflected in the building's silhouette. Although both Fifth Avenue and 42nd Street are 100 feet wide and the site is in the same zoning area, the 42nd Street wall could rise higher before being set back. One of the peculiarities of the 1916 Zoning Law was that buildings facing parks could rise higher before setbacks were required, despite the fact that trees and other living things need sunlight at least as much as people in order to flourish.

The anomaly in the zoning law translated into allowing the first setback on 42nd Street to be higher than the first setback on Fifth Avenue, resulting in the heights of setbacks varying from facade to facade. The first Fifth Avenue setbacks are nevertheless higher than the plot would ordinarily allow under the law. Salmon had acquired a long-term lease on the neighboring building at 508 Fifth, and he merged the 25-foot-wide plot with his site, essentially transferring the site's air rights to his development. Every additional square foot of rentable space is a multiple of X in a developer's calculations. Add into the equation an open-ended courtyard rising from the eighth floor on 42nd Street, bringing light and air to what would otherwise be dark interiors while creating that many more prestigious and more valuable corner offices, and that's the genius of the modern skyscraper.

The Lights of Broadway

Platform Number One at the Times Square, 42nd Street Shuttle,
Broadway and 42nd Street

This station was part of the original route of the city's first subway system, the Interborough Transit (IRT). Unlike the average metro, the subway was a four-track railroad with express and local stations for most of its run, with express stations spaced about 30 blocks apart from each other, or about a mile and a half.

Times Square was barely Times Square when the subway opened in 1904, and it was a local station. Express stations provided access to all platforms, but the average local station only provided access to a platform for uptown service and another for downtown.

Two exceptions—one at Astor Place, the other at Times Square—would allow passengers to take an under-track passageway from one platform to the other. Major buildings were being built at those stations contemporaneously with the construction of the subway, and access to the buildings was deemed important enough to warrant the passageways. The Wanamaker Store was building an annex at Astor Place, and the *New York Times* was constructing its new headquarters building on the triangular block at the crossing of Broadway and Seventh Avenue between 42nd and 43rd Streets. Three stairways and four elevators would link the Times Building with the subway level for both up- and downtown service.

In the floor of Platform One are seen the vestigial remains of the under-track passageway. The vault lights, the thick pieces of glass set into a triangular frame, allowed passive light to pass through and complement the electric lighting below. The rectangular flooring is a patch job that was originally the cut for the stairs that led to the passageway. A similar but truncated pattern is on Track Four.

In 1917, a new track configuration had the East Side line extended north on Lexington Avenue from 42nd Street, and the West Side line extended south on Seventh Avenue, leaving the main line linking the East and West Sides out of the loop. Those tracks became another kind of critical link between the East and West Sides—the 42nd Street Shuttle, operating between the original stations at Grand Central and Times Square.

The two outer tracks at Times Square had originally been for local service, the two center tracks for express. With the coming of the shuttle, the outer tracks with their platforms were retained, and what had been Track Two was metamorphosed into a boarding area for the old Track Three, which explains the lack of an active Track Two.

At the same time, a walkway was constructed across the west end of the station to link the complex, abrogating the need for the under-track passageway. If you take the walkway, you will see the original tracks making the turn from 42nd Street to Broadway.

At the turn of the 20th century, Times Square was not Times Square. It was Long Acre Square. You would think that if anyone had put forward the name change it would have been Adolph S. Ochs, who owned the *Times*, but it was August Belmont II, the president of the new subway.

Naming stations after prominent local institutions such as City Hall and Grand Central made eminently good sense, and Belmont wanted to name the station at Broadway and 42nd Street for the newspaper. The city granted that request, whereupon Belmont went one step further—he proposed to have the name of Long Acre Square changed to Times Square. With one powerful force advocating the change in the form of the man building the subway, and another powerful force in the form of a major daily newspaper benefiting from the change, the Board of Aldermen voted unanimously to approve Belmont's proposal.

August Belmont II was not a transportation professional; he was a banker. He had inherited the operation of the bank that represented the Rothschild Bank in the United States, and he came to the presidency of the Interborough because the subway's contractor needed some capital for a security bond. Belmont arranged the funds, and installed himself in the president's seat.

The naming rights for the *Times* might have meant more to Belmont than simply bestowing an honorific. Belmont had had a vested interest in the *Times* since the early 1890s, when a syndicate of bankers bailed out the failing newspaper. Belmont held $25,000 of the newspaper's $600,000 debt, and it was he and other bondholders, including Jacob Schiff and J. Pierpont Morgan, who had worked with Ochs to put the *Times* on a sound footing.

One impediment stood in the way of the Times Tower—the eight-story Pabst Hotel already stood on the site. The land under the Pabst Hotel was controlled by Charles Thorley, the florist to the Four Hundred. Thorley had built the building and had negotiated the lease with Pabst. Thorley highhandedly broke the lease with Pabst in 1902 and struck the deal with Ochs, who essentially already had an understanding with Belmont. The building came with a cellar, the rathskellar where Pabst Blue Ribbon was the beer of choice, and a sub-cellar. Part of the cellar would house the subway, with the printing presses planned for the sub-cellar.

At the turn of the 20th century, the neighborhood around Herald Square was still the entertainment district, but by 1900 the Metropolitan Opera was already on Broadway between 39th and 40th Streets, and there were four theaters along Broadway between 41st and 45th Streets, with more following.

By 1905, the Times Square station was already crowded, day *and* night. People made for it "after the theatre, walking two by two like files of soldiers," reported the *Tribune*. "Hundreds of them are to be found there waiting in line for their tickets." Soon the Great White Way—*the* lights of Broadway—had moved ten blocks farther north. Times Square was humming.

Not the Knicks' Locker Room

East end of Platform One at Times Square, on the 42nd Street Shuttle

If you had walked through this door marked "Knickerbocker" in 1906, you would have entered a fantasy world. This was the Hotel Knickerbocker, and a corridor led to the hotel's Grill Room, which was done up in the Elizabethan style. Upstairs in the lobby, the ceilings were modeled on those in the Chateau de Fontainebleau, and there were tapestries on the walls, and a fountain carved by Frederick MacMonnies. The café occupied the Times Square corner, and opening off it was an oak-paneled barroom. Hanging on the wall was a three-panel painting by Maxfield Parris of "Old King Cole and His Fiddlers Three." The Knickerbocker was another hotel in a long chain of great Astor hotels in New York.

A feature of the hotel was its direct connection with the subway. The tracks at that point curved toward the south side of 42nd Street before swinging around onto Broadway. "In making this curve," reported the *Times*, "the road really trespasses upon the Astor property, but it is said that this fact will be overlooked in view of the concession to be made by the tunnel builders in affording access to the railroad from the hotel basement."

"Affording access" should have caught in the craw of subway management. If it meant what it said, the guests at the Knickerbocker, or anyone wise enough to walk into the hotel and down into the basement, would get a free ride. The Times Building afforded access to the subway level, but not into the system itself. You still had to pay. The Knickerbocker door led directly into the system, right onto the platform without passing through fare collection. The odds of this door having ever actually been open onto the platform are pretty slim.

How an Astor came to build this hotel was as much by default as an original act of volition.

John Jacob Astor, the real-estate family's founding father, had started early in this neck of the woods. In 1803, he and William Cutting bought the 70-acre Medcef Eden farm. On today's street pattern, the property ran on a northwesterly angle between 41st and 48th Streets from east of Broadway to west of Eleventh Avenue. Astor took the high ground along Broadway as his portion, today's Times Square.

The St. Cloud Hotel had been located on the southeast corner of 42nd Street and Broadway since 1868. While far removed from the hotel district, the St. Cloud's propinquity to Grand Central Depot, which opened in 1871, proved its success.

In 1892, the 28-year-old John Jacob Astor IV took over the lease on the hotel. The young Astor's father, William Astor, had died just a few months before, and, in the Astor tradition, the power and the money passed through the male line. The young Astor came into about $50 million. In 1898 he took some of his inheritance and provided a fully equipped artillery battery to the government during the Spanish-American War, for which he was given the rank of lieutenant colonel, a title he kept for the rest of his life.

A few years later, Col. Astor decided that the time had come to tear down the St. Cloud and have the property redeveloped. He gave a long-term lease on the property to a group of Philadelphia capitalists who wanted to build a hotel. The Knickerbocker Hotel Company, headed by James B. Regan, who had managed the Pabst Hotel until its demise, would lease and operate it.

With the steel framing already up in 1904, the Philadelphians saw a potential problem with Regan's firm. Fearing that they would be stuck with a $3 million hotel and no operator, they halted construction. For 18 months the property stood idle, with the only revenue generated from the posters on the billboards around it.

By 1905, Astor had had enough. He took back control of the property, had Trowbridge & Livingston take over the design, and leased the hotel to Regan for 20 years.

The colonel went down on the *Titanic* in 1912, and his son, Vincent, took over the reins. By 1921, with barroom sales nonexistent thanks to the Volstead Act, and with liquor sales making the difference between profit and loss, the hotel was metamorphosed into an office building.

The café housing *Old King Cole* became a store. The Parrish painting bounced around, finally to be ensconced in 1935 in a place of honor at the St. Regis, another Astor hotel. And now the building has come full circle. It is a Hotel Knickerbocker again.

Not Your Garden Type Variety

Firehouse Engine 65, 33 West 43rd Street, between Fifth and Sixth Avenues

T he mythological salamander, which is not to be confused with the sweet little lizard-like amphibians found in places like Bear Mountain State Park,
was rooted firmly in the Medieval bestiaries. It happily inhabited fire, or fiery
places such as the volcano of Mount Etna where it could survive without being
scorched.

The Medieval mind believed that the goal of fire was the destruction of evil
forces, or purification. The salamander symbolized purity, even virginity and chastity. A woman who was described as a salamander, according to the Oxford English
Dictionary—and we quote, parentheses and all—"(ostensibly) lives chastely in
the midst of temptations, a kind of heroine in Chastity, that treads upon fire."

The forward-thinking King Francis I of France, who imported architects and
engineers from Renaissance Italy to help modernize France, chose this Medieval
symbol as his emblem. He stuck a crown atop his salamander, and you will find
crowned salamanders on some New York buildings such as the Francis the First-i-
fied Alwyn Court Apartments at 180 West 58th Street.

But the salamanders on this 1898 firehouse, which was designed by Hoppin &
Koen, are not the regal salamanders of Francis I. These salamanders are more in
keeping with the salamander in relief sculpture on today's Bryant Park Hotel. That
building was originally the American Radiator Building, and furnaces and heaters
were the company's products. A salamander was appropriate for its corporate
headquarters. And "salamander" also describes a grill on a professional stove.

Salamanders play a different role in in Ray Bradbury's dystopian novel, *Fahrenheit 451*. The firemen's hoses in *Fahrenheit 451* are not to spray water on burning

buildings, the hoses are to spray kerosene on buildings to feed fires, all the better to burn books and those who dare to read them. Bradbury's "firemen" wore salamanders as symbols on their sleeves, images of salamanders were etched on their "lighters," and their fire trucks, which were called "salamanders," slept with kerosene in their bellies.

All of this begs the question of why salamanders were worked into the facade of a firehouse, a building designed to house those who fight fires with water in their hoses, and whose pumpers sleep with water in their bellies. There was another angle to the mythological salamander: Salamanders were able to survive in fire because they were colder than any other creature, and when a salamander was frightened it would exude a liquid that moistened its skin, a liquid that could also extinguish fire. A salamander on the firehouse suddenly makes eminently good sense.

What's in a Name?

1619 Broadway, northwest corner, 49th Street

Today's Brill Building wasn't always called the Brill Building. It was originally the Alan E. Lefcourt Building, and the portrait bust of a young man had nothing to do with Brill Brothers, the men's clothing store that occupied the corner shop in the building that would come to bear the name Brill. Although the young man depicted is in the prime of health, the portrait is a sad reminder of the frailty of life, both human and commercial.

This office building was built in 1931 by Abraham E. Lefcourt, who by the end of the 1920s had his name on some of Midtown's grandest office- and loft buildings, including the Lefcourt Colonial, Lefcourt Marlborough, and the Lefcourt National Buildings. He made enough money in real estate to start his own bank, which his name adorned as well, the Lefcourt National Bank & Trust Company.

Hoping to cash in on his past successes, in October, 1929, Lefcourt announced the coming of a 1,050-foot-high, 85-story skyscraper for this very corner, an exiguous site at best for such a tall building. The site only measures 125.5 by 112 feet.

The plan was that the Brills, who held the lease on the property, would vacate their two-story building, which would be demolished to clear the site for the skyscraper. The timing was fortuitous for Brill Brothers. The De Pinna store was planning on vacating their building on Fifth Avenue and 50th Street and moving into a new building on 52nd Street. The Brills would take over the De Pinna building, which would give them a presence on the city's most prestigious retail avenue.

Lefcourt had lined up a major tenant for his building, a tenant "said to be one of the largest business institutions in the country," according to the *Chicago*

Tribune, but then Lefcourt was hit by a double whammy. First, his client balked after the stock market crash, forcing Lefcourt to scale back on his plans. He wound up with an 11-story building, including a penthouse floor. Then, with the building still on the drawing boards, came the death of his beloved son, the 18-year-old Alan, in whose memory the building would be named and the portrait bust installed.

Lefcourt had doted on his son. One of Lefcourt's goals had been to inculcate a sense of thrift and responsibility in the boy, especially an interest in real estate. In 1924, there was already a forerunner of today's Monopoly board game on the market, but Lefcourt went one better—he gave the 12-year-old boy title to his very own building to play with, a $10 million building that Lefcourt was planning to build on the southwest corner of Madison Avenue and 34th Street.

What happened to Lefcourt professionally in the early Thirties is summed up by Leo Rosten's fictional character, Hyman Kaplan, who was attending night school to learn English as a second language. When asked by his teacher to give the principal parts of the verb "to break," Kaplan proudly stood up and, with perfect logic, proclaimed "break, broke, bankrupt." Even Lefcourt's bank broke, amid allegations that he and his fellow officers had been siphoning off funds for their own purposes.

The Brill brothers, the property's lessees, did the only reasonable thing—in 1932, they foreclosed. Instead of moving to Fifth Avenue, they opened a store in the corner space, and they became landlords.

Leasing was slow in the depths of the Depression, but one bright light was switched on in November, 1932. The Paradise Restaurant took the entire second floor for a cabaret that combined dining with floor shows and music by the likes of Paul Whiteman and Glenn Miller. Joseph Urban, who was known for designing chic restaurants such as the Roof Garden Restaurant in the Hotel St. Regis, planned and decorated the restaurant, with the opening scheduled for New Year's Eve. A year later, Prohibition was repealed.

Repeal only allowed drinking at tables, and when bar service was legalized in New York State in 1934, a spokesman said that the Paradise would be ready. Management was planning "the most beautiful bar in New York. It'll be 100 feet long, in a new room we're going to open upstairs. The late Joseph Urban (he had died the year before) designed our main room, you know, and the new bar and fitting will be the work of the Joseph Urban Studios."

Despite the success of landing the Paradise, the building that had been planned to provide "executive office space" could only lease small spaces that appealed to one-man operations like music publicists, booking agents, and song-writers and arrangers, spaces that were more like cubicles. A desk, a chair, and a telephone were frequently the only appurtenances. The Brill Building became the new Tin Pan Alley, but the music business is not an easy one.

In 1941, the *New Yorker* writer A. J. Liebling wrote about a thinly-disguised building that covered "half a Broadway block in the high Forties" that he dubbed the "Jollity Building." By then the Paradise was a dance hall, and a pool hall was in the basement. "Eight coin-box telephone booths in the lobby of the Jollity Building serve as offices for promoters and others who cannot raise the price of desk space on an upper floor," Liebling wrote. "The phones are used mostly for incoming calls." The renting agent regretted not being able to collect rent from the "heels" in the phone booths.

Lefcourt, who died of a heart attack at 55 in 1932—some think it might have been a suicide—was probably rolling over in his grave.

Is That Symbol the Mighty Dollar Sign?

On Fifth Avenue, northwest corner of 53rd Street

The Bride's Door, the doorway to the left of the main entrance of St. Thomas' Church, was designed so that brides could slip into the church and have a moment's peace in a room of their own in which to prepare for the Mendelssohn to come.

Some of the symbolism over the doorway might have given pause to a bride or two. There is a double panel with some finely chiseled decoration in the canopy above the statue of St. Joseph, the patron saint of marriage. On the south side, the sunnier side, is a lovers' knot. On the other side, the darker, north side, is a Gothicized dollar sign. Yes, the mighty—the designers were careful not to say "almighty"—dollar sign.

The dollar sign was there from 1913 until 1921 before anybody seemed to have noticed it, but when news of its presence broke, immense crowds were reportedly going to the church, "not to worship," said the *Hartford Courant,* "but to see the little stone image carved in the Gothic arch above the door."

The relationship between the congregation's wealth and the dollar sign was not missed in headlines such as the one in *The Chicago Daily Tribune*: "Dollar Mark On 'Bride's Door' of Rich N.Y. Church." *The Literary Digest* called it a "monumental jest," but the rector was not amused, and was clearly in denial. He said that it was a "figment of the imagination."

Despite the rector's wishful thinking, the dollar sign was very real, and there was a perfectly understandable rationale behind it. The architects who had designed the church, Cram, Goodhue & Ferguson, said that the symbols were there to reflect the difference between a good marriage and a bad one. The

lovers' knot symbolized true love and the right kind of marriage. The dollar sign tells the story of the loveless marriage, the marriage for money.

The firm's head draftsman, E. Donald Robb, couldn't understand the fuss over it. Using stone or stained-glass to teach a scriptural lesson was an age-old custom, and Robb said that it was the duty of the artist "to supplement the efforts of the preacher by employing such designs as will call the attention of the people" to their shortcomings, especially to show how they comport themselves in reality.

Symbols could have been copied from venerable sources, but the architects preferred depicting the idea in a modern way. The bad marriage was shown to the Fifth Avenue congregation in its own parlance with the sign of the mighty dollar instead of the language of the dead masters.

The architects were fully aware of the history of St. Thomas'. The church that they were designing was replacing one that had burned to the ground in 1906. It had been built in 1870 and was smack in the middle of the Vanderbilts' stretch of Fifth Avenue. The church's congregants were the upper crust, and many of society's grandest weddings had been staged there, which in part might have been the inspiration for the existence of the Bride's Door.

When one thinks about money and marriage, it is usually the groom who has it, with the bride portrayed as the gold digger who wants it and will sell her soul for it. The irony is that the most famous wedding to take place in the old St. Thomas was the reverse case. It was the marriage of Consuelo Vanderbilt to the Duke of Marlborough, and it was through the Machiavellian doings of Consuelo's mother that she was obliged to sell her soul and to part with a ton of family money—her money—to a man who was title rich but land poor. No doubt the architect Bertram Goodhue had that particular 1895 wedding and others like it in mind.

The Gilded Age was awash with nubile American heiresses being sold off for titles, and their marriages provided spectacle, the circuses of the day. The police were regularly called out to maintain order at these affairs. Women had run alongside the carriage bearing Consuelo Vanderbilt and her father to the church, where an estimated 5,000 onlookers had gathered. The general populace might be lucky enough to catch a glimpse of the bride's dress as she alighted from her carriage, but that was about it. Consuelo Vanderbilt's dress was said to have cost $6,720.35, no doubt worth a look.

A wrinkle on the dowry story occurred in 1889 with the wedding of Cornelia Roosevelt and the Baron Clemens Freiher von Zedlitz. An "ante-nuptial agreement," or a "pre-nup," had actually been executed. The bride's ample fortune would remain in her name, and it would remain hers to do with as she pleased. The news spurred a keen interest in the marriage, and a large crowd swarmed about the doors. Among the guests already safely in a pew were Mr. and Mrs. Theodore Roosevelt.

Anachronism, Thy Name Is Mortarboard

University Club, One West 54th Street, northwest corner of Fifth Avenue

The architect Le Corbusier came to New York in 1935 to observe the new Machine Age Modernism, but instead he found himself admiring the more conservative buildings. The New York version of the Italian Renaissance was "so well done that you could believe it to be genuine" said Le Corbusier. "It even has a strange new firmness which is not Italian, but American!"

It all falls into place at the University Club. When the architect Charles Follen McKim was asked in the late 1890s to defend his design that included the seals of American colleges in the facade of the neo–Italian Renaissance clubhouse, McKim mounted a virtuoso dog-and-pony show that included images of shield-bearing facades from the Italian Renaissance. Even the most dubious members of the building committee walked away convinced of the propriety of McKim's decision. It didn't seem to matter that he was masking a nine-story, steel-framed building as a three-story palazzo, nor that the heraldic symbols in the originals would have been papal- or family crests and not seals of American colleges and universities. McKim had made his intellectual point.

In that respect, McKim also included something over the entrance to the club that seemed to elicit little comment regarding its propriety. McKim had written to Edith Wharton that "the designer should not be too slavish . . . in his adherence to the letter of tradition," and here is manifestation of that philosophy. In a classic

Doric frieze you might find a string of triglyphs, or vertical objects of three grooves, alternating with metopes, or circles within squares. In the entablature above the front entrance, McKim took variations on these elements and had them flanking a blank rectangular space that was presumably scheduled to have the club's name inscribed within.

William Mitchell Kendall, a senior member of McKim, Mead & White, said that the entablature was "adorned with the usual triglyphs, metopes, and mutules, *modified and enriched* [italics added] to harmonize with the ornamented columns." Instead of V-shaped grooves for the triglyphs, McKim specified cabled fluting to reflect the fluting on the columns flanking the entrance. And to strengthen the relationship between the club and education, McKim didn't have circles within his squares. He inserted mortarboards.

The members of the University Club were supposed to have at least attended a college for a few years or to have received an honorary degree, so mortarboards make sense. The primary drawback on a Renaissance-style building is that today's mortarboard is a rather recent phenomenon. The word only made its first appearance in the 1850s.

A willing suspension of disbelief might be required to accept a mortarboard depicted on a building modeled on a Renaissance-style palazzo, but we accept the seals of American colleges in all those shields, and American colleges weren't around in the Renaissance either. Anyway, the mortarboards didn't seem to elicit any comments when the clubhouse opened in 1899, and they don't seem to have elicited any since. As le Corbusier said, it's "a strange new firmness which is not Italian, but American!"

Crystal Gazing

Today's Henri Bendel, 714 Fifth Avenue, between 55th and 56th Streets

Anchored by the Vanderbilt mansions, the stretch of Fifth Avenue from 51st to 58th Streets had been the city's most affluent stretch of residences from the 1870s until the early 20th century, when all that began to change. In 1908 a pair of five-story commercial buildings was speculatively built at 712 and 714, between 55th and 56th Streets, on the site of the mansion of George J. Gould. By 1910, the Zabriskie residence at 716 Fifth was being altered for business, and on the southwest corner of 56th Street, the Baudouine house was being converted into a gallery for the Duveen art dealership.

In 1910, 714 Fifth Avenue was leased to Francois Spoturno of Paris, who headed the French perfumery firm, the House of Coty. To Sporturno, packaging was everything, and he had started having René Lalique, the jewelry and glass design maestro, design bottles for his fragrances. With his understanding of the need for appealing packaging, Sportuno asked Lalique to have a hand in packaging his store.

Coty's alterations were finished two years later, and they included something unique in the city—René Lalique's architectural glass. The windows were bas-reliefs in frosted glass, and the glass fills the Fifth Avenue window on the third, and fourth floors. As a note on the windows at Henri Bendel says, Lalique's "composition depicts flowering poppies and vines climbing skyward. The naturalistic rendering of the floral design, with more mature blossoms toward the bottom and buds toward the top, illustrates the lingering influence of Art Nouveau in Lalique's work," and it is one of the very few manifestations of Art Nouveau in the city.

By 1926, Coty decided to move its executive quarters to 55th Street west of Ninth Avenue, renting out the upper floors of their Fifth Avenue building while retaining only the showroom space. At the expiration of its lease in the 1950s, Coty itself moved out.

In the 1980s a "Going Out of Business" business that was selling electronics was occupying the space that had been Coty. The Lalique windows were all but forgotten, until the architectural historian, Andrew Dolkart, who was researching the building for the Municipal Art Society, "discovered" them. In 1984 the windows began to make the news again, and the building was designated a New York City landmark.

Despite the landmark designation, a developer was moving forward on his plan to tear down the Fifth Avenue buildings and erect a blockbuster. Similar to the rescue of the Villard Houses and the construction of Helmsley's Palace Hotel behind them, the resolution was to preserve the facades of 712 and 714, and have the 52-story tower rise from 50 feet back, with the main entrance to the office building on the side street.

The Fifth Avenue buildings would be gutted and the space leased for retail purposes. The windows were removed, restored, and re-installed, and the specialty store Henri Bendel moved in and became the beneficiary of the windows on the third floor, where a viewing platform was erected from which the windows can be viewed up close.

Gregory Gilmartin relates an aspect of this story that took place during the early talk of having a high rise on the southwest corner of 56th Street. The real-estate mogul who owned the building catercorner said that he could not imagine a tower going up on the site because it would block the view of the people who had bought apartments from him. Although there would be no financial quid pro quo, the mogul wanted his name on the project, and he told the developer that if he didn't cooperate, some political clout could be brought to bear that could tie him up forever. The mogul's bluff was called.

7

Midtown East

East 40th to 59th Streets, from Fifth Avenue East

What Was the Publisher Thinking?

220 East 42nd Street, between Second and Third Avenues

The founder and editor of the *Daily News*, James M. Patterson, was steeped in American history. His grandfather, Joseph Medill, was the founder of the *Chicago Tribune*, and young Patterson couldn't walk the hallways of his grandfather's newspaper office without being reminded of American history, with first pages of important editions lining the walls that included a "4 o'clock a.m. Extra" headlining Lincoln's assassination.

The engraved quote "He Made So Many of Them" is ascribed to Abraham Lincoln, although its provenance is not nailed down. Lincoln either said something like "God must love the common man, He made so many of them" or "The Lord prefers common-looking people. That is why He made so many of them."

The architect Walter H. Kilham, who worked on the design of the Daily News Building with Raymond Hood, assumed that the quote that Patterson had excerpted was God's love for the common man, and the implication was obvious to Kilham: God loved the readers of Patterson's tabloid. There is little substantiation that Lincoln had actually said it, and, if Lincoln did say it, the big question is why Patterson would have wanted it carved in stone. Any sensible public relations consultant would have told Patterson that it was bad corporate policy to demean your audience by describing it as "common." He was out to attract customers, and to sell newspapers.

If a good source for a quote is someone who was there when it was uttered and the quote was recorded soon after, then John Hay is a pretty good source. Hay, one of Lincoln's personal secretaries and a biographer of Lincoln, wrote a note on December 23, 1863, that "The President last night had a dream. He was in a party of plain people and as it became known who he was they began to comment on his appearance. One of them said, 'He is a common-looking man.' The president replied, 'Common-looking people are the best in the world: that is the reason the Lord makes so many of them.'" That quote certainly seems more Lincolnesque.

The *Daily News,* which was the nation's first tabloid, started publication in 1919, and it was still the brash, new kid in town when its building opened in 1930. The newspaper called itself "New York's Picture Newspaper," and lots of photographs—at least one per page in the editorial content—told the stories, accompanied by short, snappy prose. And there were catchy headlines that were frequently even greater puns (in the 1980s, "State Will Have No Truck with Tandems"), and comic strips such as *Dick Tracy* and—Leapin' Lizards!—*Little Orphan Annie.* They all contributed to make the *Daily News* the nation's largest selling daily within ten years of its inception.

A product of Groton and Yale, Patterson was hardly an upper-class twit. He took a year off from Yale to cover the Boxer Rebellion, and, while still in his twenties, Patterson had written a few plays and novels. One of them, *A Little Brother of the Rich*, said the *Times*, excoriated "fashionable society and pictured the women of his social set as excessive drinkers and vulgar exhibitionists." He later served as a legislator in his home state of Illinois, and as an editor, war correspondent, and soldier. As a captain in the Rainbow Division in France during World War I, his division commander, Douglas MacArthur, described Patterson as "the most brilliant, natural born soldier that ever served under me."

Patterson had determined to start a tabloid after a visit with Lord Northcliffe, a family friend, whose London *Daily Mirror* had a daily circulation of 800,000 in the late 1910s. It was Northcliffe who convinced Patterson that he should start a tabloid that was bright enough to entice the masses, and, sure enough, with the introduction of the *Daily News*, people who had never regularly read a newspaper were buying the *Daily News* on a daily basis.

William Randolph Hearst believed that it was a passing fad, but as the *Daily News'* circulation eclipsed the *Journal'*s at 500,000 in 1923, Hearst began to worry, and he started a circulation war. He introduced a lottery with a grand prize of $1,000, so the *Daily News* responded with its own lottery with a grand prize of $2,500. The amounts spiraled upward, each newspaper outdoing the other, until the prize had reached $25,000, at which point both publishers quit to lick their financial wounds. But Hearst had seen the virtues in a tabloid: By 1924 he was publishing *The New York Mirror*.

Times Square was where the greatest number of newspapers was sold, and Patterson liked the idea of being on 42nd Street. He might have considered the site of the future McGraw-Hill Building at 330 West 42nd Street, but that block-through site was already spoken for.

The Grand Central district was booming, in large part because of the terminal itself and its connections with the suburbs, and the subway with its connections with the rest of the city. The block front on the east side of Lexington Avenue between 41st and 42nd Streets beckoned, and it would have put Patterson right in the middle of things, but the zoning law of 1916 explains why he had to settle for a site farther east.

A goal of the zoning law was to segregate certain functions. Some zones were set aside for strictly residential purposes, others allowed a mix of retail and residential, still others allowed light industry in the mix, and so on. The zoning law only allowed light industry on 42nd Street west of Eighth Avenue and east of Third, which explains why the Daily News and McGraw-Hill buildings are where they are. Printing presses were light industry.

Patterson's site was block-through, so he could have the loading bays in the rear on 41st Street where the rolls of newsprint and barrels of ink could be received and the finished product trucked out, with a good public face shining onto the "front."

Patterson had started life left of center politically, but he started tilting further and further to the right. The *Washington Post* was diametrically opposed to just about every political stance Patterson took in his later life, but upon his death in 1947, the newspaper said that the country had lost "a genius in the newspaper world." Patterson was an uncommon man, and the Lord made so few of them.

Through These Doors to Jersey City

Just west of the entrance to the Chanin Building, 122 East 42nd Street, between Lexington and Park Avenues

The Chanin Building was on the cutting edge of modernity when it opened in 1929. Its banded, metal marquees that were rounded at the corners, for instance, were the precursors of the later iterations on the Empire State Building, the McGraw Hill Building, Radio City Music Hall, and 30 Rockefeller Plaza.

But the marquee just west of the building's entrance doesn't look anything like any of those marquees. It is more like an Art Deco take on a honeycomb, with horizontal bands filled with chevrons and broken up by vertical struts. And instead of finding a recessed entryway leading to brass revolving doors, there is a flat entrance flanked by vaguely neoclassical wall sconces.

If you had stepped into this entrance in December, 1928, before the Chanin Building had even opened, you would have found yourself in a bus depot that served the Jersey City terminal for the Baltimore & Ohio Railroad.

Until World War I, B&O passengers whose destination was New York City were ingloriously dumped in Jersey City. From Jersey City, the passengers had to take a ferry across the Hudson River to reach the city, much as the Countess Ellen Olenska had done in Edith Wharton's *The Age of Innocence*.

To save fuel during World War I, the B&O was allowed to use the tracks of the Pennsylvania Railroad and enter Pennsylvania Station. The B&O and Pennsy were bitter rivals, and by the mid-1920s, with the war over, another kind of battle

broke out—the B&O was summarily evicted. Passengers had enjoyed the through ride, and B&O management found itself flailing about trying to find a new way of delivering passengers into Manhattan.

The immediate solution was by bus, direct from the rail terminal in Jersey City. The buses would be sitting directly across the platform from the arriving train, and driven onto a ferry operated by the railroad, and across the river. From the water's edge of Manhattan, they would travel on to the original Waldorf-Astoria Hotel on Fifth Avenue between 33rd and 34th Streets.

Soon there was a second bus terminal in Manhattan, and a third, and one in Downtown Brooklyn, and they were all served by buses coming from and going to the Jersey City terminal.

The bus terminal in the Chanin Building was B&O's second. It occupied the entire western part of the main floor. It was ideally situated in the heart of Midtown, and it was luxurious. The entrance on 42nd Street led to the ticket office, a grand space with ornamental columns and a two-story-high ceiling, with indirect lighting provided by Egyptoid-Moderne torcheres and ceiling fixtures. There was a lounge, with framed photographs of national treasures on the walls, and there were potted palms, and furniture that was so modern it could have been designed by Mies Van der Rohe. After you had checked your luggage—even hand baggage—porters took it to the waiting buses, and it would be delivered directly to your seat or berth on the train.

Not only was there no extra charge for the service, when passengers boarded a B&O motor coach, they had "made their train." The train would not leave Jersey City until the coaches had arrived. Traffic jams and missed trains were already part of city lore by the late 1920s, and the B&O motor coach was the one way to beat traffic. Guaranteed.

The buses operated from the 41st Street side, and if you look at the four westernmost bays on 41st Street, you will ask where all the flowers have gone. Rene Chambellan's bronze frieze ends with a flourish four bays east from the western end of the building.

The buses operated through the two easternmost of those four bays, entering through one arch, discharging their passengers and baggage, then picking up departing passengers and their baggage, and exiting through the neighboring bay. The actual bus station was decorated in an updated Romanesque style, with variegated brickwork, and with rondels set into the walls that were cleverly masked air vents. Roman arches led to and from the waiting room, and a pair of arches separated one roadway from the other. You can still see the shape of those structural arches in the west wall of the store that occupies 117 East 41st Street.

No doubt you are wondering how the buses could maneuver in such tight quarters, and the answer was a turntable at the far end of the space. The turntable had a diameter of 30 feet, and it could make a complete revolution in one minute. It had roller bearings and was belt driven, just like a turntable for records.

The bus turntable in the Chanin Building was not the only one in the city. There was also one in the former Dixie Hotel, at 250 West 43rd Street. The Dixie was known for its "Southern hospitality," and it didn't hurt that many of the buses originating from the Dixie served Washington, D.C., and points south. The Dixie Bus Depot bucked the trend that sent most of the long-haul bus operators to the new Port Authority Bus Terminal in 1950, but by 1961, it was all over. The B&O bus service had already been discontinued by 1958.

Sic transit transit.

Flogging the Product

The Chrysler Building, 405 Lexington Avenue, between 42nd and 43rd Streets

If you build the superlative of anything, whether it's the first or biggest or longest or fastest or tallest, the odds are that whatever it is will make the news. If the thing is superlative enough, such as the tallest building in the world, the news will probably be flashed 'round the world.

In the first third of the 20th century, news of one superlative after another on the subject of the world's tallest buildings kept on flashing. First there was the Singer Building, then the Metropolitan Life Tower, then the Woolworth Building, then, in the late 1920s, there was the race between the Bank of the Manhattan Building at 40 Wall Street and the Chrysler Building.

All of those buildings had corporate names attached to them, and for good reason. Management understood that their buildings were giant billboards for their products, and the buildings kept serving that function well after the building had

opened and all the hoopla had died down. The name of the product would be in every book of records, it would come to the fore every time a tour guide pointed out the building, or whenever somebody said "Meet me on the northeast corner of Lexington and 42nd. You know, where the Chrysler Building is."

A difference between the Chrysler Building and the other record holders is that the Chrysler Building really was a billboard for the product. On the string course at the 31st floor setback are depictions of fenders and tires, with gleaming hubcaps setting off the white walls, along with an Art Deco–fied interpretation of the actual radiator cap on the Chrysler Six. The wings and hub caps, like the spire itself and other trim on the building, were made of a newly developed stainless steel that maintains its lustrous quality.

An interesting wrinkle to the story is that during all the building frenzy with the race between Chrysler's building and the Bank of the Manhattan Company, Walter Chrysler started having second thoughts, and at one stage of the game he told his architect, William Van Alen, to make the building shorter by ten stories. But then Chrysler had second thoughts about his second thoughts. Both General Motors and Ford already had office buildings in the city bearing their names. They were handsome but ordinary buildings that nobody looked at twice. He realized that the publicity value was not only in having a dazzling building with his name on it, just being in the race was perhaps of equal importance, and winning it, even if by a bit of chicanery, was worth going for. Word leaked out that work on Chrysler's building had stopped at 845 feet, so H. Craig Severance, the architect of the Bank of the Manhattan Building, called it quits at 927 feet. The leaked story was pure fabrication, and Chrysler just kept on going, plus he had an ace up his sleeve with a stainless-steel spire that was hoisted into place to serve as the capstone of the building at 1,048 feet. The title was his.

The building's reign as tallest was short, however. By the end of 1930, Chrysler found himself outfoxed. The management of the Empire State Building, headed by former governor Al Smith and John J. Raskob, the former chief financial officer at General Motors and the man who considered Chrysler an upstart, added a five-story "penthouse" to the top of their building, lifting the height of the Empire State from 1,000 feet to 1,050 feet. For good measure, the dirigible mooring mast was then added, taking the height to 1,250 feet, ensuring the title as tallest for another forty-plus years.

Something to Crow About

The eagle on Grand Central Terminal's elevated circumferential plaza, southeast corner, Vanderbilt Avenue and 42nd Street

oday's Grand Central, which was built in 1913, is the third on this site, and this cast-iron eagle, weighing in at 1.5 tons and with a 14-foot wingspan, had originally adorned the second Grand Central. That building was called "Grand Central Station," in contradistinction with the first Grand Central, a "Depot," and with today's "Terminal," so called because all trains that enter the building terminate there. When the second Grand Central was torn down in 1910 to make way for today's terminal, this eagle, along with its confreres, went missing, scattered to the anonymous winds.

Grand Central Depot was a three-story, mansard-topped Second Empire building, and it ranked among the most prominent buildings in the city when it was built in 1871. By the 1890s, its facilities could not accommodate the ever-expanding clerical staff, and the decision was to add three stories to it.

The architect Bradford Gilbert was asked to design the addition and to give the facade a more "modern" look. Elements of the old were stripped away, including the central Mansard roof. Stucco was applied over the old brick, and the overall style was changed to a more classical design with English baroque flourishes. Four small, Christopher Wren–like clock towers, or "tourelles," were added to the roofline, and at the base of those towers were the eagles.

Nobody seems quite sure how many eagles there had actually been. If there had been four at the base of each of the four tourelles, simple math tells you sixteen, but because of "facadism" there had probably been eleven. Few people could see anything from the street but the eagles along the facade, so you get three eagles on the base of each of the two towers on the corners of the 42nd Street facade, two on the base of the central tower on Vanderbilt Avenue, and another three overlooking 45th Street.

The sculptor of the eagles is unknown, ditto the foundry, and not even Margot Gayle, *the* authority on everything cast iron, had discovered anything. The basic facts are a mystery.

Few people seemed to have bothered with the disposition of the eagles until 1966, when David McLane, a photographer for the *Daily News*, stumbled on one of the eagles at the Metro-North railroad station in North Tarrytown. His curiosity was piqued, and he and other intrepid eagle seekers went on a search for more.

Their first stop might have been "Eagle's Nest," an estate on the north shore of Long Island, in Centerport. Eagle's Nest started being built in 1910, the very year that the station was being pulled down, and Eagle's Nest just happened to have been owned by William K. Vanderbilt II, a vice president of the New York Central Railroad. The eagles were essentially his for the taking, and Vanderbilt no doubt simply appropriated them without a word. Flanking the driveway to Eagle's Nest is a pair of the estate's namesakes.

The balance of the flock started turning up in some pretty unlikely places.

One of the places has a name similar to Vanderbilt's estate—Eagle's Rest, in Garrison, New York, where there are two eagles. In 1919, Col. Jacob Ruppert, the second-generation brewmeister and by then owner of the New York Yankees, bought the property, and he arranged to have the eagles transported and erected there, although how and when is a mystery. He no doubt had an affinity for eagles. His father's Knickerbocker Beer had won a prize at the centennial celebration in Philadelphia in 1876, and Ruppert's labels were soon sporting an eagle bearing a banner in its teeth that read "Centennial Prize Medal." Eagle's Rest is now part of St. Basil Academy.

Another eagle was found on Long Island's north shore, overlooking the Sound from a private home in Kings Point, and one more is mounted on a pedestal at the intersection of Routes 28 and 214 in Shandaken, New York.

A seventh eagle turned up in the backyard of the Westchester home of Laurie Hawkes and Paul Grand Pre, who found it in the hemlock bushes after they had bought their house in 1995. They were offered $100,000 for the statue by an antiques dealer, but by then they knew the eagle's provenance, and they felt a higher calling than Mammon's. They wanted to arrange to have their eagle returned to its place in history. By coincidence, their daughter was going to school with the grandson of E. Virgil Conway, the then-MTA chairman, and their eagle now sits on the roof of the food market on Lexington Avenue at 43rd Street.

The eagle on the railing here at Grand Central Terminal had been on the grounds of a monastery, and, like the first eagle to return home to roost, it was first disassembled, sandblasted, cleaned, reassembled, and painted. Unlike the original eagles, which were painted a uniformly drab color, these eagles have been painted to reflect an eagle's glorious colors, with their "tongues alive in their beaks as if in full cry," as one reporter said.

The original site selected for this reincarnated eagle was overlooking the main concourse from the Vanderbilt Avenue balcony. That plan fell through because the management of the restaurant that occupies some of the balcony space did not want to give up 40 seats to accommodate the eagle, which was a blessing. The eagle would have been a mixed metaphor—a fish out of water.

Meet Me Under the Clock

The lobby of 335 Madison Avenue, entered via East 43rd Street

"Meet me under the clock" was all you had to say if you were meeting someone in Midtown during the years 1913 to 1981. The clock was in the Biltmore Hotel, sitting atop a brass arch that led to the hotel's Palm Court, and it was in plain sight as you climbed the stairs from the main entrance on 43rd Street.

The hotel's location, complete with an entrance directly from Grand Central Terminal and within comfortable walking distance of major shops and Times Square theaters, couldn't have been more convenient, and the hotel loomed large in New York's political and social history.

The Biltmore was the traditional gathering place for the Democratic faithful—both Al Smith and Franklin D. Roosevelt used it as the headquarters for their presidential races. It was a favorite place to meet a friend on the way to somewhere else, or just to sit around and gab. And even marriages were performed there. On the third floor was the Meditation Chapel, a non-sectarian but Christian-inspired architectural gem.

The hotel was particularly popular among students, in part because they were given special weekend- and holiday rates. It was a smart marketing plan—business travelers frequented the hotel weekdays, and students filled the void in the slow periods.

In the 1920s, F. Scott Fitzgerald wrote that hundreds of girls "dangling powder boxes and bracelets and lank young men at their wrists" would be swarming about the Biltmore.

In the 1950s, J. D. Salinger's Holden Caulfield met his date at the hotel before going to the theater. "A lot of schools were home for vacation already," says the protagonist of *The Catcher in the Rye*, "and there were about a million girls sitting and standing around waiting for their dates to show up."

Joan Didion, who arrived in New York at the age of twenty in 1954, said that people who had "grown up waiting under the Biltmore clock and dancing to Lester Lanin" were, well, different, certainly different from the newly arrived who hadn't grown up with all the advantages.

By 1981, the hotel that had created a social class unto itself was declared redundant. The site was slated to be cleared and developed as an office building. The developers, the brothers Paul and Seymour Milstein, soon realized that if they tore down the 1913 building, a new building on the site would have less rentable space to the tune of about 200,000 square feet. The Biltmore had been erected before the 1916 zoning law, and even with the revised zoning law of 1961, the developers would not have such a large envelope (the three-dimensional space) in which to build. They simply wouldn't get as much bang for their buck.

"MEET ME UNDER THE CLOCK"

The management of 335 Madison Avenue does not permit photographs to be taken of the Biltmore clock that is now in the building's lobby. Hence, this matchbook.
PHOTO FROM THE COLLECTION OF JOHN TAURANAC

The Milsteins did the only reasonable thing from the perspective of real-estate developers. They gutted and stripped the building of its skin; they reconfigured it, and gave it a new granite facade. It might have cost about 25 percent more to reconfigure the building than to tear it down and start from scratch, but, with commercial rents in the range of mid-$40 a square foot in 1984, those 200,000 square feet would generate more than $8 million a year.

When the plan was first proposed, the building was on the preservation commission's docket, and a cry went up among preservationists to save at least some of the architectural features of the lobby, including the clock.

The Milsteins struck a deal with the New York Landmarks Conservancy, a nonprofit group dedicated to the preservation of noteworthy buildings. The clock and a "reasonable approximation" of the Palm Court, part of the hotel lobby and the East 43rd Street entrance, would be restored. In exchange, the Conservancy would not push for true preservation.

But look on the works of the mighty Milstein Brothers and despair. Their PR mouthpiece claimed that the original fabric of the Palm Court—the marble on the walls, the stuff of restoration—was too "grimy, and could not be cleaned properly," so the developers promised that a new Palm Court, with the "same arches as the old parlor, with mock skylights, (and with) columns and floors covered either in granite or marble and all exposed metalwork . . . of bronze," would be created. The assumption was that the wreckers had moved in, knocked down the walls, and dumped the rubble in landfill somewhere.

The architects who were to have done the restoration, Hardy Holzman Pfeiffer Associates, did the principled thing. They submitted their resignation.

Now here's the rub. Not all those "grimy" walls, brass fixtures, and the main entrance were destroyed. Key parts of the Palm Court and the entire 43rd Street entrance were carefully removed from the site, restored, and put to good use by a restaurateur at 290 Eighth Avenue.

Slabs of marble and brass fixtures and whole entrances are not anthropomorphic cartoon characters that suddenly sprout heads and legs and arms and spring to life. Inanimate objects do not remove themselves from walls and walk out the door on their own. Somebody carefully orchestrated it. If a restaurateur could afford to salvage and restore whole swaths of the Biltmore's Palm Court and re-install it, along with the brass entrance, certainly the Milsteins could have simply cleaned it all. That puts the lie to the Milsteins' claim that it was beyond salvation.

To assuage their guilt for reneging on the deal to preserve the Palm Court or to create a simulation, which the developers cavalierly came to dismiss as an "architectural contrivance," the Milsteins contributed $500,000 to a fund administered by the Landmarks Conservancy. That figure comes to about one sixteenth of the money generated in one year by those extra 200,000 square feet of rentable space.

The clock, at least, was saved and is *in situ*, sort of. The clock was installed behind glass within a niche in the wall behind the lobby's concierge desk, where it now sits forlornly about 25 feet away from its original site. It is not even a blip on the city's social radar screen. To paraphrase Yogi Berra, nobody meets there anymore, and it's not because it's too crowded.

Those Tracks Below Are the Secret to the Elegant, Swellegant Park Avenue

The second grate east of Park Avenue, on the northeast side of 49th Street

The grate that Marilyn Monroe stood on during the filming of *The Seven Year Itch* might be more famous, but the grates along Park Avenue from 45th to 97th Streets tell a more important story. It's the story of the making of one of the grandest stretches of the city.

In the 19th century, steam locomotives hauled railroad cars at grade on some of the city's streets, including whole swaths of Fourth, Tenth, and Eleventh Avenues, from the Harlem River as far downtown as Chambers Street. Whole neighborhoods fell or were never developed to their fullest because of the arrival of trains rumbling along neighboring streets.

The tracks are still on a major stretch of the former Fourth Avenue, today's Park Avenue, but they are unseen as far as 97th Street except through the occasional grate, such as the grate located only inches away from the 49th Street wall of the Waldorf-Astoria. Those tracks continue right under the hotel.

The presence of those tracks goes far in explaining a peculiarity of the Waldorf that is shared with several office buildings between it and Grand Central Terminal. You have to take a flight of stairs or an escalator up to the lobby floor in the Waldorf, and up to the mezzanine level in many of the office buildings such as 270 and 280 Park Avenue, or you are obliged to climb some steps from the street to reach the concierge level, and then up another set of steps to reach the elevator level, as in 277 and 299.

No sensible architect would intentionally design a hotel or an office building with stairs to climb or an escalator to ride to reach the lobby floor unless there was no recourse, and the Yiddish verb for carrying something that is heavy combined with the Latin noun for baggage synthesizes the reason—nobody wants to *schlep* their *impedimenta* up or down stairs, and the architects of these buildings were eminently sensible.

The reason for all this bother is that not a single building along the spine of Park Avenue in the upper Forties has a true basement. Where you would find the usual basement, you find trains and tracks instead. With no basements, the elevator housing had to be on the first floor, hence lobbies were up a floor.

The reason for the peculiar configurations is, ironically, the existence of another kind of structure that ideally has no stairs—a railroad station, Grand Central.

You can thank William J. Wilgus for this. Wilgus was the chief engineer of the New York Central Railroad at the turn of the 20th century, and it was his idea to turn what had been non-revenue-generating train yards into the city's largest real-estate venture of that time.

Until the coming of today's Grand Central Terminal in 1913, the New York Central Railroad had been operating steam engines on Park Avenue from 97th Street, first at grade, then in a partially covered cut to the open-air train yards that stretched from 50th to 45th Streets, from west of Lexington Avenue to east of Madison Avenue.

With the electrification of the railroad, trains entering the new terminal would operate in underground tunnels, since there would be no need to vent the smoke and steam. The old train yards could be declared redundant and the new train yards could be roofed over. But why stop there? Since the railroad already owned the property, Wilgus said the land could be put to better use—there could be a vast real-estate development, with grand hotels and apartment houses, with exhibition halls and office buildings above the yards, with the trains stored and operated in the basements of the buildings. The key to accomplishing this is skyscraper design. Just as you can stand with your legs straddling the tracks of a model train, so skyscrapers can stand with their legs—the columns they stand on—straddling the tracks of full-size trains.

It was alchemy, pure and simple. From the very air would come gold in the form of rents.

A twist to the larger story is inherent in the design of Grand Central Terminal itself. Grand Central is justly famous for its grand flights of stairs up to the Concourse balconies, but the terminal should be more famous for its ramps, ramps leading from Vanderbilt Avenue at 42nd Street, ramps to the lower level, and ramps down to many platforms. There is even a gentle incline from the Park Avenue entrance at 42nd Street to the concourse. Hardly any *schlepping* of *impedimenta* on stairs required.

"Plans"

The lower stained-glass panels in the St. Patrick window, the west wall of the south transept, St. Patrick's Cathedral, between 50th and 51st Streets

Unlike the subject matter of the average stained-glass window in a house of worship, such as the main window above these panels that celebrates Saint Patrick, these panels relate a mundane tale of internecine rivalry.

The window was the gift of James Renwick, Jr., the architect of the cathedral and the man responsible for the design of the window. Renwick knew good quality and he specified it, and if the luminescent blue in this stained glass is reminiscent of the great windows in Chartres Cathedral, it's because this window was made by a stained-glass maker in Chartres, Nicolas Lorin.

To understand the story as depicted requires some temporal juggling. The window has Renwick showing his plans for the proposed cathedral to Archbishop John Hughes, a scene that might have taken place in 1853, when Hughes accepted Renwick's architectural plans, or, more likely, 1858, when work was about to begin. Immediately to Renwick's left is John McCloskey, dressed in the red robes of a cardinal. McCloskey is also holding plans.

Archbishop Hughes died in 1864, and McCloskey succeeded him, not to become cardinal until 1875. Hughes and McCloskey in his cardinal robes could not have been in the same room at the same time, but Renwick wanted to make a point, and nobody can miss the cardinal's red robes. Renwick's plans for the cathedral as accepted did not come to fruition in their entirety for reasons that were in part financial, in part McCloskey, who succeeded in having some of the building altered from Renwick's original plan to his own scheme, which Renwick was then obliged to execute. The image was intentionally designed to illustrate Renwick's displeasure over McCloskey's meddlesome nature, and if what McCloskey is holding is meant to be a floorplan, it makes no sense; as an elevation, even less.

Hughes and McCloskey were long-time associates—McCloskey had even been Hughes's coadjutor, his assistant—and McCloskey no doubt had had the archbishop's ear from the outset. Complicating the issue was that completing the cathedral according to Renwick's plans was a bit of a pipe dream to begin with, but Archbishop Hughes had undertaken many projects that had come to successful conclusions, and he was a great promoter. Although finances were nonexistent at the outset in 1858 when construction began, Archbishop Hughes had faith.

Work on the cathedral was stopped in 1861 by a combination of a paucity of funds and the onset of the Civil War, but when McCloskey took over as the new head of the diocese upon the death of Hughes in 1864, there was no lollygagging. No sooner had McCloskey been installed "than he turned his attention to the unfinished cathedral," the *Tribune* reported. "Under his energetic yet *conservative management* [italics added], the work was resumed. . . . From the first he made himself familiar with the plans in their minutest detail, and seldom a week passed that he did not visit the building several times."

A few days before the consecration of the cathedral in 1879, a *Times* reporter cruelly wrote that there were "temporary shams which the architect, in an evil moment," had decided on. The "shams" that the reporter noted had been thrust upon Renwick against his will, and they were not temporary. Cutbacks had begun early, and many of Renwick's plans were chipped away, others simply abandoned.

The central spire at the crossing was one of the first to go, as evidenced by the lack of columns required to support the additional weight.

The masonry ceiling that Renwick had designed was quickly dropped as well. Over Renwick's protestations, a "sham" ceiling of lathe and plaster was substituted for the stone ceiling—the bosses, the ribs, even the capitals atop the columns, they are all plaster. And with no masonry ceiling there was no need for the flying buttresses, so that idea fell by the wayside as well.

Another "sham" the reporter had noticed was that some of the interior walls were not of natural stone, but of Beton Coignet, an early concrete masonry unit that was stamped out of a mold, which was far less expensive than cutting stone. Beton Coignet had only been patented in France in the 1850s, and it was first manufactured in the U.S. in 1872. Renwick had been trained as an engineer, and he artfully used it for arches and clerestory windows, all of which were prefabricated at a factory in Gowanus, Brooklyn, with the headquarters building still standing at Third Avenue and Third Street.

Another basic plan of Renwick's that fell by the wayside was his idea that St. Patrick's should be modeled on true Medieval cathedrals, with individual chairs that could be moved about as needed. The financial advantage of pews is that they can be rented, and the nearer the altar the more valuable the pew, so the Medieval touch gave way to the Midas touch. Within a week of the opening of the cathedral, pews started being auctioned off. Fifty-three pews were bid on at the first auction, with annual rentals reaching a high of $2,100 for a pew in the first row.

With the coming of the permanent pews went Renwick's vision of how the floor should be laid as well. Renwick had specified green and red sandstone for durability, with colored marbles worked into Gothic patterns. Instead, the floor in the nave was wood when the cathedral opened, with only the sanctuary in marble.

Perhaps the most serious alteration to Renwick's plans was his vision of how a true Gothic-style cathedral should terminate in the east end, with an ambulatory around the high altar and a Lady Chapel beyond. Although Hughes had originally accepted Renwick's plan, he early put the kibosh on the idea, perhaps at the urging of McCloskey, who was known to have advocated a flatter wall. McCloskey's plan was inherently less expensive, with the added virtue of allowing room for the future archbishop's residence and rectory, even perhaps some speculatively built housing. A centennial history of the cathedral said that the result of having the east end of the church ending abruptly in the flat wall was "a graceless form with which no one was particularly happy."

All of this might explain why Renwick is depicted with his eyes heavenward, or perhaps he is just rolling his eyes over the fact of what McCloskey had been up to all those years. Renwick might have been vain, but there is no indication that he was particularly mean-spirited or vindictive, but whatever McCloskey did was clearly enough for Renwick to make sure that something of the story was told in this stained glass.

Why Those Bolts of Electricity?

570 Lexington Avenue, southwest corner of 51st Street

This roofline is one of the most fabulous in the city, if not *the* most fabulous. The architects Cross & Cross had been designing buildings in the style of the neo-this or neo-that well into the 1920s, whereupon they started to change their style. Their first truly Modern building was 1 East 57th Street in 1930, and by 1931, when they designed this building, they had hit full stride.

John Cross intentionally built what he called "vibrant energy" into the design, and he included bolts of electricity and wave-like emanations from the head of the central figure on the building's roofline. The reason for all the trim is the client for whom the building was originally built. It is decorative trim that, curiously, would be equally appropriate for the second primary tenant.

The Radio Corporation of America (RCA) had commissioned the building, and the "forked lightning" and the bolts of electricity were there because electricity was key to powering radio sets. The central figure that you see—and there's one 50-foot-high figure on each of the four sides of the tower—is there to symbolize

the spirit of radio. The plan was that an aura of colored light would shoot out from the aluminum crown of "forked lightning" at night, as if it could find its way to all the radio sets that sat center stage in living rooms across the nation.

The copper cladding on the finials was primarily there to serve as a lightning rod—copper is electricity's most efficient conductor—and also to serve one more visible link with electricity. Electricity was so key to broadcasting in the 1930s that RCA's logo, a charming serif type face, had an electric-bolt-like squiggle under its "A."

RCA did not stay long in its new building. In 1932, RCA moved into 30 Rockefeller Plaza, Rockefeller Center's flagship building, and, as the building's major tenant, its name went up on the building in lights.

Those bolts of electricity on 570 Lexington were right up the alley of the next tenant, General Electric (GE). GE could move right in without changing anything on the facade except the name in the clock on the corner. The fist with a bolt of electricity emanating from it is repeated at street level, and terra-cotta and aluminum figures on the lower floors have heads sitting atop stylized bolts of electricity.

The relationship between RCA and GE was complicated. RCA had been sort of a corporate step-child of GE. In the 1980s, General Electric essentially "re-acquired" RCA. GE moved out of this building and into 30 Rockefeller Plaza, whereupon the naming rights came full circle. In 1988 the RCA Building was renamed the GE Building. In 2015, in yet another act of corporate imperialism, down came "GE," and up went "Comcast," plus the NBC peacock.

The decoration on Tower 570 remains its wonderful, original self, and it is virtually pristine, with any repairs reflecting the original work. Whether an aura of light ever shot out from the crown of "forked lightning" is a mystery, but in the 1950s, colored lights played from within the open, gold-leafed tracery on the roofline, adding a magical quality to the night skyline. The infrastructure for the original lighting is still in place, but today the roofline is floodlit. The twinkle is gone.

By the Skin of Their Teeth

312 and 314 East 53rd Street, between Second and First Avenues

A wood-framed house in Midtown built to the grid system is a rare house indeed. The few that were erected in the mid-19th century were built when the area was neither suburban nor yet part of the built-up city. The fear of fire is the reason.

The city had experienced one disastrous fire after another in the 18th- and early 19th centuries, with flames jumping from building to building, leaping streets and devouring block after block, until the fires had become conflagrations. You only have to read Samuel Pepys's account of the great London Fire of 1660 to understand New York's fire of 1835, when slowing down the spread of the flames could only be achieved by the same method—buildings were blown up to create fire breaks.

Under the subject "The Great Fire of ..." in the index of a book on the history of the Fire Department are the dates 1776, 1778, 1804, 1811, 1835, and 1845. After the mid-19th century you still read about terrible fires, but they were ordinarily contained to one building or to a ship, not to whole swaths of the city, and the reason was the enactment of fire laws that in part forbade wood frame houses.

By 1849, there could be no wood frame houses built south of a line that extended from river to river 100 feet north of 32nd Street. In 1860, the line was placed at 100 feet north of 52nd Street, at the southern lot line of these houses. In 1866, the year these houses were erected, the line was moved to 86th Street. The builders, Robert and James Cunningham, just snuck in under the wire.

Wood frame houses by that time were relatively inexpensive to build, thanks to two developments: the mass-produced nail had been perfected by the 1820s, and the balloon-frame house had been perfected by the 1830s. Balloon-frame houses were unlike the more traditional method of construction that required mortising together heavy lumber linked by wood pegs. Balloon-frame houses were constructed with two-by-fours nailed together to create the frame—a revolution in carpentry—which meant that they could be almost whacked together by two builders working together. They were dubbed "balloon frame" houses not because they were blown up like balloons, but because people originally feared that the houses, which seemed so flimsily constructed, could be blown away like balloons.

These houses are hardly grandiloquent, but "Second Empire" and "Italianate" are frequently the choice of architectural adjectives for describing them. Second Empire usually conjures up grand, overblown, eclectic buildings—"Ulysses S. Grant Modern"—and Italianate frequently conjures up great freestanding, be-turreted and be-towered buildings. Of course, you might simply describe the style as plain-old, vernacular architecture, the kind you might find on Main Street and be done with it.

What is amazing about these houses is that they are still single-family occupancy, and what is perhaps more amazing is that despite the very real potential for fire, they have not burned down.

The Fish Are Jumpin'

The Brook, 111 East 54th Street, between Park and Lexington Avenues

A string course with a wavelike motif, the classic Vitruvian scroll, makes eminently good sense for this men's club, the Brook, and the motif on its own would have been heuristic enough. This one comes, however, with a whimsical difference. Those fish that are swimming upbrook might just be brook trout, to drive the point home that this is the Brook.

This is not the only whimsical string course in the city—a string course depicting the race between the tortoise and the hare is on the apartment house at 1040 Park Avenue at 86th Street, and another at the Marine Air Terminal at La Guardia Airport has flying fish as a motif—"flying fish" in the form of seaplanes used to take off from North Beach Airport, today's La Guardia.

Ten-forty Park, the Marine Air Terminal, and the Brook were all designed by the same architectural firm, Delano & Aldrich, who were ordinarily *molto serioso*. Their usual designs were conservative buildings in the Federal or Georgian styles that were intentionally designed to be understated. For 1040 Park and the Brook, they subtly sneaked their whimsy into the otherwise staid buildings.

Delano and Aldrich came by it all naturally, and could pull it off with aplomb. Just think of the middle names of two famous New York personages, Franklin Delano Roosevelt and Nelson Aldrich Rockefeller. William Adams Delano was a cousin of FDR, and his partner, Chester Holmes Aldrich, was related to Senator Nelson Aldrich, hence to Aldrich's daughter, Abigail "Abby" Aldrich, or Mrs. John D. Rockefeller, Jr.

For clients, Delano & Aldrich liked to stick with their own kind. The partners designed Kykuit, for instance, the Rockefeller estate in Pocantico Hills in Westchester County, and they designed mansions galore. They designed two elite private schools on the Upper East Side, Chapin on East End Avenue, and St. Bernard's on East 98th Street. When they planned St Bernard's, Delano & Aldrich perhaps forgot what they were designing. Their original plans provided housing for servants on the fifth floor, and a wine room in the basement.

Between Delano and Aldrich, there were undergraduate degrees from Yale and Columbia's School of Mines, a graduate degree from Columbia's School of Architecture and two from l'Ecole des Beaux Arts, and they both taught at Columbia.

The partners were joiners—Delano was a member of the Brook when this building was designed, along with the University and Century, and the Piping Rock in Locust Valley, Long Island; Aldrich preferred memberships in more professionally oriented organizations, such as the Society of Beaux Arts Architects and the Société des Architects Diplomes. They viscerally as much as intellectually understood the needs and wants of club members, and their designs for clubhouses include the Union, the Knickerbocker, and the Colony.

Between 1850 and 1925, clubs seem to have been started at the drop of a club tie, and so it went with the Brook. The idea for the club was conceived in a fit of pique in 1901 when the clatter of dishes emanating from the Union Club's kitchen late one evening told Thomas B. Clarke that the waiters were telling the guests that it was time to go home. Clarke, an art dealer, was indicative of a turn-of-the-20th-century club man. At one time or another he was a member of about ten clubs in the city, but that evening at the Union led him to believe that something was rotten in the state of all of them. The Brook was established two years later, and in 1925, the club moved into this building.

The name of the club is an odd choice for a men's club. Its inspiration was the refrain in Alfred Lord Tennyson's poem, *The Brook*:

Men may come and men may go,
But I go on forever.

The clubmen wanted uninterrupted service 24 hours a day, with the doors never closed, and the kitchen- and serving staff always on hand, day and night. By employing "a duplicate set of attendants" the clubmen sought relief from what the *Times* described as "the autocratic servant problem," and by so doing escaped the problem of disgruntled servants who might want to get some sleep.

The fact that service was 24 hours a day, seven days a week, was an especial boon to the members in the summer, when a member's city abode would more than likely be shuttered. The member could find all the comforts of home at the Brook if duty called him into town at any time, since the door was always open. And if the door to a member's home had been closed in his face because of marital discord, as Mrs. William K. Vanderbilt, Jr., did to her husband in 1909, he could always find refuge and a home among his friends at the Brook.

Furthering the illusion of a home away from home, the service in the dining room was just as you would expect at home, where nobody would never think of writing down whether roasted- or boiled potatoes were preferred. There was no writing down of orders in the dining room, which obliged the waiters to remember all the details of an order until they could write them down, safely removed from the dining room and the eyes of members.

Of the roughly 50 men's social clubs that Fremont Rider listed in his 1920s guidebook, the Brook was not included. Discussing the average club, Rider said, "strangers can of course obtain access only when introduced by a member." This was one area where the Brook broke with the notion of being a home away from home. The Brook would brook no guest who was a resident of New York City— "No Local Visitors Allowed." And, added the *Times*, "caution must be exercised when out-of-town or foreign visitors are invited in."

The Brook's short membership roll further separated the wheat of the Brook from the chaff of other clubs. And then there was the way that the Brook took on new members. One did not apply. Membership was by invitation only. The invited men may come and the invited men may go, but the uninvited also serve who only stand and wait.

American Imperial

In the lobby of the St. Regis Hotel, 2 East 55th Street, on the southeast corner of Fifth Avenue

Who'd a thunk that such a thing as the humble letter box in a building lobby would be architect designed? However, given the choice between a generic, off-the-shelf letter box and a custom-designed letter box that harmonizes with the style of the building, architects were routinely including the design of letter boxes in their duties within twenty years of the introduction of the combination mail chute and letter box in 1884, and manufacturers were happily furnishing letter boxes in any style or color. The letter box just had to be made of good, strong metal and adhere to the post office department's standards.

The letter box in the 1904 St. Regis Hotel is nothing less than American Imperial, as befitting an Astor-built hotel, and clearly the hotel's architects, Trowbridge & Livingston, were having a wonderful time with its design, with the federal symbol giving a new level of meaning to spread eagle, and with all those swirls and vines and volutes, especially the capitals with their elaborate ram horns.

But where is the mail slot? The ordinary letter box has one mail slot in the front, but this letter box has two letter slots, and they are on the sides, all the better to preserve the fearful aquiline symmetry. (The "P.O.D" within the seal is an abbreviation of "Post Office Department.")

The styles of custom-designed letter boxes varied wildly, like the building designs themselves. In the Woolworth Building, they are Gothicized. In the Salmon Tower, the letter box reflects the low relief, Romanesque-y sculpture surrounding the entrances. In the lobby of the Chanin Building, the letter box is adorned by an Art Deco–styled eagle. At 29 Broadway, the letter box, like the Art Deco building itself, exudes modernity. It depicts the advances made in transportation, which is

an appropriate motif—speedy transportation by train, ship, or air translates into the speedy delivery of mail.

The combination mail chute and letter box was one of those Victorian innovations that simplified life for all involved. Instead of having to go downstairs and out to the street to find a mail box to post your letter, you only had to drop your letter down a chute from the common hallway on your floor and down it would go to a letter box on the lobby floor, there to be picked up by a postal worker on his usual rounds.

James G. Cutler, the man who was awarded the nation's first patent on a mail chute and mailbox combination, was himself an architect, and the very first mail chute was in the Elwood Building in his hometown of Rochester, New York, in 1884, a building that Cutler had designed five years earlier.

Other manufacturers could produce letter boxes, and in all likelihood the Hecla Iron Works manufactured the one at the St. Regis. Hecla manufactured custom-designed letter boxes for other buildings such as Chicago's Commercial National Bank and Philadelphia's Fulton Building, and Hecla did the St. Regis's original bronze marquee, along with the housing for the swinging doors and the doorman's sentry box. And clearly the architect Samuel Trowbridge liked the work of Hecla, which supplied the railings for Trowbridge's own house at 123 East 70th Street in 1902, two years before the St. Regis opened.

The 1927 apartment house that this writer lives in has a Cutler, and it adheres to the specifications of the U.S. Postal System. The box is distinctly marked "U.S. Letter Box," the door opens on hinges on one side, with the bottom of the door not less than two feet six inches above the floor. The assumption was that the letter box was an off-the shelf neoclassical design, complete with Federal eagle, and, sure enough, on the website for the Smithsonian National Postal Museum, the 1920 model that is illustrated is a dead ringer.

One of the beguiling touches with the Cutler letter boxes is that locks were ordinarily cleverly disguised. The lock to the Cutler in 29 Broadway is craftily disguised as the headlight of the locomotive. The lock in the letter box in this writer's apartment house is in the center of a rosette, as is the lock to the letter box in the St. Regis.

Flatiron Building: Fact and Fancy

The Fuller Building, 41 East 57th Street, northeast corner of Madison Avenue

The first bit of fancy regarding the Flatiron Building is its name, and the mosaic decorating the lobby floor of the Fuller Building provides a hint: the Flatiron Building's name was the Fuller Building. It was built by the Fuller Construction Company under the leadership of Harry S. Black, the same Harry S. Black who together with Bernhard Beinecke and others created the United States Realty and Improvement Company, the same Fuller Construction Company that built—and named—the Fuller Building in which this mosaic sits.

The second bit of fancy is the word *flatiron*. The triangular plot upon which the Flatiron Building sits is a right triangle, and the last time this writer ironed a shirt he was using a flatiron in the form of an isosceles triangle, not a right triangle. You really can't blame the building for the misnomer. The site had been dubbed the "Flatiron" by the turn of the 20th century, before the building was built.

You still have to wonder why the gore created by Broadway and Fifth Avenue between 22nd and 23rd Streets was dubbed the "Flatiron" when other comparable sites all the way up Broadway to 107th Street were not, although the site where the Times Tower was to be erected was described as the same *kind* of

flatiron as the Fuller Building stood on. Perhaps the site's claim to fame is that it was the first major example created on Broadway's northerly angled march with the right-angled streets as its setting.

Despite its name, the Flatiron Building is justifiably one of the most famous buildings in the city—it has even given rise to the name of the neighborhood— and, perhaps because of the building's fame, there are more fancies to the Flatiron Building than facts.

One of the interesting things about this mosaic is the date, 1903. A simple standard for the year a building is built is when it is first occupied. Coming up with when the first office tenants started moving in is up for grabs, but one commercial tenant was in residence on the ground floor before 1903. On December 12, 1902, the United Cigar Store ran a display ad in the *Times* announcing that, "After weeks of preparation we will open the door of our newest and most up-to-date store in the Fuller—better known as the Flatiron Building—Saturday morning at 9 o'clock."

One sure fact is that the building is indeed a true skyscraper, a tall building supported by an interior skeleton of steel or poured-in-place concrete with steel reinforcements, with its walls doing little more than keeping out the cold and damp. A skyscraper's walls do nothing to bear the weight of the structure itself. A wonderful photograph taken during the building's construction shows the frame having risen about 16 stories, with the exterior walls rising for the first three stories, then no walls but evidence of a steel skeleton for two stories, and then walls beginning again at the sixth floor and rising to about the twelfth. If those walls had been load bearing, the building as depicted would not have been. The walls are hanging off the steel structure—as some people say, like a curtain—hence the phrase curtain-wall architecture.

Thanks to the building's triangular plot, its heavily draped neo-Renaissance style, and the fact that from the north it commanded the Broadway view like a ship's prow cutting through the right-angled streets, not to forget that it was the tallest building in the neighborhood, the Flatiron captured the imagination of natives and visitors alike and served as a symbol of the dramatic new age of skyscrapers in the early 20th century.

More fancies than its name have floated about the building for years, and despite what some "authorities" might say, the Flatiron Building was hardly New York City's first true skyscraper, nor is it the city's oldest true skyscraper. The city's first completely steel-framed building was Bruce Price's American Surety Building at 100 Broadway, which went up in 1896. Likewise, the Flatiron Building was never the world's tallest building, nor was it ever the city's. By 1899, 15 Park Row had already risen 29 stories, to 391 feet; the Flatiron, at 21 stories, is 300 feet high.

Adding to the building's story is another great fancy—that the phrase "Twenty-Three skidoo" originated because of a phenomenon occurring on Fifth Avenue and 23rd Street. It is a fact that the prevailing winds from the west had to go somewhere when they hit the building. The resulting downdrafts, and the consequent updrafts as the wind hit the sidewalks, raised ladies' skirts and men's hopes at a time when a glimpse of stocking was looked on as something shocking. In 1907, the Ashcan artist John Sloane wrote in his diary that "a high wind this morning and the pranks of the gusts about the Flatiron Building at Fifth Avenue and 23rd Street was interesting to watch. . . . And a funny thing, a policeman to keep men from loitering about the corner." And what the police at the corner of Fifth and 23rd started saying, goes the story, was "Hey, you on Twenty-three, skidoo," which was soon reduced to "Twenty-three, skidoo." (*Skidoo* was probably derived from *skedaddle*, or "get away.") There are many possible leads for the combination of *twenty-three* and *skidoo*, but as the authority of New York slang, Irving Lewis Allen, said, "The phrase was popular before the Flatiron was built." Fancy that.

Cladding, Thy Name Is Fast

460 Park Avenue, northwest corner of 57th Street

This office building might not look so remarkable today, but it was a world record holder when it opened.

You might have been tipped off that something big, or at least something fast, was about to happen if you had been on the corner of Park Avenue and 57th Street early on the morning of June 21, 1954. You would have seen the steel frame of this building topped out at 22 stories, but you would have seen no cladding, no walls. Ordinarily, builders will begin to clad a steel-framed building once the frame is about ten stories high. The sooner a building is enclosed and

protected from the elements, the sooner the interiors can begin to be installed and the finishing trades can do their work.

But the Tishman Realty & Construction Company and the architects Emery Roth and Sons had a little something up their sleeves.

The speed at which buildings could be clad was ever increasing, and making news. In 1848, to every observer's astonishment, it took three days to clad James Bogardus's cast-iron facade for the Milhau Pharmacy at 183 Broadway. The building was 20 feet wide, and five stories high.

Fast forward 105 years and Tishman was in the record books for enclosing a much larger building. Tishman clad 99 Park Avenue, a 26-story building with a 200-foot frontage, in six and a half days, and they wanted to best that record. The plan was for the walls to go up in one extended workday.

Work was to begin at 6:00 a.m., and Norman Tishman, president of the construction company, had planned on blowing a whistle to start the assembly job. To his horror, a whistle was the one thing that was not in place. An obliging policeman lent his whistle to Tishman, and, at its sound at 6:02, the first of the 676 aluminum panels—each an eighth of an inch thick, four and a half feet wide, two stories high, and weighing 200 pounds—was hoisted into place by one of the four six-man crews. By 4:00 that afternoon, with a half hour out for lunch, the job was done.

The day all this took place was the summer solstice, the day with the longest daylight. Whether it was serendipity or the result of high-level planning, the directors wanted everything in place for one long take when they shouted "Action." The cameras would be rolling.

Directors, lighting, cameramen, this doesn't sound like your average grist for the public relations mill. This sounds more like Hollywood, and, in fact, it was a bit of Hollywood. There was even a Beverly Hills lawyer representing the interests of the property owner. This was the Davies Building, as in Marion Davies, the actress and former mistress of William Randolph Hearst and San Simeon. Although she might have been portrayed as a dumb blond in *Citizen Kane,* the real Marion Davies knew her Shinola.

In 1925, only nine years after having become a Ziegfeld girl, Davies's personal property assessment in New York City was already $50,000.

In the 1930s, she started to buy real estate on the advice of Arthur Brisbane, Hearst's chief editor who doubled as his real-estate adviser. Brisbane had built the Ritz Tower on the northeast corner of Park Avenue and 57th Street in 1927. Davies followed suit and purchased the 100-by-135-foot parcel across the avenue, on the northwest corner of 57th Street. In the best Astor tradition, she then sat on the property until the time was ripe. In 1953, with the post-War building boom in full swing, she went into action.

The Davies Building Corporation, a subsidiary of her Cosmopolitan Corporation, leased the property to Tishman, who would improve the property. Tishman already had a major ground-floor tenant lined up in National City Bank (CitiBank is still there).

In addition to this property on Park Avenue, Davies owned the 34-story Squibb Building at 745 Fifth Avenue, a seven-story office building at 19–21 West 57th Street, a five-story building at 28 West 58th Street, and a 25-foot-wide, five-story, limestone row house on Riverside Drive that she called home. From 1953 to 1955 she invested in the musical *Kismet* and tripled her money, bought the Desert Inn in Palm Springs, held the lease on the land upon which a 17-story office building was going up at 545 Madison Avenue, and leased the property to Tishman at 460 Park.

Some dumb blond.

Plenty of Plenty

The Evangeline Wilbour Blashfield Memorial Fountain, on the north side of 59th Street, between First Avenue and Sutton Place

Evangeline Wilbour Blashfield believed that public markets in New York should be as inviting as their European counterparts, and in the 1910s she noticed that the market under the ramp at the Manhattan end of the Queensboro Bridge had only one unsightly water faucet for all the vendors. She proceeded to arrange for a granite fountain with a mosaic as the central feature for the market. She had Charles Stoughton design the fountain, Eli Harvey sculpt it, her husband, Edwin Blashfield, paint the cartoon, and, although the Municipal Art Society was credited with having given the fountain to the city, it was Mrs. Blashfield who paid for it. And she modeled for it.

The fountain was to be named *Abundance,* with the fruits and vegetables flowing from the cornucopia reflecting the bounty in the market, and the date on the fountain—MCMXVIII—was when the fountain should have been installed. Unfortunately, pneumonia killed the 60-year-old Evangeline Blashfield before the fountain could be installed. The decision was to postpone the installation until 1919, and to name it in her honor.

Evangeline Wilbour Blashfield, said Kate Douglas Wiggin, the author of *Rebecca of Sunnybrook Farm,* "possessed a greater amount of knowledge about a greater number of subjects than any woman of [her] acquaintance. [She] illuminated any topic of conversation not only with . . . wit, grace, and distinction, but with clear vision and fine judgment." Her expertise included arcanum such as the position of the ancient Roman woman before the law, and among her many talents, Blashfield wrote both plays and non-fiction. She wrote articles for *Atlantic Monthly* and *Scribners,* and a collection of mini-biographies of women called *Portraits and Backgrounds.* Together, she and her husband wrote *Italian Cities,* and they edited and annotated one of the most famous art-history books, Vasari's *Lives of Seventy of the Most Eminent Painters, Sculptors and Architects.*

Evangeline Blashfield came by it all naturally. Her mother, Charlotte Beebe Wilbour, was from a venerable New England family. She was a charter member of

Sorosis, a women's society created in 1868 because the journalist Jane Cunningham Croly had been barred from a New York Press Club dinner honoring Charles Dickens. Croly was a member in good standing in the New York Press Club; she just wasn't a member of the Old Boys' Club. Sorosis set out to represent the interests of professional and self-supporting women. It was Wilbour who dubbed the group "Sorosis," a botanical term for plants with a profusion of flowers that bear fruit, a word that, coincidentally, has its roots in the Latin word for "sister," *soror*. By 1870, Wilbour was the president.

With her interest in equal rights, Wilbour was naturally active in the suffragist movement. It was she who read the platform at the 1869 Convention of the Woman Suffrage Association that demanded the ballot, arguing that if women were to be subject to a government, women had to be able to participate in it.

Evangeline's father, Charles E. Wilbour, was no slouch either. He had attended Brown, had been a reporter for the *New York Herald*, and he was proficient enough in French to translate some of the works of Victor Hugo, including *Les Miserables* in 1863, the translation that was the Modern Library standard until 2008. He headed printing and stationery companies in New York City, and by the mid-1870s he and his family were living in Europe, and he was on his way to becoming a renowned Egyptologist, whose collection would be bequeathed to the Brooklyn Museum.

Edwin Howland Blashfield, Evangeline's husband, was born in Brooklyn in 1848. He is simply described on this memorial as "Painter," but he wasn't just any old painter. Blashfield was one "of the leading American painters of the Gilded Age," said the art historian Robert Hughes, "the dean of American mural painters," said Jeff Greene, the art restorer.

Look on his works and be bedazzled. A stately dome at Chicago's Columbian Exposition of 1893, the ceiling of the ballroom in the original Waldorf-Astoria Hotel, the decoration in the Library of Congress in Washington and the Appellate Division on 25th Street, the mural in the Great Hall of City College, and on and on.

Blashfield's mother had trained as a portrait painter, and she thought that Edwin should follow his natural inclinations and become an artist; his father wanted him to be an engineer. To placate his father, Edwin went to MIT, but he chucked it after his second year, and in 1867 he took off for Paris to study art. With an annual income of $700 from an inheritance, he could afford it.

Evangeline Wilbour and Edwin Blashfield were married in Europe, and they returned to New York in 1882. Their apartments—the first in the Sherwood, the "artists' Bohemia" at 58 West 57th Street, their second at 49 Central Park South— were said to be the only true salons in New York at the turn of the 20th century.

In 1893, Edwin Sullivant Vanderbilt Allen, a fellow artist and neighbor in the Sherwood, told them that he wanted to establish an organization that would contribute the kind of municipal art to the city that the City Beautiful movement was advocating. The result would be a more livable city, with the benefits far outweighing the expense of incorporating public art.

Allen wanted the Blashfields to start the bandwagon rolling, and it was Evangeline who rallied a group of influential architects, artists, and businessmen that led to the creation of the Municipal Art Society. She even provided the society with its motto— "To make us love our city, we should make our city lovely." The irony is that it took her more than 20 years to break the society's gender barrier and become the first woman on its board of trustees.

The question remains why the Wilbours, Evangeline's intelligent, successful, and socially entrenched family, had precipitously left New York City for Europe in 1874 to become expatriates, and the answer is that Charles Wilbour was on the lam. He had gotten himself mixed up with the Tweed Ring, and every time some printing business was thrown Wilbour's way, both he and the Ring profited. And there was a lot of business. The *Times* reported that no printer in the country had amassed a fortune of like proportions in such a short period. In a little over two years, Wilbour succeeded in raking in nearly $2 million from the city alone.

You could also marvel at Wilbour's work ethic. Despite Wilbour's responsibilities as the active head of a major printing and stationery firm, he found time to be a stenographer in both the Supreme Court and the Bureau of Elections, and an examiner in both the Tax Commissioners' Office and the Surrogate's Office. His no-show jobs took in about $18,000 a year, when the average skilled laborer might have been making $650 a year.

Wilbour had it, and he flaunted it. "During the palmy days of the Ring," *The Times* reported, "Wilbour might be seen nearly every morning driving his 'span' of horses (a matched pair) down Broadway." And nobody could have expected him of skullduggery. He flaunted "his affiliations with a clique . . . too elevated and aesthetic (for him) to be for one moment suspected of stealing city funds."

By 1874, with the law coming down on the necks of the Tweed Ring but before Wilbour could be implicated, he fled, taking his family with him. Eight years later, Evangeline Blashfield returned, seemingly unscathed by the scandal. Wilbour died in Paris in 1896, and four years later Mrs. Wilbour returned. It seems that all was forgiven. Her name is carved in the Women's Health Protective Association fountain that was installed in 1910 on Riverside Drive at 116th Street. She was on the board of directors.

A note on why the fountain is where it is today: During the renovation of the space that made way for Bridgemarket in 1999, the fountain was restored and relocated to the east end of the public plaza on 59th Street.

8

The Upper West Side and Morningside Heights

Between West 59th and 110th Streets,
West from Central Park West, and West from
Morningside Drive from 110th Street to 125th Street

Best Bib and Tucker

65 West 70th Street, northeast corner, Columbus Avenue

It was either George W. Rogers, the developer of the Tuxedo Apartments, or his architect, Arthur Donovan Pickering, who in 1890 was privy to recent goings on in society with a capital S. It's the only explanation for the name of this apartment house.

The Tuxedo apartment house was erected as part of a building boom that resulted from the coming of the Ninth (Columbus) Avenue Elevated railroad to the Upper West Side in 1879. The El was the area's first rapid transit connection with the business and retail districts, and it proved the axiom that population follows transportation. The side streets, especially the park blocks between today's Central Park West and Columbus Avenue, started filling up with row houses for the upper middle classes.

With trains rattling by the front apartments on Ninth Avenue every few minutes, the bloom was off the rose of development on the avenue itself, but many of the avenue's multi-family buildings had pretensions of grandeur. This apartment house, with its rusticated brownstone on the first floor that was designed to blend in with the neighboring row houses, was a cut above the average.

The building's namesake was the residential country club in the Ramapo Mountains just north of the New Jersey–New York border. The resort was named for a word derived from the Lenape language meaning "crooked water" or "crooked river," and it has been memorialized by the short, formal dinner jacket that some of the elite started sporting in 1886 after they had concluded that—inspired by the Prince of Wales—a more casual look than tails was appropriate for dinner in the rustic setting. The resort had been started by Pierre Lorrillard IV, a descendant of the man who had started the tobacco company.

Lorillard held about 600,000 contiguous acres, and in 1885 he told his friend, the architect Bruce Price, that he wanted to develop an exclusive resort that would include year-round outdoor activities, and a clubhouse with a ballroom. If there wasn't to be a dance on a Saturday evening, concerts would be scheduled. Lorillard wanted Price to lay out the plans, and he also had Price design some of the original buildings, including the railroad station.

The link between a resort for the rich and this apartment house for the middle class is most likely explained by the fact that the building's architect, Arthur Donovan Pickering, who struck out on his own in 1886, had worked with—small world—Bruce Price.

The Tuxedo coat of arms seen here, with its breast plate and crossed halberds and visored helmet, is pure fabrication. If Lorillard's Tuxedo had had a coat of arms, it might have been a pair of crossed fishing rods flanking a jeroboam of Lafite-Rothschild astride an English riding saddle, or perhaps simply a short dinner jacket with silk lapels.

No Crown for Oliver

The Oliver Cromwell Apartments, 12 West 72nd Street, between Central Park West and Columbus Avenue

A cartoon by Ellison Hoover, "The Algonquin, By One Who Has Heard All About It," ran in *Judge* in the 1930s. The cartoon had both contemporary and historic figures lounging about in the hotel's lobby, and among the historic figures was Oliver Cromwell, a bit of an inside joke. The Algonquin had originally been called the Puritan, but Frank Case, who came to operate the hotel, believed that the name was "cold, forbidding, and grim," and that it contradicted "the spirit of inn keeping." You can only imagine what Case thought when the Oliver Cromwell Apartment Hotel opened in 1927.

The developers, the brothers Irving and Julius Dworfman of Brooklyn, might have simply overlooked the fact that Cromwell was a Puritan and everything that *Puritan* connoted. They might have remembered only that Cromwell was English. England is perhaps the best source for hotel- and apartment-house naming in Manhattan—with a Buckingham, four Cambridges, two Marlboroughs, seven Mayfairs, two Wellingtons, four Windsors—more than 60 names in all.

The Oliver Cromwell Apartment Hotel should have fit right into this naming scheme, with the seal seemingly an appropriate emblem. However, Cromwell lived by the words of John Bunyan from *Pilgrim's Progress*:

To cast the Kingdoms old
Into another mold.

Cromwell was a regicide and a tyrannicide, and in the 1650s this sometime tyrant himself was a Puritan with a capital "P," a Puritan to such a degree that he banned the celebration of Christmas because it had become too celebratory, too pagan.

The Puritan Revolution cast out a king and established a commonwealth, and you would think that symbols of royalty had gone with the monarchy. Nevertheless, the seal of the Lord Protector of the Commonwealth that is above the entrance inexplicably includes a crown. That seal was not Cromwell's. Cromwell had refused the crown when it was offered to him, and his personal seal—his banner—was the same seal, minus the crown. No crown for Oliver.

The apartment hotel was an artful design by Emery Roth that deftly made the transition between a base on a relatively small plot and a freestanding tower, much like his design for the Beverley that was going up at the same time on Lexington Avenue. The building was tall for its time and place, and it had expansive views from its upper floors, and because of its form, the lucky apartment dwellers at the setbacks had roof gardens that were reached through elegant French casement doors. The apartments were luxurious, all equipped with the latest fixtures, and on the lobby floor were more amenities, including a residents' lounge, a restaurant, and café.

The overall style was the Mediterranean Renaissance, complete with tiled roofs, which raises the question of why the Dworfmans didn't name the building something more appropriate, something Mediterranean. Too bad about the name, and that crown.

Why "The Dakota"?

1 West 72nd Street, at Central Park West

Two stories explain why Edward C. Clark, who built the Dakota Apartments, called it "The Dakota." First, the probable one.

Clark was a lawyer who represented the sewing-machine manufacturer, Isaac Merritt Singer. Clark's workload became so great that he gave up practicing law as a general practitioner to represent Singer exclusively. He became Singer's partner in the late 1870s, and assumed the presidency upon Singer's death. Clark himself died in 1882, two years after work had begun on the apartment house, and he died a very rich man. His estate, some of which was in West Side real estate, was valued at $25 million.

Before building the Dakota, Clark had built the Van Corlear Apartments on the west side of Seventh Avenue between 55th and 56th Streets. The six-story Van Corlear was big for its time. It measured 200 by 100 feet, and it had a large, open-ended courtyard to assure light and air for all the apartments, some of which were as large as nine rooms. The Dakota, a square doughnut of a building, was bigger. Its footprint was twice that of the Van Corlear, it was half again as high, and some of its apartments had 20 rooms and living rooms as big as 24 by 49 feet.

When Clark announced that he was building a luxury apartment house that was huge for its time that would come with apartments that were huge for any time, people called it "Clark's Folly." The idea of apartment-house living for the *haute bourgeoisie* was a novelty in the early 1880s, when few "proper" New Yorkers would willingly share a common roof with other families. Luxurious apartments were considered foreign, risqué. They were "French flats."

Clark, however, was determined. As a member of the West Side Association he was always boosting the area, encouraging others to buy into it and to build in it, even to change it somewhat. He liked American names, especially Western and Indian names, and he believed that the avenues on the Upper West Side should have a Western twang—he liked Montana Place, Wyoming Place, and Idaho Place for Eighth, Ninth and Tenth Avenues.

He built an apartment house named the Wyoming on the southeast corner of Seventh Avenue and 55th Street (the present apartment house with the same name on the site was built in 1906), and, on the southwest corner of Seventh Avenue, he built the still-standing Ontiora at 200 West 55th Street, an Indian name for the Catskill Mountains (*Onti Ora* means "clouds of the sky"). Naming the apartment house "The Dakota" was simply in keeping with this motif.

The other story is certainly more beguiling, and although it was first related years after the fact, one should never let a bad fact get in the way of a good story.

With 59th Street the northern border of the developed city in 1880, the question for Clark was who would willingly live as far removed from civilization as West 72nd Street. "Why," he was told, "they might as well be living in the Dakota Territory." Clark, a genial man with a sense of whimsy, named the apartment house after the territory.

Clark thereupon instructed his architect, Henry J. Hardenbergh, to embellish the building with Western details, and on the eighth floor above the entrance on 72nd Street is this portrait of a Native American, probably a Sioux—one of the dialects of the confederacy of tribes that comprised the Sioux nation was "Dakota."

Soon naming apartment houses after places in the American West or those associated with Native Americans took hold. The city has seen the Colorado, two Montanas, a Nebraska, three Nevadas, a new Wyoming, a Cherokee, Cliff Dwellers, even a Yosemite.

For the record, the year 1881 that encircles the Indian head is overly optimistic. The building did not open until 1884.

The "Poseidon" Station

Northwest corner, 72nd Street–Central Park West

This subway entrance could only have been the brainchild of the architect Squire Vickers, who had become the chief architect of the subway when art and decoration were starting to fall out of favor. This was complicated by the fact that when this station opened in 1932 he was obliged to work within an ever-tightening budget. In the design of this entrance, Vickers saw his opportunity for combining his love of architectural detail with the necessity for belt tightening.

The Dakota Apartments still has a dry moat around it, with cast-iron fencing that includes wonderfully evocative depictions of fantastical dragons or sea monsters,

with the railing itself clamped firmly in their jaws. One authority describes the man's head as that of a "wise man," another as "a fierce old man," but the odds are it's Poseidon. If those are sea monsters, and if the moat had been filled with water, the god of the sea would have been the logical choice.

If a standard subway entrance had been employed, this marvelous bit of artwork would have been destroyed, and that would have been anathema to Vickers. His decision was to incorporate the railing as part of the entrance, thereby saving it for posterity and saving the city some money at the same time. (This was the IND, the subway that was built by the City of New York. Unlike the first two subway undertakings, which had been built as private enterprises, the IND was "INDependent" of private money.)

Along with the railing, Vickers would salvage and incorporate the stone bases. The only non-salvage was some ironwork that was required to fill the gaps in the railing, and a pair of fluted, neoclassical columns flanking the ironwork. That was where Vickers broke even more with custom. Those columns are not standard IND issue.

The standard IND entrance had a pair of squared-off columnar lampposts that were gently tapered, with flanged tops and geometric set-ins that hint of the Art Deco. The 1930 design was by Vickers' fellow Cornell graduate, William Herbert Dole, and Dole's design became almost as much a hallmark of the IND as the cast-iron kiosks had been for the IRT. Dole might have had a hand in designing some of this entrance as well. The geometric patterns flanking the salvaged Dakota piece provide a hint.

The Dakota railings and statuary that Vickers saved are part of his legacy, and although very little has been written about them, they are perhaps the most beguiling in the city. They were manufactured by Poulson & Eger, an ironworks factory in Brooklyn. The quality of the work by Niels Poulson and Charles Eger certainly appealed to Henry J. Hardenbergh, who incorporated the firm's products again in Beinecke's Manhattan Hotel in 1896. By then, Poulson & Eger were calling themselves the Hecla Iron Works, and they were so proud of the Dakota fencing that they had a sample of it prominently displayed in their showroom.

The Work of a Master Forger

Originally, the Central Savings Bank, 2100 Broadway, between 73rd and 74th Streets

Banks in the 1920s were frequently modeled on Italian Renaissance *palazzi*, and for good reason. The Medici and their ilk needed to hole themselves up in buildings that were defensive in nature to keep their enemies at bay, and their *palazzi* doubled as *castelli*. They were designed to be as easily defended as they were palatial.

Five centuries later it seemed perfectly appropriate to design banks in the same style, with great thick walls and iron-framed doors and defensive grilles at the windows to keep the Bonnies and Clydes at bay, with palatial interiors that belied their defensive exteriors.

But what do you make of these whimsical animal heads atop the grilles? They are every bit as practical as more traditional spear-fence gates—you wouldn't want to be entangled on those pointy ears—they are simply friendlier, more pleasing to the passing pedestrian, and passing pedestrians far outnumber potential bank robbers.

The grilles are made of wrought iron, or iron that is literally worked by hand, and they are the handiwork of Samuel Yellin, who described metalwork as "the salt and pepper of architecture." Yellin was raised in Eastern Europe, where he attended a school that specialized in the arts and crafts. After an apprenticeship, Yellin was a master craftsman by the time he was 18. Two years later, in 1906, he settled in Philadelphia. His first major commission was for the gates of the estate of the banker J. P. Morgan, Jr., in Glen Cove, Long Island. In 1917 he worked with Cass Gilbert on the Allen Memorial Art Museum at Oberlin College in Ohio.

In the early 1920s, Gilbert recommended Yellin to the architects York & Sawyer, who were making a pitch to design the Federal Reserve Bank of New York. Gilbert called Yellin "the master worker in ornamental wrought iron."

York & Sawyer got the Federal Reserve job, and Yellin got the ironwork job, and he went on to design the ironwork on this bank for the same firm, and on the Cunard Building, and on Church of St. Vincent Ferrer, and on and on.

Yellin called himself a "blacksmith" or "ironworker," never a "craftsman" or "artist," although he understood architectural styles, and he designed and executed his creations to harmonize with whatever style a firm might use. He would first work out the solutions on paper, and his first sketch would be to put everything in perspective to ensure harmony. Then, one sketch after another would be created, each one more finely delineated than the last, until the sketches were full size. But it wasn't until he was actually smithing, working his iron at a forge by twisting and bending and weaving his chosen medium that Yellin could be fully satisfied.

Proof is at the Cloisters, where you will see delicately wrought handrails and window grilles and iron-framed doors, even a weather vane. They are objects that you would swear could only have been salvaged from some Medieval ruin, but they are the original work of the 20th century's master forger.

Not Your Usual Tenement House

302 Columbus Avenue, between 74th and 75th Streets

This red-brick apartment house looks like the usual tenement house that went up in the city in the late 19th century, but on closer look you will see subtle differences.

For starters, this building is only three windows wide, when the average tenement house is four, with two of those windows lighting the front room of one apartment fronting the street, the other two lighting the front room of the neighboring apartment. The same pattern was flopped and repeated in the rear, with the living-room windows overlooking a 10-foot-deep backyard.

The average tenement, even one with storefronts on the main floor, ordinarily has the entrance in the center, because that's where the stairs and hallways are, all the better to accommodate four apartments to a floor. The entrance for this building is on the side. And not many tenements have wood-paneled entrances more akin to the vestibule of a town house, and not many are given brickwork around the Roman-arched windows and delicate filigree-like terra-cotta string courses and dentils like the ones here.

And "The J. M. Horton Ice Cream Company" in the pediment? Tenement-house developers might have honored family members in pediments, with some exotica such as "Salome" thrown in, but a commercial name is rare.

One theory is that the name was installed as a rooftop advertisement designed to catch the eye of passengers on the Columbus Avenue "El." The sign could only be comfortably seen by passengers traveling uptown, and only those on one side of the train, which would rule out the bulk of your viewing audience. Not such a good media buy.

The building's architects were not your usual tenement-house architects. They were Robert N. Cleverdon and Joseph Putzel, who designed one of the most elegant row houses in Harlem's Mount Morris Historic District, and an elegant row of houses in the Carnegie Hill Historic District. They also designed the grand buildings at 583 and 648 Broadway, as well as at 382 and 400 Lafayette Street.

By now you've probably figured out that this building was not a tenement house at all. It was a depot for the J. M. Horton Ice Cream Company—a warehouse where ice cream was stored awaiting delivery, with perhaps an ice-cream parlor occupying the shop on the main floor.

Horton's ice cream wasn't just any ice cream. In the last quarter of the 19th century, James Madison Horton was to the wholesale ice-cream business what Bernhard Beinecke was to the wholesale meat business. Horton's was the ice cream served at the inaugural balls for Presidents Benjamin Harrison and Grover Cleveland. It was said to furnish three-fifths of all the ice cream served in the city—practically every public institution was supplied with it on a daily basis. Every steamship leaving New York harbor was said to have enough Horton's in its hold to satisfy the ship's passengers, going and coming. At seaside resorts you found Horton's served in paper packages of a handy shape that was described as "a triumph of civilization," and its name was so associated with ice cream that when one little girl was asked how to spell "ice cream," she responded "H-o-r-t-o-n."

James Horton lived in Harlem at 112 West 126th Street, and he was a civic booster. He was a director of the Mount Morris Bank and a major player in the real-estate field, which goes far in explaining why he would know the work of Cleverdon & Putzel. He served with the likes of fellow Harlemite Mayor Thomas F. Gilroy on philanthropies such as the Harlem Charity Balls, and he was invited to places such as the White House to visit with Theodore Roosevelt. Sweet work, and Horton got it.

What Is an Ancient Symbol of Christianity, the Chi Rho, Doing on an Apartment House?

2166 Broadway, between 76th and 77th Streets, Today's Opera Apartments

The scene could have been out of a Mickey Rooney and Judy Garland movie, where the kids decide to put on a show to save Pop's drug store. The setting, however, was the Manhattan Congregational Church in the late 1920s, and the kids were adults. They were saying "Hey, gang, let's tear down our old non-revenue-generating church building and put up a money-making apartment hotel on the property. We can install the church within, outsource the management, and soon we'll have lucre pouring in and we will save the church."

Their church had been built in 1901 on this mid-block site, and, sure enough, the congregation tore it down and put up the 28-story Manhattan Towers, with the church ensconced within. That should put in perspective the monogram of Chi

(X) and Rho (P), the first two letters of Greek *Khristos*, and the date. The cornerstone commemorates the original church on the site, not today's building.

The fact that a church was incorporated within the premises also explains why the architects, Tillion & Tillion, Gothicized the facade on the lower three floors and added faux buttresses. It also explains the two separate entrances on Broadway, one to the residences, the other to the church.

Topping off the building was an enormous gold cross, which made for one good news story. In 1930 the *Times* reported that the blessing that concluded "the first wedding to be performed in the new skyscraper edifice of the Manhattan Congregational Church was bestowed . . . on the 24th floor, directly under the large gold cross surmounting the tower."

Despite the cross atop the building and the church below, the building was hexed. The cornerstone had been laid almost a month to the day after Black Tuesday and the beginning of the Crash. And not all the news stories could have pleased the congregation.

Within the first year, one man was arrested for maintaining a gambling house on the premises, with three dice throwers charged with disorderly conduct. But worse than some high rollers and bad press was yet to come. By 1931, the Manhattan Tower's management had fallen behind in its payments to the tune of $120,000, and, at about the same time, the church's minister went missing. The shepherd had abandoned his flock and absconded with an unreported sum of money from the till. The church folded, and the building fell on hard times.

The former sanctuary was revitalized in 1969 as the Promenade Theater, where wonderful off-Broadway fare such as Steve Martin's *Picasso at the Lapin Agile* was presented. The railing leading downstairs to the theater still had its Gothic motif in those days. Today, with a health club in residence, there is a nondescript replacement.

The idea of erecting revenue-generating buildings with a church ensconced within was abroad in the land on the cusp of the 1930s. Sometimes the idea worked, sometimes not.

One of the first of the money-making schemes took place at the Chelsea Presbyterian Church at 208 West 23rd Street. The old church was torn down, and the 18-story Carteret was built on the site, with the new church in the rear. That congregation is gone.

The Church of the Strangers had occupied its church on West 57th Street since 1898, and 30 years later that congregation decided to cash in. Now the Gothic arch at 311 West 57th Street that originally led to the church leads to an event space, with its 35-foot-high "cathedral" ceiling celebrated as a feature.

The Baptist Tabernacle Church had stood at 160 Second Avenue since 1850, but by 1930 that congregation replaced its old church with a sixteen-story apartment house. The Tudor-arched entrance under the name Baptist Tabernacle led to the religious facilities. That congregation too is gone.

Several undertakings have actually succeeded, including the Second Presbyterian Church at 6 West 96th Street, Calvary Baptist Church at 123 West 57th Street, and the Madison Avenue Baptist Church at 129 Madison Avenue.

A variation on the success theme is found on the northwest corner of Park Avenue and 34th Street. Stretching for more than half a block is 10 Park Avenue, a 26-story apartment house that architect Harvey Wiley Corbett designed for the Community Church of New York, which had stood on that corner since 1867. The original plan was to have the church occupy the lower floors of the building itself, but wiser business heads prevailed. Real-estate values are lower on the side streets, and greater revenue can be generated from Park Avenue. The actual church building wound up around the corner on 35th Street, with a cathedral-like entrance to the church from an entrance on Park. Today, that space is a restaurant. The church around the corner is going strong.

The Rice Children

The Porte Cochere, Villa Julia, today's Yeshiva Ketana, 346 West 89th Street, southeast corner, Riverside Drive

Julia Barnett, M.D., and Isaac L. Rice, LL. B., were married in 1885, and in short order they had six children—four girls, Polly, Dolly, Molly, and Lolly, or Muriel, Dorothy, Marion, and Marjorie, and two boys, Isaac, Jr., and Julian. The children and their mother are the subjects of the sculpture group on the family home that was built in 1903. The classical temple provides a hint of the parents' interests.

The sculptor of the group is a bit of a mystery. When the Rice house was built, there was no mention of a sculptor or a sculpture group, and the sculptor's identity is only guessed at, although there are some major hints.

This writer had his money on Henry B. Herts or Hugh Tallant, the architects who designed the house. They were both talented artists and sculptors in their own right, occasionally embellishing their own architectural work with their own sculptural work.

Herts came by some of his design sense by osmosis—he was from a family of decorators—and although he studied architecture at Columbia and l'Ecole des Beaux Arts, he never bothered with getting a diploma from either of them.

He might have gotten off the academic track when, as a junior at Columbia, he entered a competition for the design of a temporary arch to be erected at Fifth Avenue and 59th Street as part of the Columbian quadricentennial. As many as 50 practicing architects entered the contest, and Herts won.

Herts was already interning in the office of Bruce Price, who agreed to consult with him on the project, while Stanford White and other members of the jury offered to give him "all the assistance in their power." One of the things that worried Herts was the deadline. He had six weeks to complete it, from September 1, 1892 until October 12, 1892. And he pulled it off.

For the capitals of the columns, Herts imitated the models of the Temple of Castor and Pollux that he knew from the architectural hall in the Metropolitan Museum of Art, and the great eagle topping the arch was copied from casts at Columbia's School of Architecture. Bas-relief panels chronicled the life of Columbus, with the crowning feature an allegorical group of 12 figures arranged in and around a boat, with the "Genius of Discovery" standing and trumpeting. The figures on the arch were made of plaster and papier mâché, and Herts modeled and constructed all the ornaments and allegorical groups that embellished the arch. He was both sculptor and architect.

Unlike Herts, Tallant was an academic overachiever. He majored in engineering and math at Harvard, and he graduated in 1901 with both a B.A. and an M.A. Tallant was awarded prizes for literary essays, he was an editor at the *Lampoon*, for which he also contributed illustrations, and, thanks to Harvard's Kirkland scholarship, he studied in Paris at the Beaux Arts, where he won the Grande Medaille d'Honneur, the medal awarded to the student at the top of his graduating class.

Herts and Tallant were both on Paris' Left Bank when talk of "the new art," or *art nouveau,* was in the air. Evidence of its influence is in their 1903 design of the New Amsterdam Theater. Tallant even carved a panel called *Progress* for the theater's foyer.

All bets are off.

Down in the bottom right hand corner on the frame of the sculpture is a monogram, "L St L," and the odds are that those initials belong to Louis St. Lanne, who arrived in the United States from France in time to work on the Columbian Exposition in Chicago. That monogram is the only evidence linking St. Lanne to Villa Julia, but there is a trail leading from the house.

Isaac Rice died in 1916, and, as a memorial to him, Julia Rice donated a gateway and fountain for the Betsy Head Playground, in Brownsville, Brooklyn. St. Lanne was the sculptor of the fountain, and Herts the architect. Then, in 1923, Julia Rice presented the city with an enormous athletic complex in Pelham Bay Park that included a 7,000-seat concrete stadium designed by Herts, capped by a Greek temple. In front of the temple stood a colossal statue, *The American Boy,* by St. Lanne, for which the New York Society of Architects awarded him the bronze medal. Julia Rice knew her stuff.

The Stones of Rouen

The statue of Joan of Arc, between the Lower (Main) Roadway
of Riverside Drive and the Upper Drive at West 93rd Street

Although the reins on this horse are loosely held, the horse's raised foreleg, the angle of its head, and its tense muscles all convey energy. And Joan of Arc stands forward in the saddle, the visor of her helmet raised, her eyes on the hilt of the sword she holds on high with the cross-guard of the hilt creating a cross, the perfect symbol for Saint Joan.

In the spirit of true Gothic architecture, the pedestal is light, almost airy, yet it too is strong. It was designed by John V. Van Pelt, who taught architecture at both Cornell and Columbia, but he did not always practice what he preached. Using an anachronistic style of architecture was a mistake in both logic and taste, he would say, but there were exceptions. "For a Roman Catholic cathedral," he said, "Gothic might still be an appropriate expression." Consider this monument Joan's cathedral.

Plans for the statue were announced on the 500th anniversary of Joan's birth in 1912, and the timing was fortuitous. The fortress in Rouen in which Joan had been imprisoned was about to be excavated, and the committee thought that the stones from the *donjon* would be just the thing to serve as the pedestal. In June, 1914, 229 blocks left Rouen for New York. Those stones you see within the arches of the pedestal are just some of the stones of Rouen.

The committee members were all highly motivated. They were also all wealthy in varying degrees, and their names resonate with interconnectedness.

George F. Kunz, the committee president, had his fingers in many pies. For his day job, Kunz was the head of the diamond department at Tiffany & Co. He was the nation's foremost expert on precious stones, an honorary curator at the American Museum of Natural History, a vice president of the New York Academy of Sciences, and a special agent of the U.S. Geological Survey, which might explain why Mohegan granite had been used as the framing of the pedestal. He and his family summered near the Mohegan quarry in northern Westchester. A graduate of Cooper Union, Kunz was a patron of the National Sculpture Society, a member of the City History Club, and president of the American Scenic and Historic Preservation Society, a pioneering group that set out to identify structures worthy of preservation. He knew the city, and he knew sculpture and the stuff it stands on.

Another member was McDougall Hawkes, the director of the nascent Museum of French Art. Eva Van Cortlandt Morris of Morrisania was Hawkes's wife, and in 1912 he hosted a luncheon at the Metropolitan Club honoring a French delegation to celebrate the Champlain Tercentenary. The luncheon was followed by a visit to the Fifth Avenue mansion of another committee member, Senator William A. Clark, where six paintings of Joan of Arc by Bernard Boutet de Monvel hung on his walls. A year later, Hawkes hosted a reception for the French ambassador at the Ritz-Carlton. Along with other wealthy New Yorkers were Senator Clark and J. Sanford Saltus, the committee's honorary chairman.

Saltus was a patron of the arts in general and numismatics in particular, and he could afford to be—his father owned and operated Saltus Steel. His benefactions include the bust of Edgar Allan Poe at NYU's Hall of Fame, and medals with cash awards presented by the American Numismatic Society, the National Academy of Design, and the Art Students League. Like many of his confreres, Saltus was a Francophile. In the early 1920s, he listed a bank in Paris as his address in the *Social Register.*

Statues don't come cheap, and Saltus contributed $20,000 to the cause. To drum up more funds, he arranged for the American Numismatic Society to host what was billed as the most extensive exhibition of material relating to Joan of Arc that had "ever been brought together anywhere in the world." It included about 1,000 articles—more than 50 reproductions of statues of Joan, paintings that included one of Senator Clark's Boutet de Monvels, and medals and coins from prominent collectors such as J. Pierpont Morgan and Rodman Wanamaker.

Saltus contributed a collection of medals—12 gold, 93 silver, and 97 bronze—that he had specifically acquired for the occasion.

No sculpture competition was ever officially held, but sculptor Anna Vaughn Hyatt seems to have been the odds-on favorite from the outset. She had exhibited a *Joan* at the Paris Salon of 1910, and Saltus had been there to see it.

Hyatt's father was a zoologist, and her natural predilection was to sculpt animals. In 1900 at about the age of 25, she came to New York to study with Gutzon Borglum and Herman MacNeill. Animals are not easy to find in the city, so she spent a lot of time at the Bronx Zoo.

By 1906, one of her animal sculptures was already in the Metropolitan Museum of Art, she was selling pieces through the Gorham Galleries, and she was living abroad. Hyatt became fascinated by Joan of Arc while in France, and she immersed herself in all things Joan, not just reading about her, but visiting places associated with her life.

Creating an equestrian statue of Joan was right up Hyatt's alley. When the time came to begin the actual work for the Paris salon, she just needed the right horse as a model, the kind of horse that could bear the weight of armor. In the stables of the Magasin du Louvre in Paris, Hyatt found a Percheron, a breed that was popular for hauling streetcars and wagons.

With only a female assistant, Hyatt completed the life-size plaster cast in four months, including the heavy work of building the armature and covering it with more than a ton of clay. She was given honorable mention. Some jurors admitted that Hyatt would have taken first place if only they "had been convinced that a woman had really done the work."

Saltus had no question. Hyatt went to work in a studio on her family's vacation property in Annisquam, Massachusetts, where she reworked and refined her original Joan. She enlarged the scale, and she used her niece as the model for Joan, having her straddle a barrel. And again she found a Percheron, this time at the East Gloucester fire station.

Bashford Dean, the curator of armor at the Metropolitan Museum of Art, was the consultant on the armor, and every detail was historically correct. The armor was 15th-century Italian, the finest period of the armorers' art, and the model came from Dean's private collection. (Dean was another who had married into New York royalty. His wife was Alice Dyckman.)

Dean had been fascinated by armor as a boy, but he started his professional life as a zoologist. He would wow his students at Columbia with his ability to take a piece of chalk in each hand, go to the blackboard, and, working simultaneously with both hands and with equal dexterity, draw an armored fish of the Devonian period. For Dean, the study of armor was a logical extension of zoology, making his journey to the Metropolitan Museum a natural segué.

By the time the statue was unveiled in 1915, there was a war on, and the statue became a propaganda tool. The dedication began to the thunder of cannon mingled with *La Marseillaise,* and the French ambassador told the assemblage that a bit of shell-shattered pilaster from the cathedral at Reims had been incorporated in the base with the stones of Rouen, along with letters from eminent personages such as President Woodrow Wilson, all grist for the propagandist's mill.

A protagonist who unwittingly set the stage for some of this story was Archer Milton Huntington, the stepson of the railroad man Collis P. Huntington, and heir to his fortune. It was Huntington who provided the land on upper Broadway for Audubon Terrace, the setting for the Hispanic Society, which Huntington had founded, and the American Numismatic Society, the site of the Joan of Arc exhibition.

In 1922, Huntington wanted to have a medal cast to honor the Argentine statesman, Bartholmé Mitre. Huntington knew Hyatt's work, but he had never met her. When they did meet to discuss the project, something seemed familiar about her, and he asked if they had ever met. "On the train coming to New York from Westchester," she said. "We see each other every day." A year later, she and Huntington exchanged vows in her studio at 49 West Twelfth Street.

A Forgotten Pieta

The Firemen's Memorial, Riverside Drive at 100th Street

The scene is familiar—a mourning woman holding a male corpse. Whether the woman represents the dead man's mother or his widow, the grief is the same. This sculpture group is *Sacrifice*, and it depicts mere mortals—a wife who has become a widow and a firefighter fallen in the line of duty, a soldier in a war that never ends.

The woman is not gazing on the face of the fallen, she is looking away, as if wondering what the future holds, and the group on the southern side of the memorial tells us. Here is *Duty*, the woman in the role of a mother with her child—their child—depicting her future responsibilities, the duty of a single parent, a reality known to too many.

The memorial is powerful not merely for its idea but for its execution. The threesome that created the composition—the architect H. Van Buren Magonigle, the sculptor Attilio Piccirilli, and the model Audrey Munson—also teamed up to create the *Maine Memorial*. Both were finished in 1913, despite the "XCMXII" on the east flank of the tablet.

Magonigle had worked in the office of McKim, Mead & White, whose influence is evident in the memorial's neoclassicism, and he had his finger in various design pies, including book and magazine covers, typography and page illustration, and furniture design. In his spare time he served as the president of the Architectural League from 1917 to 1919.

Attilio Piccirilli was already an accomplished carver and sculptor, and in the same year that this memorial was finished, he was commissioned by Daniel Chester French to carve the statues of *Manhattan* and *Brooklyn* for the Brooklyn approach to the Manhattan Bridge. Piccirilli's work on this memorial includes not

just *Sacrifice* and *Duty*, but the nineteen-foot-long, eight-foot-high relief on the west wall depicting a horse-drawn fire engine racing to a fire.

Munson was the "American Venus," the *model* sculptor's model whose ability to strike and hold just the right pose for the idea she was embodying was her gift. She was the model for French's *Manhattan* and *Brooklyn*, for A. A. Weinman's

Civic Fame atop the Municipal Building, for Augustus Lukeman's *Memory* in Straus Park, and on and on.

The idea for the Firemen's Memorial grew from a proposal originally put forward by Episcopal bishop Henry C. Potter to commemorate Deputy Chief Charles W. Kruger, who had died fighting a fire. The idea was soon expanded to a memorial for every member of the New York City Fire Department who has died in the line of duty, a role it still touchingly plays.

As public art, the memorial fell under the auspices of the Art Commission, a ten-member board that consisted of four ex-officio members, three laymen, and a painter, a sculptor, and an architect. The heads of city departments could serve as acting commissioners if something under their jurisdiction was the subject, and Fire Chief Edward F. Croker served. His early criticism was that Magonigle's design was not altogether satisfactory, although he did not elaborate, and he did soften. A criticism that made the *Times* was that the monument's purpose should not be an abstraction, that the statue should be more obvious so that everyone "would know its meaning." A fireman in full regalia was more like it. That suggestion was ignored.

The memorial's site would be on Parks Department grounds, and several sites were proposed, only to be rejected for one reason or another. Croker particularly liked the way the statue of General Franz Sigel was situated on Riverside Drive at 106th Street, and 100th Street was settled on. The difference in the sites is that 106th Street is 100 feet wide, and the 60-foot wide 100th Street lacks the grand approach from the east. From the west, however, the 100th Street site was grander, with its broad steps leading up to the summit of a knoll.

An estimated $50,000 was needed, and the public subscription began with a benefit performance at the Metropolitan Opera House that was directed by the Association of Theater Managers. The performers included Anna Held, of milk-bath fame; George M. "Give My Regards to Broadway" Cohan; and Eddie Foy, before the seven little Foys. By the time the memorial was unveiled in 1913, the estimated cost had practically doubled to $90,000. Sizable donations came from the likes of Isidor Straus of Macy's and the banker J. Pierpont Morgan, with the $40,000 difference from the Board of Estimate.

In 1930, Piccirilli wrote a letter to the *Times* on the subject of both the Maine Monument and the Firemen's Memorial. Under the headline "Monumental Vandalism," Piccirilli's letter said that both monuments were suffering, and he questioned what the Municipal Art Commission and the Park Commission had been doing to protect the city's public monuments, and what the National Sculpture Society intended to do.

Some of the vandalism was natural. If you take any fragile object that is executed in marble and erect it in the open air, said the sculptor Eli Benedict, "sooner or later that eternal vandal, the weather, will destroy the most artistic work with a robustness commensurate with the rigors of the climate." Despite the fact that marble had been the classic medium for statues, the only truly suitable material for outdoor art was granite or copper.

The government started to act on preserving what it had. In 1935, with funds from the Federal Emergency Relief Bureau, artists such as Jackson Pollock were employed by the Parks Department to scrub down monuments, including the Firemen's Memorial, but it wasn't enough. Parks Commissioner Robert Moses established the Monuments Section, whose principal chore was the preservation of the city's 360 monuments. The bronze plaque you see on the west flank of the Firemen's Memorial had originally been marble, but by 1950 it had weathered beyond recognition, and the Monuments Section was at work reproducing it in bronze, with Piccirilli himself working with Parks Department artisans on the plaster mold.

But deterioration continued on the memorial itself. The Tennessee Pink Limestone veneer had not been properly attached to the brick that was supporting it, and water had seeped in. By 1991, and $2.1 million later, the monument was whole again.

This "P" Is Found in Some Pretty Big Haystacks

895 West End Avenue, southwest corner of 104th Street

The architect Gaetan Ajello frequently had his name carved into the walls of the buildings of his design, along with the date of the building's construction (see the limestone slab on the left corner of 895). He also enjoyed honoring his patrons by incorporating their monogram in escutcheons. Here you will find a "P" in an escutcheon above the entrance, three more P-bearing escutcheons above the fifth floor, and another three just below the cornice.

The "P"s are there to honor the Paterno Estate, two brothers, Charles and Joseph, who had taken over the real-estate operation of their father in 1899. Together the Paterno brothers were responsible for some of the grandest apartment houses on the Upper West Side that went up in the first two decades of the 20th century, and Ajello designed a good number of them, including the threesome at 885, 895, and 905 West End Avenue.

Ajello's facades are distinctive. He liked white brick and great cornices, and coining and string courses and balconies and French windows, all the neoclassical trim in his arsenal, but never overdone, always in perfect balance and harmony.

Ajello's predilection was to make the ground floor ceilings especially high—some as high as 20 feet—to create a grand entrance. An elaborately balustraded staircase in the lobby would create the illusion that it led to the piano nobile, or the reception rooms in a private home, all in an effort to create an illusion of domesticity. What is truly astonishing about buildings such as 895 West End is that it is twelve stories plus a half basement above ground, but it is as high as the 16-story building diagonally across the street. The difference is in the height of the ceilings. Even with the same square footage, the apartments with the higher ceilings are

more spacious and elegant. Their cubic footage is simply that much greater.

Ajello has never achieved the fame of other residential architects, and you won't find his name trumpeted in real estate ads the way you will find Rosario Candela's. Candela's name is synonymous with apartments with grand, flowing layouts, especially some of the Park Avenue apartments that he designed in the late 1920s. The problem is that sometimes a Candela facade can look like any other. Another difference is that Ajello's buildings always bore the initials of his patron in the escutcheons. By 1924, Candela's ego was swelling. At 875 West End, you find an "R C" in the escutcheon above the entrance.

More Manhattan Valley than Loire Valley

P.S. 165, 234 West 109th Street (view from 108th Street),
between Broadway and Amsterdam Avenue

I n the 1890s, C. B. J. Snyder was a busy superintendent of public schools. For the 50 years before his arrival on the job, school buildings in New York City had been built on the same old plan. That started to change with the arrival of mayors who liked public works for the betterment of the public instead of their wallets, mayors such as Thomas F. Gilroy and William L. Strong, who saw the necessity for improved design. It was only then, in the 1890s, that the Board of Education was finally made to see that the "old school" school buildings—plants that were poorly designed, ill lit, and lacking basic educational services such as laboratories and auditoriums—were not up to snuff.

PHOTO BY JOHN TAURANAC

In 1898, when P.S. 165 was ready to open, there were about 40,000 children attending half-day classes in the city, and over a thousand children who could not be accommodated in any classes at all. Snyder was racing to accommodate them all. There were 21 new buildings or annexes in the course of construction that year.

A hallmark of Snyder-designed schools is the H-plan, buildings that could be built mid-block, where real-estate values were generally lower than avenue sites. By virtue of his H plan, the sites provided room in the open-ended courtyards for playgrounds, accompanied by over-sized windows that flooded the classrooms with light and air.

P.S. 165's steel-frame construction was new world, although its facade might look old world. Snyder chose the architecture of Francis I of France, the style associated with the hunting lodges and palaces of the Loire Valley or, more precisely in this case, the Hotel de Cluny on Paris's Left Bank.

The scale is different, but the elements are the same, right down to the rounded turrets in the corners, and the *chien-assis* dormer windows in the sloping roof (in the Middle Ages, when glass was prohibitively expensive, *chien-assis* windows were unglazed to provide light and ventilation for attics in barns). For good measure, Snyder added a flèche. The flamboyant dormer windows are festooned with crests, and here is another difference between P.S. 165 and Cluny, whose crests celebrate the religious aristocracy. Snyder's seals celebrate the City of New York, with windmills and barrels, and the United States of America, with the stars and stripes. The images are perfectly appropriate. State-funded public education is the path to good citizenship.

The Works of Man, Saintly and Mundane

The Synod House, northeast corner of Amsterdam Avenue
and 110th Street (Cathedral Parkway)

T he architects Heins & LaFarge won the competition to design the Cathedral Church of St. John the Divine in 1891, but soon after Lewis Heins's death in 1907, the architect Ralph Adams Cram was asked to step in and finish the job. By 1911 he was at it, but before starting any of the projects on the mammoth building project, the Synod House came first. There was a time factor involved. A synod, a council of church officials, was scheduled for New York City in 1913, and the pressure was on for a building to be ready in time to house the convocation.

For stylistic precedents, Cram opted for the French Gothic, especially Mont St. Michel. In the six niches flanking the doors are statues of kings and emperors and czars who defended the faith, and standing alone as the central figure and representing the United States is George Washington. Washington is part of a *trumeau,* the central support of a medieval doorway. Perhaps this is a political statement. Without George Washington and his ideals, all might collapse.

Within the Gothic-style arch are three ranges of niches, each with its own set of statuary. The top range is the saintly part. The mundane is ringed in two ranges below, and the statues represent individual trades and professions, especially in New York. As the nation's publishing center, book binding is represented, and the city was the nation's greatest port so navigation is here, and the textile industry is here, and sculpture and literature and industrial art and music are all here for the obvious reasons that New York was the center of all those endeavors.

Architecture is represented by a square-jawed and distinguished-looking man clutching rolled-up plans in one hand and a model of a Gothic-style tower that smacks of one of the cathedral towers. The statue depicts the architect himself, Ralph Adams Cram.

Cram makes no mention of his likeness having been worked into the statuary group in his autobiography, and whether it was done without his knowledge and designed to come as a surprise we don't know. It's not the only statue in the city showing an architect with a model of his work. In the lobby of the Woolworth Building is a corbel depicting Cass Gilbert cradling a model of the building.

The sculpture group was designed and executed by John Evans & Company, and you have to wonder if John Evans depicted himself as the representation of sculpture. Evans was not above little jokes of that nature. He worked the monogram of Henry Hobson Richardson into one of the capitals for Glessner House in Chicago.

John Evans was one of the most successful architectural sculptors of the late 19th and early 20th centuries, and, according to Cram, Evans provided "the very thing we ourselves were struggling to accomplish (in the cathedral), the

combination of the fundamental principles of Medieval art with the quality of contemporaneousness that would redeem our products from archaeological sterility and give them a measure of life."

Upon Evans's arrival in New York City from Wales in the early 1870s, he went to work for Ellin & Kitson, and Robert Ellin, who knew talent when he saw it, promptly dispatched Evans to Boston to execute the carving on Henry Hobson Richardson's "New" Old South Church on Copley Square. Evans worked with Richardson on the sculpture for the Brattle Street Church, and on the porch of Trinity Church, and he wound up doing so much work in Boston that he became known as the "Boston sculptor."

The idea for the Synod House was sparked in 1907 when the banker J. Pierpont Morgan determined that a "suitable" building was required so that the clerical and lay delegates might comfortably gather for the council meeting scheduled for 1913. The Synod House, minus the organ, was ready on the appointed day.

Neither William Bayard Cutting, who chaired the committee, nor Morgan lived to see the Synod House come to fruition. Cutting died in 1912, Morgan in 1913. Their estates, reported the *Times*, "cheerfully accepted the pledges made by the two men" that underwrote the construction. The pledges came to about $200,000 apiece.

Armageddon on the East River

Sculpture that is second on the right, the central portal of the Cathedral of St. John the Divine, Amsterdam Avenue at 112th Street

This apocalyptic vision has a collapsing Brooklyn Bridge taking down a bus and some cars with it into the East River. A building that strongly resembles the stock exchange is already in the drink, along with people who seem to be blithely going about their lives—a woman is playing a piano, diners are at a table—and all accompanied by skeletons and phantasmagorical creatures that are straight out of some of the more hellish images in Gothic art. Safely removed from all the mayhem and barely visible is the Statue of Liberty, tucked in nearest to the wall.

This carving and the other eleven flanking the main door are relatively recent in the scheme of things. The subject matter of the sculpture flanking the main door was not even discussed until the 1920s, and by the mid-20th century the cathedral was already being called St. John the Unfinished, for the simple reason that it was (and still is) unfinished. As the former dean of the cathedral, the Very Rev. James Parks Morton, said philosophically, "That's the thing with cathedrals. Wars, famine, people run out of money—work stops."

In 1978, Dean Morton began Cathedral Stoneworks, an apprenticeship program that was housed in a studio on the cathedral grounds. Work on the south tower actually began, and every so often the fortunate passerby could glimpse a piece of stone that had been carved and was waiting to be hoisted up to the tower to become an integral part of the cathedral.

In 1988, another project was the carving of the blank blocks of stone for the Portal of Paradise. To guide the work was the English sculptor, Simon Verity, whose experience included the restoration of Gothic structures in England and Europe.

Working with apprentices was uncharted territory for Verity, and the notion of teamwork was "a risky experiment," he said, but he was sanguine. "In medieval times the best buildings were experiments."

When Verity and his six apprentice sculptors started work on these carvings, the collapse of some of the city's bridges was a very real possibility. In 1986, engineers discovered that half of the steel in the anchorage of the Manhattan Bridge had rusted away, and the bridge was in danger of collapse. Two of the four subway tracks and two of the seven lanes of traffic were closed on the bridge while work progressed on saving the structure.

In 1988 engineers discovered that the Williamsburg Bridge was in even worse shape. The cables that supported the bridge's center span were fraying. Hundreds of broken wires were visible, and the cables had lost a third of their original strength. Further investigations by the chief engineer, Sam Schwartz, showed that the beams supporting the deck were suffering the same type of corrosion that had caused the collapse of the West Side Elevated Highway, and two of the steel bars had actually fallen into the East River. The bridge was closed. This dystopian vision carved into the cathedral was a very real possibility of a hell on earth.

A Scarred Facade

The Regnor, 601 West 115th Street, the northwest corner of Broadway

In 1912, the architect Gaetan Ajello and the Paterno family again teamed up, this time to create three apartment houses on the west side of Broadway between 115th and 116th Streets: the Luxor, the Regnor, and the Rexor. Luxor was the ancient Egyptian city known for its palaces; Regnor and Rexor appear to be neologisms, implying a queen or king, a ruler or sovereign.

The three apartment houses shared the same regal DNA, and it shows. Their facades typically had ornamental terra-cotta bands between floors, neoclassical terra-cotta trim framing the windows, along with escutcheons, double-height framed windows on the upper two floors, and neoclassical cornices as the capstones.

On the lower three floors of the 115th Street facade of today's Regnor you will still see the original rustication and neoclassical trim, the egg-and-dart motif and dentils, neoclassical columns, angel-bearing shields, and escutcheons inscribed with the monogram "JP," for Joseph Paterno.

Above the third floor, however, you don't see a hint of Gaetan Ajello. All you see are scars. New brickwork, whose color does not match the old, runs up the corners of the facade where the original coining had been, and the same mismatching brickwork is at the roofline because the cornice is gone, and the same brickwork surrounds the windows in place of the neoclassical framing, and it runs across the facade where balconies had once been.

It was all brought about by a tragedy on Broadway that occurred in 1979—a lintel fell from the eighth floor of the Regnor, fatally injuring a Barnard student. The result was a sensible law, Local Law 10, which was passed in 1980 and later revised as Local Law 11, but the law carried with it unanticipated results for the urban fabric.

The law said that every five years an architect or engineer had to inspect buildings that were taller than six stories and within 25 feet of any public spaces, and to certify that "a building's exterior walls and appurtenances thereof (were maintained) in a safe condition."

The inspections usually required scaffolding, and the owners were obligated to pay for it all, and to repair any dangerous conditions. If ignored, the landlord or co-op board could suffer criminal- as well as civil penalties. The New York Chapter of the American Institute of Architects saw to the heart of a problem—whether landlords would resort to pulling down ornamentation on general principle rather than spend the money for restoration work—and the AIA was on to something.

The landlord of the Regnor was Columbia University, and Columbia had hardly been cavalier about its property. The building had been "thoroughly" inspected every other year, but there had been a leak in the exterior wall of an apartment three floors above the one from which the lintel had fallen. The leak had been repaired, but Columbia decided to take no chances. The very day after the accident, the university hired a contractor to carry out repairs on the building.

Columbia, like many landlords and co-op boards, concluded that it was far more sensible to remove "appurtenances" than pay to maintain them and still run the risk of having them fall and injuring someone. They figured that it was cheaper to strip off any potentially hazardous ornamentation, so "appurtenances" were ripped untimely from their mothers' breasts. It explains why so much trim landed in the junk heap, and why we have been left with so many scarred and mutilated buildings. But there is one bright note. In 2016, the board of 905 West End, one of the other Ajello-Paterno trio, bucked the trend, and had its balconies recreated. That facade is beginning to look whole again.

These Eagles Might Do

Grant's Tomb, Riverside Drive at 122nd Street

The great pair of stone eagles that flanks the stairs to Grant's Tomb were not original to the tomb. As the former parks commissioner, August Heckscher, said, they were rescued "from some doomed post office."

The post office in question wasn't your run-of-the-mill old post office. Standing in the southern end of City Hall Park, the Post Office was one of the most prominent buildings in the city when it was built in the 1870s, and it was huge, the largest post office building in the world. It housed not only the central workings of the postal system for the whole city, which included the requisite space for pneumatic tubes that delivered mail to sub-post offices, the federal government also larded it with courtrooms and other bureaucratic necessities.

The style of the post office was the Second Empire Baroque, the florid mansard style of the Tuileries in the Paris of Napoleon II. It was one of several buildings designed by Alfred B. Mullett, the supervising architect for the U.S. Treasury Department, who probably did more to popularize the exuberant style in the U.S. than any other individual. The post office, however, was not well regarded by critics. By 1874, while the post office was still a-building, the architectural critic Montgomery Schuyler weighed in. Schuyler said that Mullet had "already piled incongruous dormers on his pediments, and crowned his dormers with irrelevant fowls, and reared pavilions above his eagles, and crowned his pavilions with iron crests, and culminated his crests with domes, and surmounted his domes with cupolas."

These eagles, each with a wingspan of more than 8 feet, were some of those "irrelevant fowls." We don't know who the sculptor of the eagles was, but Mullett's role as the supervising architect of the Treasury Department brought him into close contact with some of the nation's greatest practitioners. Daniel Chester French, for instance, designed sculpture groups for the post offices in Boston, Philadelphia, and Saint Louis. Whomever Mullett chose was certainly up to the task—the eagles are pretty good—and Grant's Tomb, where the eagles landed, needed all the help it could get.

The architect of the tomb was John Duncan, and his original plan for the tomb, from the top down, had a quadriga atop the dome, a sculpture group atop the base with urns at all four corners, four statues atop the portico to represent the armies under Grant's command, and an equestrian statue of Grant himself in front of the tomb. The plinths for the four statues atop the portico were installed, but the only sculpture that actually made it onto the tomb is John Massey Rhind's pair of recumbent figures bearing a plaque with the message "Let Us Have Peace," flanked at the corners by federal symbols supported by eagles. Contributions to the building committee had not poured in.

In the 1930s, while the post office in City Hall Park was being torn down, the Federal Works Progress Administration was gussying up Grant's Tomb in anticipation of the tourists visiting the city for the 1939 World's Fair. The federal government offered to salvage the eagles from the post office and donate them for use on the tomb to gussy it up even more. Nobody knows whether anyone questioned the aesthetics of having the heads of both eagles turning to the left instead of toward each other and creating balance, but any eagle in a storm.

Shades of Greenwich Village All Over Again: West 125th Street, Meet West 129th Street

125th and 129th Streets, west of Broadway

Once upon a time, a street called Manhattan Street, having escaped the maw of the street commissioners of 1811, followed a northwesterly angle from Manhattan Avenue at 124th Street to the Hudson River in the village of Manhattanville. At the river's edge in the early 20th century were piers for Hudson River Dayliners and ferries to Fort Lee, New Jersey, and a streetcar to serve them. The westbound streetcars operated from the East Side on 125th Street, and then, where West 125th Street intersected Manhattan Street at Morningside Avenue, the tracks followed Manhattan Street to the piers.

The ferry passengers insisted on calling the streetcar "The 125th Street Streetcar," whether it was operating on 125th Street or Manhattan Street. To reflect the reality of the common usage and at the urgings of the Harlem Board of Commerce, in 1920 the Board of Aldermen determined that the venerable name "Manhattan Street" should be changed to West 125th Street.

The board sensibly thought it unwise to have two West 125th Streets west of Manhattan Avenue, so the old 125th Street became La Salle Place. Then the council realized the lack of wisdom in having the new 125th Street intersecting the old 126th Street, so the single block of 126th Street between Amsterdam Avenue and Broadway became Moylan Place, and 127th Street became Tiemann Place, and the rump end of 129th Street became St. Clair Place.

None of this pleased the *Times*, which complained that the Board of Aldermen had substituted "four new places of somewhat doubtful nomenclature in so far as local traditions or associations are concerned and obliterated one good old name which has been associated with that district from time immemorial."

The *Times* called La Salle Street a "high-sounding French name," but it certainly came with local associations. Manhattanville College had been on the southern slope of Hamilton Heights since its establishment in 1853, and had given rise to the name Convent Avenue. The college had been established by the Christian Brothers, the order founded by Jean Baptiste de la Salle.

Moylan Place commemorated Pvt. William A. Moylan, who went off to World War I and never returned. He was the son of William Moylan, who lived on the block for years (Moylan Place was demapped with the coming of the Grant Houses); Tiemann Place was named for Daniel Tiemann, the former mayor whose house and paint factory had been in the neighborhood; and St. Clair Place was named for little St. Clair Pollack, whose burial place is up the slope on Riverside Drive.

The aldermen also changed the name of the street that paralleled Manhattan Street to the north, so Lawrence Street became the new West 126th Street, which resulted in a morass at Broadway. Because of its angle, it practically bumps into 128th Street east of Broadway, and west of Broadway it practically intersects 129th Street.

House numbers on the affected streets had to be juggled, new stationery had to be printed, street maps had to be revised, even the name of the subway station at Manhattan Street had to be changed.

And the new West 125th Street? It does indeed meet West 129th Street west of Broadway.

9

The Upper East Side

East 59th to 96th Streets, from Central Park East

A Quiet Ode to St. Cecilia

In the vestibule of the Sherry-Netherland Hotel, 781 Fifth Avenue, northeast corner of 59th Street

This relief panel of six girls singing and playing musical instruments faces another relief panel of seven boys carrying large plumes. The subject matter is celebratory and welcoming in nature, in the best tradition of hostmanship, and, by extension, the hotelier. The panels also serve as an ideal complement to the decoration of the lobby, which exudes the aura of a palatial Italian Renaissance hall. Both panels are by Karl Bitter, and they were originally diagonally across the plaza on the south side of 58th Street. They decorated a porte cochere that was part of the grand entrance to the house of Cornelius Vanderbilt II, work that was executed under the direction of John Donnelly of Woolworth Building fame.

House is a modest term to describe the mansion of Vanderbilt, who, in 1885, came into $67 million upon the death of his father, the railroad man William H. Vanderbilt. First built in 1880, the 60-plus-room house on the northwest corner of Fifth Avenue and 57th Street had swollen to 137 rooms when it was extended north and west in 1893. If the math is right, it was the city's largest single-family residence ever.

With the extension, the mansion overlooked the Plaza. The original front entrance on 57th Street was reduced to the everyday entrance, having been far eclipsed by the glory of the new, ceremonial entrance on 58th Street. The setting of the house with Central Park at its feet presented an air of the country in the city, and adding to the ambience was a garden, the first mansion in the city to have such an approach. A fence with a pair of wrought-iron gates opened onto a driveway arcing through the formal garden to the porte cochere, and facing out from the bases of the columns were six panels by Karl Bitter.

Bitter was a court sculptor of the Vanderbilts—he contributed to George W. Vanderbilt's Marble House in Newport and to Biltmore in North Carolina, to William K. Vanderbilt's Idle Hour in Oakdale, Long Island, and he sculpted these panels adorning the pedestals of Cornelius Vanderbilt II's carriage porch.

When the widowed Alice Vanderbilt sold the house in the 1920s, she was under no illusion that the real-estate purchase had been made for the house, but for the property upon which it sat. The house would make way for Bergdorf-Goodman.

She donated some objects such as a mantelpiece by Augustus Saint Gaudens to the Metropolitan Museum of Art, and sold other *objets d'art*. Two of the sculptural groups were salvaged and installed in the vestibule of the new Sherry-Netherland Hotel in 1927, presumably for a price. Whatever happened to the other four is a mystery.

To Hold Out, or Not to Hold Out, That Is the Question

134 East 60th Street/750 Lexington Avenue, between Lexington and Park Avenues

I n acquiring a site big enough to be developed efficiently, developers frequently run the risk of encountering a holdout. Someone might be betting that the offered price will keep rising if enough pressure is put on the developer, or it can mean that someone likes where he already is, thank you very much, and simply refuses to budge, despite the best efforts of law firms whose specialty is "de-leasing" and property owners who do not tremble at the word harassment.

The average successful holdout usually sticks out like a sore thumb, but not the holdout in the flank of 750 Lexington, which is perhaps New York's most overlooked holdout. Here a tenant named Jean Herman, who believed that she could never find such a centrally located and affordable apartment again, stubbornly refused to leave her rent-controlled, walk-up apartment in the mid-1980s for which she paid $168 a month. This, despite the fact that the other five tenants in the building had moved out, and the developer, after having been unable to satisfy her requirements for a comparable apartment *rent free*, was dangling $650,000 in front of her. No deal.

The economic solution for the Cohen Brothers was to accept the fact of Ms. Herman. While Ms. Herman was still in residence in the brownstone, the developers sheared off the top floor, put in a new roof and re-installed the cornice, gussied up the facade whose color would be akin to the spandrels in the new building, leaving Ms. Herman as the sole tenant in the building. Ms. Herman's victory, however, was short lived; she died in 1992. The windows overlooking 60th Street today are grayed out.

A Venerable Practice Revived

143 East 62nd Street, between Lexington and Third Avenues.

New York used to be chockablock with shop signs cantilevered from walls, and the good ones synthesized the product sold by the retailer, as exemplified by the sign at Tender Buttons. There were wire-rimmed spectacles for opticians, and signs in the outline of a shoe for shoe-repair stores, even a pistol suspended from a brace in front of a gunsmith's shop across from the old police headquarters on Centre Market Place. And there was the ubiquitous pawnbroker's symbol—the three balls—for hock shops.

Stores whose products defied easy recognition and were difficult to synthesize in a single image resorted to saying the obvious. Rappaports Toy Bazaar on Third Avenue had a sign overhanging its entrance with its message stacked vertically: "TOYS." Lascoff Pharmacy on Lexington Avenue did the same: "DRUGS." Some of the restaurants in the Longchamps chain of restaurants had vertical signs attached to their walls, as did Luchow's on 14th Street at Irving Place.

The artful and tasteful sign cantilevered from shop walls used to be rare enough—*schlocky* was the operative description for too many—and in 21st-century New York, artful and tasteful signs are becoming fewer and farther apart, rarer and rarer, which is why the Tender Buttons sign is such a joy. In the tradition of the best signs, the image tells the story.

The store was started in 1964 by the late Diana Epstein, who was joined the second day of the store's operation by Millicent Safro, who is still the store's leading light. When the store moved to its present site, the partners conceived of a simple sign, and up went the first of them. It was stolen, to be discovered broken and beyond repair on Third Avenue. The second sign crumbled—it self-destructed, as Ms. Safro described it—and its replacement, today's gold-leaf sign, was installed in 2013.

The partners had always enjoyed signs such as the opticians' classic glass rims, and there are some signs decorating a sanctum sanctorum in the shop, including one sign that synthesizes the cataloging and shelving of thousands of buttons: the sign is for the New York School of Filing.

Buttons might be small and seemingly insignificant, but, as the management says, they are also "richly varied, often exquisitely crafted, imaginatively designed, and made of valuable materials. In their making, they reveal our impulse to enhance even the most familiar and minute details of everyday life," just like their sign.

Easier than a Trip to St. Peter's

The Pieta in the south aisle, St. Vincent Ferrer Church, southeast corner of Lexington Avenue and 66th Street

There are countless paintings and sculpture pieces depicting the descent from the cross with the Virgin Mary mourning her son. Michelangelo sculpted four iterations on the theme, and his most famous, and one of the most famous statues in the world, is the Pieta that is enshrined in the Basilica of St. Peter in the Vatican. You can save yourself a trip to Rome by visiting this church.

A real advantage in viewing the statue here is that you can stand right next to it and take in all the details, unlike viewing the original at St. Peter's, where you are kept at a distance. And viewing this copy is infinitely better than the only time the Vatican has ever made a loan of the original, when it was the central feature at the Vatican Pavilion at the 1964 World's Fair. The planners for the pavilion were concerned with crowding, so they devised a plan for traffic control that was based on a fixed viewing time. The viewing area was stepped, with four tiers that were about 5 feet apart. On the lower three tiers there was no lingering, no time for contemplation. The visitors were on glorified conveyor belts. They caught a fleeting glimpse of the statue as they were whisked by. The topmost viewing area was stationary, designed for visitors who wanted a "leisurely view of the *Pieta*." Nobody saw the statue from any closer than 16 feet, with the statue about 36 feet from the top tier.

The setting was designed by the stage and lighting director, Jo Mielziner (*Annie Get Your Gun, Carousel, Guys and Dolls*, etc.). Here, the lighting was subdued, reverential. Four hundred flickering lights that were suspended from the ceiling in tight concentric rings created a "halo."

There is nothing hokey about viewing the *Pieta* in St. Vincent Ferrer. The statue is omnipotent, and it holds you in its power. The copy is about two-thirds the size of the original. It sits on a base that is 48 by 21 inches and is about as high as the base is wide.

Although it was not customary for sculptors to sign their works in the Renaissance, in the original you will find Michelangelo's name carved on the cincture of the Madonna's robe. Soon after the statue's installation in 1499, Michelangelo overheard some tourists ask each other who the sculptor might have been, and the belief was that it was their fellow Milanese, Cristoforo Solari. Michelangelo didn't appreciate the idea that his work was being attributed to another sculptor, so "one night he repaired to Saint Peter's with a light and his chisels, to engrave his name on the figure," as the Blashfields described in their translation of Vasari's *Lives*. And he didn't just sign his name. He defiantly carved "*Michaelangelus Bonarotus Floren Faciebat*," or "Michelangelo Buonarroti, a Florentine, made this." This iteration simply shows the cincture, and nowhere is to be found the name of the sculptor who made the copy either.

Also missing are Christ's wounds on his hands and feet, and the Virgin's left thumb has been repaired.

X-rays made of the original during the statue's stay in the city showed that pins had been inserted into the fingers of the left hand of the Madonna and into the little finger of the right hand of Christ. This copy might bear more verisimilitude to the original than anyone ever suspected.

78th and Where?

P.S. 158, southeast corner of York Avenue and 78th Street

PHOTO BY JOHN TAURANAC

Y ou're probably used to thinking of Avenue A as part of Alphabet City on the Lower East Side, but here it is on the Upper East Side. It's explained by the street commissioners who laid out Manhattan's streets on the gridiron plan in 1811. The north-south avenues were numbered from One to Twelve, and progressed numerically from east to west. But the commissioners began their numbering system arbitrarily, and there were four avenues east of First Avenue that were left over. To those avenues the commissioners accorded letters, and they had the letters progressing alphabetically from west to east. No rationale was offered for this dual naming system.

The street commissioners might have wanted to distinguish between avenues that were uninterrupted by natural topography such as a changing shoreline, intending that the lettered avenues would flag the fact that an avenue might begin or stop at the water's edge, sometimes to be picked up again wherever land reappeared. It's a nice theory, but it doesn't hold water. When the map was published in 1811, First Avenue dropped off for about 5 blocks between 98th and 103rd Streets. Tenth did not begin until about 21st Street, Eleventh at about 34th Street, and Twelfth Avenue made a brief appearance between about 112th and 128th Streets. Avenues C and D permanently dropped off the map north of Tenth and

Eleventh Streets. Avenues A and B are two of the lettered avenues that reappeared, but we know them under different names north of Stuyvesant Town.

It can come as a surprise to learn that East End Avenue was originally Avenue B, and that Pleasant Avenue and Sutton Place were originally Avenue A, as was York Avenue. In fact, if you were to tell a parent whose child attends P.S. 158 that the kid is going to school on Avenue A, you will probably have one confused parent.

P.S. 158 was built in 1898, 30 years before the name of Avenue A changed to York Avenue north of 60th Street. The name did not honor the Duke of York, for whom the city was named, nor did it find its roots in Yorkville, the local neighborhood. The name honors Sergeant Alvin York, the World War I hero. York had no swagger about him, no bluster. At the outbreak of World War I, he was a conscientious objector, but he went to war saying that he would do the best he could, and he did pretty well. He won the Congressional Medal of Honor.

After the war, this modest man returned to his Tennessee hills, and despite all the hero worship that was thrust upon him, and all the parks and streets that were named for him, his head never became swollen. In fact, it seems that he did not attend a naming ceremony for York Avenue, if, indeed, there even was one.

Full Disclosure: the author attended P. S. 158, grades 1 through 4.

The Initials Are A. C., Not C. A.

1014–1018 Madison Avenue, between 78th and 79th Streets

This is no ordinary monogram. Only an artist would have extended the base line of the "C" to act as the horizontal bar for the "A." Despite the artistry involved, the fact remains that the "C" comes before the "A" when it should be the other way around. The initials stand for Alexander Calder. Call it artist's license.

This sidewalk artwork came about in 1970 by a combination of a bad thing in a good place. The bad thing was that an ordinary sidewalk was in terrible shape, and the good thing was that the bad sidewalk was in front of three buildings that housed art galleries, including the gallery of Amelia and Klaus Perls, who just happened to be Alexander Calder's agents.

The Perlses talked with the owners of the buildings that flanked theirs, Robert Graham, of James Graham & Sons, and Morton Rosenfeld, whose building housed several art galleries. They all agreed that since they needed a new sidewalk, they might as well have one that was different.

Calder was intrigued by the challenge. It wasn't a mobile, it wasn't a stabile—it was something different. Calder would accept no fee for the design. He did it because the Perlses were not just his agents, they were friends, and he thought it would be fun.

The sidewalk is about 75 feet long, the width of the three buildings. There are sets of vertical and horizontal black parallel lines in front of 1014, crescents at 1016, and lines fanning out from the entrance of 1018, so arranged that they subliminally serve as directional pointers leading to the entrance of the galleries. The sidewalk's material is not the usual cement, but rustic terrazzo, a mixture of marble chips and concrete, with zinc strips defining the three patterns.

The construction company that made the first installation—the current sidewalk is a replacement, the first iteration having fallen victim to wear and tear—employed Italian-Americans who were experienced in work of this nature, and Calder told them not to worry about perfect symmetry. He said the design would be enhanced by a few irregularities.

Upon seeing the finished product, Calder said "It's a little stiff, but it's too late now," as Peter Benchley reported in the *Boston Globe* in 1970. Calder had felt no need to visit the site preparatory to making his drawings, as was the case with much of his work, nor was he usually on hand for the installation or fabrication. He liked to say that he made objects that were stronger than their surroundings.

In the 1970s, you could have crossed Madison Avenue and walked four blocks south to the Whitney Museum to see his point. Just inside the entrance was *Calder's Circus,* a theater piece with wire creatures that Calder actually used to play with, with him playing the ring master. The Breuer building is not an easy thing to upstage, but even static, Calder's little circus succeeded.

No Head for Facts

In the lee of the stoop, 52 East 80th Street,
between Madison and Park Avenues

Nobody is quite certain who sculpted this head, but the odds are pretty good that it was either the Austrian Franz Barwig or the German Henry Kreis. The head was borne on the shoulders of one of the two statues that flanked the original Ziegfeld Theater on the northwest corner of Sixth Avenue and 54th Street. Although the sculptor might be a mystery, the building's architect is not. It was Joseph Urban, a one-man dynamo who combined artist, set designer, interior designer, and architect in one package.

In the early 20th century, while still in Vienna, Urban was a leader in the Hagen-bund, a confederation of Secessionist artists, and a show of Franz Barwig's work was mounted under Urban's aegis. Twenty-plus years later and Urban and Barwig were collaborating on Mar-A-Lago, the estate of Marjorie Merriweather Post in Palm Beach, a period that paralleled the design and construction of the Ziegfeld Theater. Mar-A-Lago opened in January 1927, and the Ziegfeld a month later, but whether they worked together on the Ziegfeld is speculative.

Whether Urban and Henry Kreis joined forces on the Ziegfeld is equally speculative, but the timing was equally good, and Mar-A-Lago enters the scene again. Urban needed a foreman to oversee the work of the 15 sculptors on the job, and Kreis was given the assignment.

Fortune magazine's art director, Francis Brennan, described Kreis as Urban's "protégé," and Urban tapped him to sculpt the figures representing the arts for the Hearst Building on Eighth Avenue between 56th and 57th Streets, which bore a strong resemblance to the Ziegfeld in many of its details and opened precisely one year after the Ziegfeld.

How Urban came to design the Ziegfeld Theater is the confluence of two powerful forces—the impresario Florenz Ziegfeld and the newspaper publisher and movie producer William Randolph Hearst. The *Ziegfeld Follies* of 1917 was a "memorable" *Follies* wrote Hearst's biographer, W. A. Swanberg, with "dreamy sets by Joseph Urban" and an even dreamier Marion Davies on stage, and with William Randolph Hearst in the audience. Hearst hired Urban to design sets for his movie studio, Hearst Productions.

Hearst was also a real-estate investor, and Sixth Avenue was ripe for speculation. The spur of the Sixth Avenue El that operated between 53rd and 59th Streets was removed in 1926, and the roadway was widened, making upper Sixth Avenue desirable. Hearst owned the bulk of the property on both sides of the avenue between 54th and 55th Streets. On the northeast corner of 54th Street he built the Warwick Hotel, which opened in December, 1926, with a tea honoring Florenz Ziegfeld that was held after the laying of the cornerstone for the theater.

A theater bearing Ziegfeld's name across the avenue could only be good for the Warwick, and, the Ziegfeld was just the ticket. The *Times* said that the theater was the "most artistic in design, a setting of ineffable luxury." Urban's ideas for the murals were executed by Lillian Gaertner, with whom Urban would collaborate on the decoration of the Plaza Hotel's Persian Room, and they depicted "gay figures of young lovers, some kissing, some running, some dancing, some hunting . . . [all] to throw the audience into the spirit of the thing."

As with all things bright and beautiful, age took its toll, and with changing times came changing tastes. In 1967, at age forty, the Ziegfeld was torn down by a new generation of developers, the Fisher Brothers, and in its place went 1345 Sixth Avenue, another banal box by Emery Roth & Sons.

This head got here thanks to an offhand remark. Zachary Fisher and the theatrical producer Jerry Hammer were passing the theater when Fisher said he was going to tear it down. Hammer pointed to the limestone head and, half in jest, asked Fisher if he could have it. Four months later it arrived at his doorstep, unannounced. Hammer moved out in 1998, but he mercifully left the head behind for us to speculate on.

One of the Signers

116 East 80th Street, between Park and Lexington Avenues

Lewis Morris, a wealthy Barbadian transplant, arrived in New York in the 1670s and he purchased the 500-acre farm that had belonged to Mr. and Mrs. Jonas Bronck—the Broncks, for whom the borough is named. The Morrises might not have a borough named for them, but there are the Bronx neighborhoods of Morrisania and Morris Heights, and there is Morris Avenue, which starts at about East 138th Street and goes north.

The Morris clan purchased early, and held onto their holdings long. The Morris Land Company sold one tract of land in Morris Heights to William Astor in 1883. A piece of property that they had acquired in 1754 and had been the site of one of the family's mansions was sold in 1950, by which time the two corners involved in the sale were described as 149th Street and the Grand Concourse. A Dodge- and Plymouth automobile dealership was slated for one corner, a service station for the other.

Morrises abound in New York history, including the Morrisania-born Gouverneur Morris, who was a delegate to the Continental Congress, and his half-brother, another Lewis, who was also Morrisania-born as well as a delegate to the Continental Congress. That Lewis was a major-general in the rebel army. He was in large measure responsible for having the route of the original Boston Post Road "re-mapped" to run through his property, but he was most famous for having signed the Declaration of Independence, and the face in the pediment of this row house is his.

The house was built by yet another Lewis, Lewis Spencer Morris, in 1923, and whenever a story about him ran that was of a social nature, this sentence or a variation on it invariably appeared: "Lewis Spencer Morris, a member of the Morris family of this city and the eighth in descent from Lewis Morris, a signer of the Declaration of Independence . . . ." The phrase "Descendant of Declaration of Independence Signer" even made the headline in Morris's 1944 obituary in the *Tribune*.

In 1907, while still at Princeton, Lewis Spencer Morris became engaged to Emily Pell Coster, whose father was a partner at J. P. Morgan & Co., and whose mother was the daughter of Clarence Pell and Emily Claiborne, names that still resonate—the Claiborne Pell Bridge spans Narragansett Bay. In addition to the usual blurb about Morris' patrimony, the engagement announcement said that the affianced were among the best-known members of the younger set in society. (Other Morrises included Dr. Lewis Rutherford Morris, "one of the Morrises of New York," who married a daughter of Senator Edward Clark, and Eva Van Cortlandt Morris "of Morrisania," who married McDougall Hawkes.)

When Lewis Spencer Morris decided to build a home for his wife and himself in 1922, he had the architects Cross & Cross design this elegantly detailed, neo-Federal, red-brick mansion with the face of his forebear in the pediment.

Morris had entered the family law firm, which specialized in trust- and estate administration. With his pedigree and business acumen, he had an entrée into all the right clubs—he was the president of the Down Town Association, a governor of the Knickerbocker Club, and a member of the Princeton Club, the Brook, the Racquet & Tennis Clubs, and the State and City Bar Associations. He served as the treasurer of St. John the Divine, and he was the president of the New York Society Library. Under his watch, the library bought and moved into its present home at 53 East 79th Street in 1936.

In the 1910s, Morris was one of three trustees governing the income of Henry Astor, the brother of William, who had bought the Morris Heights property. According to Astor standards, Henry had married beneath his station. He was excommunicated socially, but not financially. Much of his income was derived from what the Astors still quaintly referred to as the "Eden farm," or Times Square, which in just the three years, from 1914 to 1917, earned the outcast Astor $760,000.

In 1939, Morris handled the sale of his in-laws' former home at 50 Park Avenue, a red brick mansion that retained the air of Murray Hill's old "marble-hall era." Two years later, as an indication of how well he handled financial matters, the estate of Emily Pell Coster was given a federal tax return of $244,635.

Morris did some work for the Fulton Trust Company, which also took a special interest in real-estate investments, and he wound up the chairman of the board. In 1930 came the announcement that the Fulton Trust was planning uptown quarters at 1002 Madison Avenue, between 77th and 78th Streets, which would be more convenient for the trust's Upper East Side customers than having to travel down to the Singer Building at 140 Broadway. The architects again were Cross & Cross, who designed what their client had in mind. The building was residential in scale, the style was neo-Federal, and within the pediment would be a familiar face—the Morris who signed the Declaration of Independence.

Scenery Flats

1001 Fifth Avenue, between 81st and 82nd Streets

You expect to find scenery flats creating the illusion of a building on the stage, but the theater is theater, where illusion is king. Fifth Avenue is meant to be built of more substantial stuff, and you do not expect a scenery flat topping off a Fifth Avenue apartment house. Nor do you expect the neighborhood's upper-class residents to have been manning the barricades and acting as agitators, but agitate they did when this building was originally proposed.

There had been three Beaux Arts–style town houses where 1001 Fifth now stands, and those three, plus the Duke mansion on the corner of 82nd, were the perfect complement to the Metropolitan Museum of Art across the street. And south of 1001 Fifth is 998 Fifth, one of the grandest, if not *the* grandest, of the Fifth Avenue apartment houses. When the 12-story Renaissance-style building opened in 1911, it had all of 15 apartments, one as large as 24 rooms and nine baths.

Along came Sol Goldman in the 1970s, who kept a low profile but was a high roller. The *Times* ranked Goldman up there among the real-estate titans Harry B. Helmsley and Seymour Durst. Goldman, by himself or with his sometime partner Alex DeLorenzo Jr., controlled about 450 properties in the 1970s, including the jewel in his crown, the Chrysler Building, where he kept his offices.

Goldman did not get where he was by going gently into the fray. Like a more famous New York real-estate operator, one aspect of his modus operandi, said the *Times,* was that he "did not mind paying off subcontractors more slowly than they would have liked."

One of Goldman and DeLorenzo's properties was the Amherst, a 21-story apartment building at 401 East 74th Street. In 1971, about 100 Amherst tenants claimed that the building was rife with prostitution and drug dealing, coupled with a diminution of service and maintenance. The landlords' goal, alleged the tenants, was to drive them out in order to attract more undesirable tenants who would pay higher rents.

The apartment house at 101 West 55th Street, on the west side of Sixth Avenue between 55th and 56th Streets, was also in their portfolio. In the early 1970s, the pair leased the site to a British developer who planned on knocking down the rent-controlled apartment building and erecting a 30-plus-story office building on the site. That plan was nixed, so a new one evolved. Gut the interiors and create all new apartments that would not be subject to rent control. In 1976, by which time both the British company and Goldman had junked the property, the building was still vacant. It made the perfect setting for the scene in the movie *Network* where residents hung out the windows and shouted "I'm mad as hell, and I'm not going to take it anymore."

The original plan for 1001 Fifth made the neighborhood residents mad as hell, and they were not going to take it, period. The plan called for a 25-story building with a tacky facade. Worse, a preponderance of the apartments was to be studios. High-rise buildings with studios frequently attract unsavory tenants, and with Goldman's track record, nobody was willing to take any chances. This was clearly not the stuff of Fifth Avenue.

The apartment tower was to be designed by Philip Birnbaum, another faceless player with great swathes of New York under his belt. "Banal" was among the kinder words used to describe Birnbaum's designs, and "gracious" was never applied to his interiors. Birnbaum's layouts were efficient. Said one admirer, the man responsible for Trump Plaza on 61st and Third, "Not all (Birnbaum buildings) were great, but they all made money."

By 1977, Peter Kalikow had taken over the project, and the three town houses came down. A pyrrhic victory was the creation of an historic district centered on the Metropolitan Museum of Art, and, as a sop to the protests, the height of the building was reduced to 23 stories.

Kalikow knew money-making layouts when he saw them, and he retained Birnbaum for his interiors. There were about 80 apartments in all, and still some studios. Gracious dining was out. The larger apartments had combined living/dining rooms.

An ostensible victory came when Kalikow hired the firm of Johnson/Burgee to redesign the facade. Philip Johnson and John Burgee opted for Post Modernism, and they decided to play off the neighboring 998 Fifth. They used rusticated limestone at the base with the obligatory Renaissance-style lanterns at the entrance, and they continued the line of 998's molding, varying it by stopping short of the edges of 1001. They also continued 998's terminating cornice, only with windows poking through. The 12th-floor roofline on 998 is the 15th floor on 1001, the difference explained by the heights of the ceilings.

Bowing to the Duke mansion next door with its real mansard roof, 1001 is topped off with an imposter that is blatantly fake. It's just a scenery flat, with a difference. In real scenery flats you don't see the supporting struts.

The Stones of the Met

The Metropolitan Museum of Art, 1000 Fifth Avenue, at 82nd Street

It's surprising to think that the august Metropolitan Museum of Art, the greatest treasure house of art in the western hemisphere, would have four piles of unfinished stone on its facade, but there they sit.

The museum began life in 1870, and the names of many of the founders resonate still, including William Cullen Bryant, the artist John F. Kensett, the sculptor John Quincy Adams Ward, the publisher George P. Putnam, the park designer Frederick Law Olmsted, and the architect, Richard Morris Hunt.

Their goal was hardly modest. The collection would constitute objects illustrative of the history of art from the earliest beginnings to the present time, and it would depend on quality, not quantity—only models of established excellence would be accepted. Their notion on the potential attendance was as modest as their goals—they bandied about the numbers of visitors to the Louvre and the British Museum.

By 1872, the collection was housed in a gallery in 681 Fifth Avenue, and if the trustees' goal was to increase attendance, they were on to something—first they opened the gallery on Saturdays, then they opened on Monday evenings.

Eight years later and the Met had a building of its own in Central Park that was underwritten in part by the city and sitting on land donated by the city. First there was one extension, then another, and still the place was overflowing with newly acquired treasures. A major new wing, dubbed the East Wing, would front on Fifth Avenue and would theoretically solve the space problem. The city agreed to underwrite its construction to the tune of $1 million, and the museum's own Richard Morris Hunt was selected as the architect.

Hunt was the first American to attend Paris's l'Ecole des Beaux Arts, and its preachings included the idea that sculpture was an integral part of architectural design. Hunt's sculpture-adorned Administration Building at Chicago's 1893 Columbian Exposition, which Edwin Blashfield described as a "colossal object lesson," was a case in point. Sculpture was in, and Hunt's design for the Met was a poster building for the Beaux Arts ideal.

Hunt's plan called for three great arches, each flanked by 42-foot-high paired Corinthian pillars. Those piles of stone on the lintels only begin to make sense when you realize that Hunt's plan included allegorical sculpture groups up there, each one representing one of the great periods in art—Ancient, Medieval, Renaissance, and Modern.

The sculpture was to be carved *in situ*, and Hunt left the selection of the sculptors to the National Sculpture Society. By having the work doled out among different sculptors, Hunt hoped to avoid being criticized for having given all the other work to Karl Bitter.

The East Wing was finished to the point where it could be opened in 1902, but the million dollars had run out, and we are left with the piles of stone. The allegorical statues never were installed. In the eyes of this writer as a little boy, those piles of stone were pyramids, up there because of the Egyptian art within. At least one of the periods of great art, the Ancient, made it to the facade of the Met in the imagination of one kid.

The Creatures from Cleopatra's Lagoon

At the base of the obelisk in Central Park, southwest of the Metropolitan Museum of Art, between 81st and 82nd Streets

Astronomers in Ancient Egypt understood that it took 12 lunar cycles for the sun to return to its original position, and the astrologers took it from there. The crab is the sign in the zodiac for Cancer, the period when the Nile begins to rise, bringing with it water for the fields and bounty to the land, and that's one of the reasons that you find crabs lurking in each of the four corners of this obelisk.

The crabs, however, were not there when this obelisk was first erected in about 1450 B.C. in today's Cairo, where it stood beside the Nile until thieves struck.

This obelisk originally had a base with rectilinear corners, but now the corners are soft. Its base had been ringed by precious metal, and thieves wanted to abscond with it. They failed in their attempts at prying it off, so the ingenious fellows decided to melt it. The unexpected consequence was that the heat was so great that it cracked the stone at the corners and some of the stone fell away. With the demise of its supports, the obelisk toppled.

About 12 years after Egypt's conquest by the Romans in 30 BC, the Romans decided to re-erect the pyramid in the capital city of Alexandria. They dug it out and floated it downstream, and that's when the crabs were added. The Roman engineer, Pontius, realized that support had to be added at the corners if the obelisk were to stand in its victimized state, so he bolted together the pedestal and shaft, with the crabs cleverly masking the bolts while doing supplementary duty aesthetically.

Philosophy also entered the scene. In today's parlance, the Romans had excellent community relations with their vanquished populations. They tried not to offend the beliefs of the conquered Egyptians, especially when related to something such as the obelisk that was as much a venerable monument as a divine symbol. The use of crabs, the sign in the zodiac that applied to bounty, was a natural extension of the Roman philosophy of co-existence.

How the obelisk, a gift from the Khedive of Egypt to the United States in the 1870s, came to be in Central Park in 1881 is a classic. The fact that it would be in New York never seems to have been questioned, and everyone who had been instrumental in having the obelisk brought to America favored the site where it wound up, but there was one suggestion after another for different sites.

The president of the West Side Association suggested the circle at Eighth Avenue and 59th Street, and if that scenario had gone forward we might have Cleopatra's Circle. Another suggestion was 42nd Street between Fifth and Sixth

Avenues, with the Egyptian Revival reservoir framing the perfect backdrop. One idea was that the obelisk should be placed in front of the Museum of Natural History, because the obelisk belonged more to science than the domain of art. Parks Commissioner Andrew Haswell Green thought that the site should be the plaza at Fifth Avenue and 59th Street, citing the column at Place Vendome in Paris as a wonderful example of a shaft in a small open space surrounded by buildings. The park designer Calvert Vaux, also a commissioner, said that the obelisk could be just about anywhere but Central Park.

A final meeting was held by the park commissioners to determine the site, and, by some legerdemain of bureaucratic maneuvering, an "executive committee," on which neither Vaux nor Green served, was to give the final word. The committee took a carriage ride through the park, stopping first at the plaza at Fifth Avenue to show their objectivity, and then on to the knoll just southwest of the museum, the predestined ideal spot.

The museum benefitted more from the placement of the obelisk than mere propinquity. Only two of the four original crabs could be salvaged in 1880, and Lieutenant Commander Henry H. Gorringe, U.S.N., who, as an independent contractor on leave from the Navy had transported and erected the obelisk and who too had advocated that the obelisk be placed near the Metropolitan, donated the original two crabs to the museum. Today's crabs on the obelisk are reproductions that were manufactured at the Brooklyn Navy Yard, arrangements no doubt also made by Gorringe.

The gift from the khedive came with one string attached. The recipient had to pay the cost of shipping and construction, and William H. Vanderbilt volunteered to underwrite the $100,000-plus expense. Vanderbilt could well afford it, and for his contribution, he got his name inscribed on the replicated crabs. Vanderbilt had been on the Met's board since its founding.

For the record, Cleopatra had nothing to do with the creation of the obelisk, or with the crabs. Cleopatra had wanted this obelisk and its mate moved to the temple at Alexandria that she had built and dedicated to the memory of her lover, Julius Caesar. Hence, *Cleopatra's Needle,* the same nickname given to the obelisk on the bank of the Thames in London.

A Hint of a European Town Square

455 East 83rd Street, northwest corner, York Avenue

New York doesn't have a clock that attracts tourists the way the glockenspiel on the town hall in Munich attracts them or the astronomical clock in Prague at Wenceslaus Square. Since 2005, however, New York has had a contender. Tucked away and out of sight of the average tourist is this trompe l'oeil mural of a clock by the master magician of visual trickery, the all-powerful fooler of the eye, Richard Haas.

Nobody can say that Haas doesn't have a sense of whimsy. On Prince Street in SoHo he took an exposed brick wall overlooking Greene Street and painted a "faux-cade" that simulates the cast iron facade on the front of the building. At Peck Slip and South Street he took another wall and painted the view of the Brooklyn Bridge that you would see from that spot if the wall weren't there. You are presented with a view of the bridge through an opening of a neoclassical building of his own invention.

This tenement house wall that Haas took as his canvas in 2005 had been graffitied, and when the Cielo Apartment house, a 28-story condominium, was built across the street from it, the developer, Jules Demchick, started hearing complaints about the graffiti. Demchick thought he had the solution. He talked with the owner of the tenement, George Papoutsis, who was more than happy to have his property spruced up, and Haas went to work. Twelve years after the fact and Papoutsis, with a twinkle in his eye, said that the wall has been graffiti free ever since.

The clock, the likes of which you would see on the town hall in Munich, is the star. Instead of a lord and lady being entertained by musicians and jousting knights, you see a pair of mounted New York City policemen, and you see the clock's exposed workings. Just as you half expect to see the gears whirling, so you expect to see the mounted policemen riding around every hour on the hour.

This painted "glockenspiel" might be an *homage* to the predominately German population of pre-war Yorkville, but the whimsical Richard Haas might also have been thinking of a skit on *Your Show of Shows* that had the comedic foursome of Sid Caesar, Imogene Coca, Carl Reiner, and Howard Morris playing herky-jerky mechanical figures who appear each hour on a large clock in a German village. By the third hour the springs have sprung and everything has gone haywire, and the skit goes on, all performed completely deadpan and with clockwork imprecision.

But there is more to Haas's mural than just the clock. On the York Avenue corner was and still is a dry cleaner's establishment, and Haas extended the image of the dry cleaner down the side street. You see the image of clean clothes neatly

hung on racks in two of Haas's windows, and a model's dummy in a third. And then there is the row of oriel windows, capped by an arch that reflects the arc of a clock, and all placed so that the east windows line up with the fire escape.

At street level are gargoyles, including a reader hunched over a writing table, and a cook licking his finger to test the concoction in the pot he is stirring. These two characters did not spring whole from the master's mind. They are reinterpreted images of actual gargoyles on 527 West 110th Street. You can *trompe* all *les yeux* some of the time, and you can *trompe* some of *les yeux* all the time, but you can't *trompe* all *les yeux* all the time.

Giddy-Up

The mounting block on the east side of the bridle path, just north of the Fifth Avenue entrance to Central Park at 90th Street

Mounting blocks might be considered effete when you think of all the Westerns you've seen where John Wayne–types stick their left-booted foot in a stirrup, grab the pommel, and hoist themselves up into the saddle. Mounting a horse in that fashion twists the horse's spine, leading to serious injuries, and a mounting block eases the pain for everyone, man and beast alike, especially the 19th-century woman. The equestrienne who was obliged to ride sidesaddle not only had to raise her left leg very high to place one foot in the stirrup and hoist herself up, she then had to navigate the right leg around the hook-like pommel, all the while wearing a lady-like skirt that was frequently so long that it fell below her boots. Mounting blocks somewhat eased the first step, and made eminently good sense, especially since horseback riding was considered a primary form of exercise in the 1850s, when Central Park was conceived.

The avowed object of the park was to preserve and improve health, and nobody was talking about playgrounds or tennis courts or skating rinks or ball fields or jogging tracks. They were talking about a civilized drive in a carriage, or a horseback ride, or a stroll. Two of these forms of exercise were specifically designed for citizens affluent enough to maintain a horse or a horse-and-carriage, or at least have the financial wherewithal to rent.

A design contest had been put out to bid for the park, with a Parks Commission to advise and confirm. The admirable plan by Calvert Vaux and Frederick Law Olmsted that was adopted, Plan 33, raised one question.

Vaux and Olmsted had built separation of function into their traffic plan. Pedestrians were separated from the bridle path and carriageways, horseback riding from carriages in a limited way, and all were segregated from the east-west transverse roads.

If horseback riders wanted to ride on a path that was exclusively for equestrians, they had the bridle path around the reservoir. If they wanted a longer ride, they had to share the roadway with carriages. Commissioners Robert J. Dillon and August Belmont maintained that the bridle path should be longer.

Dillon was the son of the first president of the Emigrant Savings bank. He was a lawyer, and, for several years, he had been the city's Corporation Counsel. Belmont was a banker, the American representative of the Rothschild Bank. With their personal finances, both Dillon and Belmont would have kept horses and carriages in the city for pleasure driving, but Belmont was in a class by himself in things equine.

Belmont's name is linked with one of the nation's most famous horse races, the Belmont Stakes, and it was Belmont who prevailed in having the bridle path extended from the west side of the reservoir to 60th Street, and from the east side of the reservoir to loop around at about 104th Street, extending the bridle path to about 4.5 miles. He might also have succeeded in getting two more mounting blocks along the bridle path on the west side between 74th and 77th Streets.

Clearly Belmont was onto something. In 1864, before the park was officially even open, 100,397 equestrians were counted.

Her Own Private Driveway to Her Own Mansion in the Sky

1107 Fifth Avenue, on East 92nd Street

You will find portes cocheres, or covered driveways, on a few New York apartment houses, but this one is different. This *porte cochere* was a private driveway that led to a private entrance that led to private elevators that

whisked you to what was tantamount to a 54-room private house on the top three floors. There has never been anything like it in New York City history.

The 1920s witnessed a seismic change in the living habits of New York's wealthy. Apartment houses were on the rise, literally and metaphorically, and the Buildings Department reported that something occurred in 1927 that had not happened in the previous 100 years. Six months had passed without a single application for a private house. The triplex in this apartment building would have gone unrecorded as a three-story private house, although by any definition it was one. It was just perched on the top three floors of an apartment house.

Marjorie Merriweather Post, the cereal heiress (she inherited Post Toasties, and acquired Bird's Eye) and her husband, E. F. Hutton (of "& Co." fame), were living in the mansion on this site that they had bought from the widow of I. Townsend Burden. By the 1920s, Mrs. Hutton wanted to escape the traffic hubbub, and a mansion that was somehow elevated would be ideal.

The Huttons could have heeded a suggestion made by Alfred Ely Beech in the 1890s, when City Hall was declared too small and antiquated to meet the city's future needs, and talk of demolition was in the air. Beech, the editor of *Scientific American*, tried to placate both the nascent preservation camp and the demolish-and-replace camp. He said that an iron pan could be slipped under City Hall, which would then be lifted into the air hydraulically and kept there by temporary supports. A skyscraper could then be constructed below it, and, when ready, City Hall would be lowered onto the top of the skyscraper. City Hall would be preserved, it would be on its original site and performing its original function, and the expanding bureaucracy would be served.

John Reed Kilpatrick, the former Yale sports hero and Phi Beta graduate, had just joined the Fuller Construction Company, and he had what might be considered a more practical solution. He was keen on erecting a luxurious, 14-story building on the corner where the Huttons' house stood, and he wanted to purchase their property along with some neighboring property. He offered to build a triplex penthouse apartment designed to their specifications if they agreed.

Although cooperative apartment living was becoming the norm for luxury apartments in the 1920s, this apartment house was to be a rental, and the Huttons were offered a 15-year lease at $75,000 a year. It was a relative bargain. The Huttons would profit from the sale of their house, their new digs would be customized to their tastes, and, with the exception of the library paneling and dining room mantle that Mrs. Hutton salvaged from the mansion and had installed, everything would be brand new. It was an offer they could not refuse. In 1926, a year after the apartment house was officially open, the Huttons moved into their mansion in the sky.

The apartment was served by four elevators, two dedicated to the family and visitors, the other two for service. The passenger elevators opened directly onto elevator vestibules in the apartment, the service elevators onto the service areas in the rear.

The apartment had ten wood-burning fireplaces. Occupying the Fifth Avenue side of the frontage on the 12th floor was the "grand foyer," which was about 40 feet wide and doubled as a ballroom. It came with coat rooms for ladies and gents, along with the usual necessaries. (The foyer is marked on the facade by the Palladian window, flanked by the coat rooms.) On the 92nd Street corner was the drawing room, with the library at the south end. The dining and breakfast rooms overlooked the south, and no neighbors were peeping in. Immediately to the south was Otto Kahn's five-story house, then Andrew Carnegie's four-story house, and so on.

The rest of the 12th floor was given over to service. There were cold-storage rooms for flowers and furs, a temperature-regulated wine room, a linen closet, a silver room, a larder, the butler's pantry, the kitchen, and a receiving room. There were seven servants' rooms, two servants' bathrooms, a butler's room with bath, a staff dining room, and a staff sitting room.

On the floor above was a sitting room overlooking 92nd Street. Overlooking Fifth Avenue in the 92nd Street corner were a guest room with bath and a private balcony, then another guest room with bath, another sitting room, and, in the south corner, Mrs. Hutton's bedroom with a bathroom and "gown closet," plus a balcony. Next door and looking south was Mr. Hutton's bedroom, bathroom and walk-in closet. Off Mr. Hutton's bedroom was the closest thing that the Huttons had in common with tenement dwellers in the days before air conditioning—the poor had fire escapes, the Huttons had a sleeping porch. In the southeast corner was a child's room with a bathroom and sun porch, and the rest of the space was given over to basic necessities and housing of more staff—a cedar closet and linen closet, a secretary's work room, two valets' rooms, six maids' rooms plus one for Mrs. Hutton's personal maid, two rooms for laundresses to do their work, a storage room, a servants' hall, and a small kitchen.

The penthouse floor was set back and ringed by a tiled roof, which was filled with plantings. A sitting room overlooked 92nd Street. Overlooking the avenue at the corner was a bedroom, and the secretary's bedroom next to it, both with baths, then another sitting room. There were bedrooms with walk-in closets and private baths for each of the three daughters (there were two by Post's first marriage, and another by Hutton—the actress, Dina Merrill), and the list went on to include a maid's room, an extra servant's room, a linen closet, a pantry, a laundry, and a servants' laundry. At 54 rooms, this was the city's largest apartment of all time.

Fewer and fewer apartment houses were being built with ten-plus room apartments in the 1920s, and this apartment house, with some 17-room apartments, was an exception to the rule by 1925. The Post-Hutton apartment was the exception to any rule.

Marjorie Merriweather Post gave up the triplex upon the expiration of her lease in 1941. It remained vacant for ten years, whereupon it was divided into six apartments.

Push Ahead

Madison Avenue, between 94th and 95th Streets

"**B**outez En Avant," French for "Push Ahead" or "Press Forward," is the message on this wall of the Squadron A Armory. A French motto might sound effete for a military unit, but the men of Squadron A were hardly your run-of-the-mill GIs. Squadron A was originally formed in 1884 by "gentlemen equestrians," and they originally called themselves the First New York Hussars, although they were not affiliated with the military in any way. It was little more than a thinly masked social club. *De rigeur* were busbies and tunics, bandoliers, swords, and riding boots, all of which the members paid for out of their own pockets. They rented quarters at Dickel's Riding Academy on West 56th Street, where they stabled their horses and had a rink set aside for their exclusive use at certain hours.

By 1889, the quasi-military unit had become a real military unit. It was mustered into the New York National Guard as Troop A; by 1895 it had expanded into Squadron A. The National Guard in late 19th-century New York was an anomaly. The troops were self-supporting, whereas the armories were underwritten by the government, and the Armory Board spent $132,000 for stables and a dirt-filled arena for Squadron A by extending the Eighth Regiment Armory on Park Avenue westward to Madison. On January 31, 1896, the troops "celebrated with a formal reception and elaborate ball."

There were no standard uniforms for National Guard units at the time, and Squadron A kept theirs. In full regalia, they participated in the Fifth Avenue parade in 1899 celebrating Admiral George Dewey's victory in the Battle of Manila Bay.

Squadron A would put on displays of horsemanship in a series of competitive games, or gymkhana, for charity affairs. Potato races would have the horsemen racing their horses full tilt up to a bucket filled with potatoes at one end of the field, grabbing one of the potatoes, and racing back to deposit the spud in a bucket at the other end. A series of pursuit and wrestling contests followed, where the pursuer tried to capture a ribbon tied about the arm of his opponent. And then came "a mounted melee," according to the *Times*. Ten members wore red plumes atop heavily padded helmets, and ten members wore green plumes atop similar helmets. "Each man had a stout stick for a sword, and the game was to knock off the plumes from one another's heads. The scrimmage was a battle royal."

Games of a different sort continued. Polo was the game of cavalry officers in the British army, and Squadron A was no different. They took it up officially, and they did it with the blessing of the C.O., who said the obvious—playing polo made you a better horseman.

But *Boutez En Avant?* For the members of Squadron A, French was the *lingua franca,* and although there is no documentation on how "Boutez En Avant" came to be on the wall, it was the family motto of Herbert Barry, who had joined the organization in 1891 and rose through the officer ranks to become the regimental colonel.

Barry was indicative of the social status of many Squadron A members. A lawyer who started practicing in New York in 1889, his father's Massachusetts family had fought in the American Revolution, and his mother's family was descended from New York's first aristocracy, the Stuyvesants. Barry had the right entrées and qualifications for all the right associations, and in the 1890s he was also a very eligible bachelor, who enjoyed "delightful evenings of informal dancing" at the homes of young society leaders. One more formal party at Sherry's ballroom had the cotillion continuing until one in the morning, at which time supper was served.

It's a mystery how so many society leaders in the late 19th century could seemingly party all night and go to work the next day and still be productive, while at the same time be in such good physical condition that they could participate in strenuous physical activities in their spare time, but they did it.

Whatever shape these cavalrymen were in, cavalry charges came to be considered too suicidal even by the bloody standards of World War I, and the mounted troop was reorganized as a machine gun battalion. The arena continued to be used for the occasional small-scale polo match into the 1960s, with polo teams having three players. The arena was a diminutive 90 by 200 feet versus the standard polo field that is 200 by 300 yards.

By the late 1960s, Hunter High School was scheduled to move into a new building on the site, and we are lucky that the wall bearing Captain Barry's family motto is with us still, since the rest of the armory, which was designed by John R. Thomas and was so wonderfully evocative of Carcasonne, is resting in some landfill. In a last-ditch effort to save some of the castle-like building, the Madison Avenue wall was preserved. Harmon H. Goldstone, the then-commissioner of the Landmarks Preservation Commission, said that it was "the most interesting part of the building from an architectural point of view." It's about all he could say about this sad bit of preservation, since by the time the Madison Avenue facade had been designated it was too late to save anything else, and we are left with this shell. Once more unto the breach, dear friends. *Boutez en avant pour le patrimoine.*

10

Harlem and the Heights

Harlem, from East 96th Street North to the Harlem River
and from the bluffs on the western edge from 110th Street
north to the Harlem River

Details. Details. Details.

The Museum of the City of New York, 1220 Fifth Avenue,
between 103rd and 104th Streets

t is said that either God or the devil is in the details, but whoever is in them, details can be especially pleasurable when an eminently sensible and ordinary object is made aesthetically pleasing, and these drainpipes rank right up there. Some early 19th-century-buildings on South Street have drainpipes with hourglass figures, but the likelihood of finding dentils atop them is pretty slim (dentils are the band of small, square or rectangular blocks that look like teeth, a great mnemonic), the same as finding raised lettering on them and a date, although this date was optimistic. The museum did not open until 1932.

The brickwork here is also different, and something else to behold. Bricks come in different qualities, and let's just say finished and unfinished. The average brick wall is two bricks thick, with unfinished brick hidden on the inside, and the more expensive finished brick on the outside for all the world to see.

On the exposed part of this wall, each horizontal course consists of finished bricks laid lengthwise to expose their sides (stretchers) alternating with finished bricks laid so that their ends, or heads, are exposed (headers). Vertically, each header is centered on the stretchers above and below, repeating the marvelously rhythmic pattern.

This style is Flemish bond, and it is not called "bond" for nothing. The system admirably binds the brickwork together. The headers bond with the unfinished stretchers behind, making the structural advantage every bit as valuable as the aesthetic one. Flemish bond was only considered for grand buildings such as the museum and 895 West End Avenue. If finished bricks are used as headers, only half of the finished brick is exposed, the other half essentially wasted. The economic disadvantage was compensated by the added structural strength.

The idea for the Museum of the City of New York began to evolve in 1924 as an idea for Gracie Mansion, which had been built in 1799 by Archibald Gracie and was by then owned by the city and functioning as a restroom. Archibald Gracie's great-granddaughter and some other high-born New Yorkers thought that a more appropriate use for the mansion would be to have volunteers dressed in early-19th-century costumes welcoming visitors as if a reception were being held.

A more visionary concept was put forward by one of the city's great chroniclers, Henry Collins Brown. He advocated that Gracie Mansion should house an institution that was "wholly and exclusively devoted to the task of preserving and collecting material" pertaining to the city, much like the London Museum and Paris' Museé Carnavalet. He was proposing the Museum of the City of New York.

Brown's idea won out, and the museum started with Brown at its head. Soon the city's treasure hunters needed a bigger building. The city provided the land on Fifth Avenue, and $2 million were raised in contributions.

Five architects, traditionalists all, entered the competition in 1928, with Joseph Freedlander, a graduate of MIT and l'Ecole des Beaux Arts, taking the prize. One reporter archly reported that the building was "an impressive pile in the early republican style of adaptation from the Georgian." Freedlander's model, minus the balcony, was basically Federal Hall, which had stood on the corner of Wall and Nassau Streets. The building had been New York's City Hall, but in 1789, with the federal capital in New York, Major Pierre l'Enfant metamorphosed it into the nation's all-purpose building. George Washington stood on the balcony to take the oath of office, he and his cabinet had offices in the building, and the first Congress met there. Federal Hall reverted to being City Hall with the federal government's move to Philadelphia, and in 1812, just as soon as the plaster was dry on the new City Hall, the city tore down Federal Hall, the single-most important building in the nation's short history.

Freedlander was best known at the time for having designed one practical object, and about to design another. In 1923, the Fifth Avenue Association sponsored traffic towers that would sit in the middle of Fifth Avenue, with police officers manually operating the traffic lights from on high. Freedlander's neoclassical extravaganzas, unfortunately, were out of view of crosstown drivers, hence failures as traffic signals, complicated by the fact that they were an impediment to the flow of avenue traffic that they had been designed to speed up, and down they came.

In 1931, Freedlander was back at it. He designed bronze traffic signals in a slimmed down, *moderne* form of classicism that were topped by a statue of a Mercury-like figure cast by the Tiffany Studios. Mercury was raising his right hand, as if to say "Stop," and in his left hand he carried a winged wheel. Those electric traffic signals were fully automated, and they were placed on the sidewalks at intersections, out of harm's way and visible to all. By 1964, they too were gone. The museum, up to the "task of preserving and collecting material" pertaining to the city, has one of the statues, a marvelous link with the architect of the building.

Egyptian Prettiest

Today's New York French-American Charter School, 311 West 120th Street

This building was built around 1903 by the Schinasi Brothers, who were tobacconists by trade. Whoever designed the building knew all the tricks of the architectural trade, but two plaques and some trim are about all that's left that is original.

The top floor had dormers flanking an arcade with a central carved panel. Today's blank crests originally bore emblems, and the name "Schinasi Bros" ran across the building where there is now a blank horizontal band, and beneath it, "Cigarette Manufacturers." And the upstairs floors had rows of windows because the workers needed light, with ten cigarette-rolling machines lumbering away on the fourth floor, and about 300 women packing the cigarettes on the third floor.

Two plaques at street level remain. "Egyptian Prettiest" was the Schinasi's most popular brand, and the plaque with the bust of a nobleman represented their second biggest seller, "Noble."

Solomon Schinasi did not arrive in this country the classic penniless immigrant in 1892. He arrived from Egypt with Turkish tobacco of the highest grade that he tried to sell to cigarette makers, who would have no part of it. Virginia tobacco was the tobacco of choice for cigarettes in the United States. Undeterred, Schinasi determined that if others wouldn't produce cigarettes made of Turkish tobacco, he would. He rented a small shop at 48 Broad Street, and proceeded to manufacture cigarettes in the window.

Morris Schinasi, Solomon's brother, joined him, and the firm of Schinasi Brothers was formed in 1895. The taste for Turkish leaf tobacco soon caught on, and the sale of Schinasi's brands started growing. First this factory was built, then a seven-story factory at 32 West 100th Street in 1907. In 1915, when they were manufacturing about 250 million cigarettes a year, the partners became a subsidiary of the Tobacco Products Corporation.

The brothers had good taste in things architectural. Solomon bought the Villa Julia from Dr. and Mr. Rice, and Morris had William B. Tuthill, the architect of Carnegie Hall, design a freestanding marble-clad neo–Francis I beauty on the north corner of Riverside Drive and 107th. Those two freestanding mansions are the only two still standing on the Drive.

In 1912, the Schinasi brothers bought the eight-story Hotel St. Andrew on the northwest corner of Broadway and 72nd Street, and to advertise it, they bought space on the cover of a pocket map of the city. A photograph showed the 72nd Street IRT control house in the foreground, setting off "the Uptown Hotel that is quickly accessible to Downtown Theatres, Shops and Business Districts, via the Subway Express at Door of Hotel."

When the Schinasi heirs announced in 1937 that they were going to tear down the St. Andrew and put up a two-story taxpayer with shops and offices on the site, the *Tribune* described the hotel as a "landmark of upper Broadway." It had opened only nine years after the Dakota, and if landmark designation had existed, the hotel would no doubt have been on the list. The control house, like the Schinasi houses, is blessedly still there.

A Star of David on a Baptist Church

Mount Olive Baptist Church, 201 Lenox Avenue (Malcolm X Boulevard), the northwest corner of West 120th Street

You might not think of Harlem as a Jewish quarter, but in the early 1900s there were one-fifth as many Jews living in Harlem as in the Lower East Side. The Jewish Harlemites were hardly urban villagers. They were solid middle- and upper-middle class, many were progressive, and today's Mount Olivet Baptist Church was one of the neighborhood's many synagogues.

The congregants that built the synagogue had already broken with the tradition of segregating the sexes, and they then went one radicalized step further—they held services in English. That was 1873.

The congregation built this temple to designs by Arnold W. Brunner in 1907, and if it looks more like a bank than a temple, you can thank the archeologists who in the early 20th century were unearthing venerable buildings. As Brunner pointed out, the architectural norm is to design buildings in the reigning style of the day, and temples that were going up in Jerusalem in the Roman period were going up in the Roman style. Synagogue architecture, he said, consequently had "no traditional lines of expression."

Brunner had already designed Congregation Shearith Israel on Central Park West in a Roman neoclassical style, and it appealed to Temple Israel's congregants, who saw a virtue in having a synagogue that could be integrated into the cityscape and adhere to the contemporaneous architectural norm.

But neighborhoods change, and what might be Jewish one decade might be Protestant the next, and what might be White one decade might be Black the next. By the 1920s, most of the temple's congregants had moved on. The building was put on the market, and the congregation of Mount Olivet bought the temple in 1925, lock, stock, and Star of David.

Mount Olivet had been on 53rd Street between Sixth and Seventh Avenues, and the parishioners were much like the parishioners of Temple Israel. They were clearly fairly prosperous, and they were in the social vanguard. Soon after the congregation had moved to 120th Street, the NAACP held its annual meeting in Mount Olivet's new home, and in 1927, Mount Olivet's minister, the Rev. William Preston Hayes, inspired by A. Philip Randolph, the head of the Brotherhood of Sleeping Car Porters, was preaching on behalf of better working conditions for the working class.

Before the move uptown, the congregants had given a trip to Europe to the Rev. Hayes and a traveling companion in recognition of the pastor's good work. Upon his return, Hayes gave a series of lectures based on his travels, the proceeds going to the financial campaign for the new property.

Hayes was frequently introduced at the talks by his traveling companion, the Rev. Adam Clayton Powell, Sr., the minister of the Abyssinian Baptist Church. The avenue one block west is named for Dr. Powell's son, Adam Clayton Powell, Jr., who also served as the pastor of the Abyssinian Baptist Church as well as an eleven-term congressman. That church has become a mandatory stop for politicians aspiring to higher office.

Stanford White, Move Over

One West 123rd Street (aka 31 Mount Morris Park West),
on the northwest corner

Nancy and John Dwight, who had this house built in 1890, both grew up in Massachusetts, she in Foxboro, he in South Hadley. Nancy Shaw Everett was attending the Mount Holyoke Female Seminary in South Hadley, today's Mount Holyoke College, where they met. They were married in 1841, moved to New York in the late 1840s, lived in Harlem from the 1860s on, and summered in South Hadley.

The Dwights made benefactions to institutions such as the Metropolitan Museum of Art, the Hampton Institute in Virginia, and the American Seamen's Friend Society, and Nancy Dwight's collection of engravings by Elbridge Kingsley would be donated to Mount Holyoke College, along with a building to house them.

The Dwights could well afford their philanthropies and this large, five-story house. John Dwight headed the firm of John Dwight & Co., manufacturers of bicarbonate of soda, the same miracle product that is probably in your kitchen cupboard—Arm & Hammer Baking Soda.

The Dwight house was on the cutting edge of design in 1890. It has a serene, aesthetic look, like the art of the early Renaissance, exemplified by clean lines and avoidance of over-ornamentation. The bricks are long, narrow, light brown Roman brick, far from the traditional red brick or brownstone. The window framing is neoclassical, and there is an elliptical projecting corner in the west end that adds interest to the otherwise four-square building. The street-level entrance is a major break with the tradition of stoops on private houses, anticipating the American basement plan to come by the turn of the 20th century. And then there is the portico. This hooded doorway, with the pediment over the front door that is distinctly Renaissance in origin, is closest in spirit to the elaborate portal at the church of San Alessandro that was built in Lucca in 1480.

All the key words used to describe the features of the Dwight house above were lifted from sources describing two houses in Boston that were designed by McKim, Mead & White—the 1886 Alexander Cochrane House and the 1888 John L. Andrew House—plus the firm's Judson Memorial Church on Washington Square that was going up in 1888, but not finished until 1893.

You'll find other hooded doorways in the city. There's one just down the block from the Dwight house at 23 West 123rd Street, and one at the Manhasset Apartments at 301 West 108th Street, and another at 936 West End Avenue, but they pale in comparison.

The portico on the Dwight house is particularly glorious. The coffered hood is filled with floral rosettes in ornamental panels, and the mosaic consists of pieces of inlaid colored marble with a beribboned laurel wreath around the oculus, the ensemble supported by freestanding Ionic columns. It is a dead ringer for the portico on Judson Memorial.

The building design is ascribed to the architect Frank Hill Smith, who was headquartered in Boston. What he is known for is his painting and interior decoration. He was trained as an artist, and a Smith painting of Saint Mark's in Venice hung in Boston's Museum of Fine Arts, and frescos by Smith adorn the walls of the Massachusetts state capitol.

One of his important interior-decoration commissions was for the Opera House in Holyoke, which might explain how he and the Dwights came to know each other. Smith also designed the decoration for the dining room of Young's Hotel in Boston, and, in 1881, he did the preliminary painting and ornamental moldings for the dining room of the Union League Club on Fifth Avenue and 39th Street. Short of the picturesque Sunflower House in Beacon Hill and one unbuilt project, little is known about Smith's other architectural projects, even if there were any.

All of this raises the question of Smith's proficiency at designing the Dwight house. If the general form, design, trim, and materials on the Dwight house are similar in so many ways with projects by McKim, Mead & White, you might begin to wonder. Was there a mole in the office of McKim, Mead & White, or was someone moonlighting?

As talented as Frank Smith might have been, with no other substantive architectural designs to his credit, the likelihood of his pulling off such a wonderful design without help seems pretty slim. If Smith did indeed do it on his own, Stanford White would have met his competition.

An Open Book

Nine West 124th Street, between Fifth and Lenox Avenues
(Malcolm X Boulevard)

A s the dog-eared pages of the books in the cornice indicate, this is a library, a house of books. Of course, a true classical cornice would not have included bound books, which only became affordable in any quantity in the 19th century. Like the mortarboards on the University Club, it was the symbolism that counted.

While still almost a separate village, Harlem already had its own library. In 1820, the Harlem Library, one of the first of the publicly accessible libraries in the city, had been established. By the early 1900s, there were about a dozen general neighborhood libraries in the city, but what was needed was a network of libraries in every neighborhood that offered inter-library loans. Onto the scene walked the steel man, Andrew Carnegie.

The creation of United States Steel had garnered Carnegie $492 million, and in 1901 he had an annual income that was estimated at $30 million, and he set out to share the wealth. After mulling over the numbers with John Billings, the director of the New York City Library, Carnegie inquired whether 65 branch libraries at about $80,000 per building would do the trick.

The offer came with two strings attached: The city was to provide the land, and the city was to accept responsibility for the upkeep and maintenance of the buildings, just as it had agreed to do for the Main Branch. The city did not look the gift horse in the mouth.

Three architectural firms—Carrère & Hastings, McKim, Mead & White, and Babb, Cook & Willard—would jointly set the standards on the design and construction of the branch libraries. The goal was to have them residential in scale to blend in with the neighborhoods, to be clearly institutional but not cut from the same neoclassical cookie cutter, and all identifiable as Carnegie libraries. The Harlem Library, today's Mount Morris Library, became part of the branch library system, and in 1909 it moved into this McKim, Mead & White building.

The tablets in the cornice are not cut from the same mold. They are cut by hand, and all are just a little different. Some of the words appear scrambled, which might be the result of weathering, but there might be a message in the madness.

To help make sense of some of the phrasing, some punctuation has been added here, and some missing letters have been filled in. Each of the left-hand pages begins with the alphabet, has some text, and ends with a variation on "This New York Public Library, No. 37, Will Contain Wholesome Books," which gets to the essence. The main message on the right-hand page charmingly says, "What Boy Cut Letters On These Pages To Give Texture To the Surfaces," and three of the four pages end with "Why Does It Matter. Drawing The Whole. Lamkin Robson," followed by however much of the alphabet would fit. The ending on the western-most book is "Does It Matter? Drawing These, Patrick Clune. Where Does Reason Commence [Illegible] Does End."

And there are more oddities. In some of the text on the left side of the spreads you find the word "Paddy," in others "Benny." "Paddy" can be an affectionate name for "Patrick," as in the carver, but it is ordinarily a pejorative for the Irish. "Bennie" is a nickname for "Benjamin," a Jewish name, and there are typographical tricks.

Medieval manuscripts, much like the design of this book, frequently had the initial letter of a lead paragraph straddling two or three lines, but only referring to the first. Here, the second time the device is used, the letter serves as the first letter twice. The "R" on the sixth and seventh lines on the left-hand page is the first letter of both "Rats" and "Rags," which might be associating both Paddy and Bennie with some of the grimmer realities of immigrant life.

The symbols on the capitals of the pilasters are even more mysterious. It would be nice to think that the symbolism relates to alchemy, the transformation of something base into something precious, which is, after all, the goal of a library, but the architects were showing their erudition another way. Three of the four symbols are printer's marks from the Italian Renaissance. The "H" with the circle in the center of the horizontal bar might have been paying homage to a school. By the time this building was being designed, William Mitchell Kendall was running McKim, Mead & White, and Kendall, like McKim, had studied at Harvard. The "H" just might be Kendall's way of honoring his alma mater with a made-up printer's mark. Whether actual or invented, printers' marks are wonderfully appropriate.

And, for the record, today's Morris Park branch library was the city's 37th, as the "No. 37" informed us.

A Porch Good Enough for William McKinley

Astor Row, 8 to 62 West 130th Street, between Fifth and Lenox Avenues
(Malcolm X Boulevard)

Presidential candidate William McKinley, famous for having waged his 1896 presidential campaign from a front porch in Canton, Ohio, would have felt right at home here. His comfort factor might have been somewhat mitigated, however, by the uniqueness of this row of houses compared with his home town, where probably every other house came with a front porch. In Manhattan you can count on one finger a string of houses with porches like the 14 pairs on Astor Row.

The row was developed by William Astor, grandson of the founding father of the real-estate dynasty. You might not equate the name Astor with a charming row of brick houses such as these, but in 1883 there was only a smattering of urban life in the neighborhood. The 28 brick houses were simply an investment, and, typical of the Astors, these houses were not built for sale. They were rentals.

The houses are semi-detached, allowing natural light to fill the interiors on three sides, and they came with gardens and porches in front and small gardens in the rear, and with interesting brick cornices, and porches that are intricately spindled and bracketed. In 1920, the *Times* called this block the "Block Beautiful," a "picture of domestic tranquility and comfort which few other dwelling blocks in the city possessed."

The city's Black community was primarily centered in the West Fifties when these houses went up (the neighborhood where Mount Olivet had been), and by the 1910s the Black community was essentially moving uptown to Harlem. In 1920, the estate of William Waldorf Astor sold the row of brownstones that backed on Astor Row, 1–25 West 129th Street. That same week, 20 of the 28 Astor Row houses were sold by William Astor's son, Vincent Astor, to James H. Cruikshank, a realty operator, who sold five of the houses within the first week. The houses never did rent at bargain rates, and there had been waiting lists.

With the financial and sociological changes that came to the city by the 1970s, Astor Row was suffering. By the 1990s, you could have called it Desolation Row. The buildings were designated landmarks, but only a huge infusion of capital could save them. Help came in the form of various philanthropic and governmental organizations, and joining the forces was Brooke Astor, Vincent's widow.

The Astors had had their pick of architects when they decided to build, and they chose Charles Buek, who is not all that well known today, but who was very much the professional. He was serving on a committee that had been established to suggest changes and amendments to a proposed state building law in 1883, and he was becoming a real-estate entrepreneur. In 1883, Buek and his wife sold a major piece of property on the northwest corner of Madison Avenue and 60th Street for $65,000 to the editor of the *New York Sun*, Charles A. Dana, and it seems that Buek not only designed the Dana house, Charles Buek & Co. erected it.

Buek did a lot of work on the East Side, but by the turn of the 20th century, the property was getting too pricey and building sites were getting too few. By then the Upper West Side had been beckoning. Buek had already set up an office on West 72nd Street in 1888, where the West 72nd Street Association, a booster group, held its first meeting.

Buek developed and designed several row houses on the Upper West Side, including the elegant 49 West 70th Street with its triple bay window on the second floor, and the bow-fronted brownstone at 230 West 72nd Street, which he sold before it was even finished. No Astor, Buek, but a first-class developer nevertheless.

A City-Planning Breakthrough: Go Slow. Hold Your Horses.

The King Houses, both sides of West 138th and 139th Streets, between Powell and Douglass Boulevards

The average block of row houses in Manhattan has one house cheek by jowl another, house after house, with no break in the wall until you reach the corner. The King Model Houses, with their two block frontages, are different. There is a pair of breaks, each 24 feet wide, in each of the four rows.

The street commissioners of 1811 had made no allowances for service areas, and the "business" part of housekeeping, from putting out the trash to receiving deliveries to loading a moving van, was all done curbside. The passageways in the King houses lead to rear service areas, and they represented the first allowances for off-street pick-ups and deliveries in Manhattan, an idea that was lauded when the houses were put up for sale in 1892—the necessary dirty work of day-to-day living could all be done without observation, preserving a Victorian sense of privacy while keeping a decorous streetscape.

The developer of these houses, David H. King, Jr., couldn't fiddle with the street pattern and make his blocks deeper in order to achieve his goal of constructing a service road in the rear of the houses. He scrapped backyards, and substituted service buildings and paved service roads enclosed by ornamental iron gates, complete with the admonition to "walk your horses." A by-product of King's plan is that the mid-block service entrances provided more corner lots, and corner lots have more light and air than a mid-block lot, hence are more valuable.

King was by trade a contractor (a builder) and he was one of the best. He built the base of the Statue of Liberty, and the Mills Building on Broad Street, the Times Building at 41 Park Row, and Bennett's Herald Building, and on and on.

King's houses came with three different styles, alleviating the problem "of unvarying brownstone fronts, ranged in grim rows like Egyptian sepulchers," as the *Tribune* described the 1890s streetscape in New York. He divided the work among three architects, two of whom he had already worked with. King had built an apartment house at 21 East 21st Street in 1878 that was designed by Bruce Price, and he gave Price the plum assignment of designing the north side of 138th Street and the south side of 139th. Price's contribution was the neoclassical, mellow yellow-brick houses.

For the north side of 139th Street, King had Stanford White design the Renaissance-y facades with rusticated sandstone for the American basements and variegated brickwork above, all complemented by neoclassical balconies and rosettes in a pinkish terra-cotta.

King had worked with White as the contractor for both Madison Square Garden and Washington Arch, and it was King who saved the Garden from mediocrity. The 300-foot tower that was modeled on Seville's Giralda was to be the Garden's crowning glory, but when construction costs started to rise, investors started to balk. King volunteered to put up half the needed $450,000, which tipped the financial scales, and the balance was raised. Washington Arch was another project that ran short of cash, and *it* was dependent on the kindness of contributors rather than the business acumen of investors. White waived his commission, and King waived his fee.

James Brown Lord designed the houses on the south side of 138th Street with the boxed stoops. There, on the basement and parlor floors, you find the only brownstone. Red brick is above.

By arranging the development in this fashion, a passing pedestrian was presented with one style of architecture on one side of the block, another on the other. The styles were different, but they created a harmonious and architectural whole.

King was clearly good at what he did, and he was equally accomplished at public relations, or at least at hiring good flack. It was a rare occurrence for New York's two major newspapers, the *Times* and the *Tribune*, to report the same "soft" news on the same day, but on March 14, 1892, both newspapers told the same story with many of the same words.

Both newspapers described the plumbing as "executed under the direction of Charles F. Wingate, the sanitary expert." The *Tribune* reported that "these houses have been constructed in such a thorough manner that they will stand for years with hardly any need of repairs." The *Times* said that the houses "have been so substantially constructed that they will stand for years with hardly any call for repairs." Both newspapers described the site as on the "west side," which is true—it was west of Fifth—but the *Tribune* capitalized it, indicating the neighborhood west of Central Park. Both stories described the project verbatim as "not far from the proposed site of Columbia College and St Luke's Hospital," which was a stretch. Columbia and St Luke's would be more than a mile south, three numbered north-south avenues west, or about another half mile, and up a hill of almost 100 feet.

An ad ran in October, 1892, with the headline "Over $42,000 Sold in the Last Four Days," with copy claiming that the purchasers had canvassed the entire market and had "bought without hesitation." In December, a two-column ad showed the alley as a wide promenade with elegantly clad women strolling with their children. "Open for inspection at all times. If you arrive late they will be lighted with gas."

Despite all the press and all the advertising, only a few of the houses sold, and the Equitable Life Assurance Company closed on the property. By the 1920s, Equitable was renting King's houses to successful Black residents. Those living in the houses were regarded as devoting themselves to a better life, and the houses became known as "Strivers Row." The name has stuck.

Not During the Renaissance

The Claremont, 3330 Broadway, southeast corner of Broadway and 135th Street

A mid this Renaissance-style, terra-cotta facade, with its classic triple arch and its properly proportioned columns and pilasters and its garlands of fruit, you will find a curious object depicted within an escutcheon in the place of honor on the roofline. It is a hand-cranked moving-picture camera on a tripod.

This 1914 building was built as the Claremont, a photoplay theater. The corner had early attracted the eye of investors as a good site for some kind of entertainment, and Rebecca Mayer, who owned the two eastern Broadway block fronts between 133rd and 135th Streets, had planned an open-air theater designed by the architect J. M. Felson for this site. Felson, who was brought to the United States from Russia as a child, had graduated from Cooper Union in 1910. The freshly minted architect went on to design dozens of buildings—he specialized in apartment houses—but some real-estate negotiations got in the way of his open-air theater being built.

The real-estate developers Arlington C. Hall and William H. Hall, Jr., also liked the 135th Street corner, and in 1913 the brothers struck a deal with Mayer. In exchange for her two block fronts that were valued at $2 million, they would give her the Hamilton Apartments, an elegant 13-story apartment house at 420 Riverside Drive that they had built. She took the deal.

The Hall brothers' real estate business had begun upon Arlington's graduation from the Lawrenceville School in 1895, and his younger brother, William, joined three years later. Typical of real-estate firms, they operated under different corporate names, including the Wayside Realty Company, the Penatoquit Point Realty Corporation, the Trelaw Holding Corporation, and the straight-forward A. C. & H. M. Hall Realty Company.

The Hall brothers were not averse to a little self-promotion, and they liked to see their initials on their buildings. The "H" in the escutcheon over the entrance to the Hamilton Apartments was not there for Hamilton, it was there for Hall. You will also see an "H" within the escutcheons of 645 West End Avenue, another Hall project. The architect who designed the Claremont and both apartment houses for the Halls was an architect known for his neoclassical facades, for his use of terra-cotta and white brick, and for embellishing buildings with the initials of the builders. Their architect was Gaeton Ajello.

When the Claremont was built in 1914 there were already far larger and grander theaters that combined moving pictures and vaudeville in residential neighborhoods. On Broadway between 96th and 97th Streets were the Riverside and Riviera Theaters, both with 100-foot frontages on Broadway, and both designed by Thomas W. Lamb. The Riverside opened in 1911, the Riviera in 1914. On Broadway and 146th Street, you find the still-standing Hamilton Theater, another Lamb design, which opened in 1913, and by 1930, movie palaces such as Loews 175th Street were opening.

The Claremont building housed more than a theater. On the second floor were a large restaurant and a ballroom that sometimes doubled as a venue for dance classes ("La Salle de Danse"), and there was a roof garden. By 1933, the theater was closed, the interior metamorphosed into an automobile showroom at the corner, with the roof garden used for additional showroom space.

By the late 1920s, the brothers had already sold the property, but they did not give up on movie theaters. With the advent of "talkies," the average American was going to the movies about once a week. In 1933, the Halls built the Midtown Theater, on Broadway between 99th and 100th Streets. It was not a "palace," but a modest, mid-block, Art Deco theater .

Despite the Depression, Arlington Hall was doing okay. In November, 1934, he and his wife Laura were described as "members of the winter colony" in Miami, and they reopened their home in Florida "after passing several months in New York City." They also owned a 38-acre estate in Ridgewood, New Jersey, and Hall built 315 Riverside Drive in 1931 to designs by Boak & Paris, who would also design the Midtown. Another apartment house that Hall built was the 19-story 22 Riverside Drive in 1933, where he and his wife occupied a triplex apartment, and where she lived until her death in 1955 (he died at 72 in 1948 in Miami). The prestigious Plaza Galleries managed the sale of some of their belongings, and the estate started divesting itself of some of its holdings. Maybe the estate should have listened to the wisdom of Mark Twain: "Buy land, they're not making it anymore." Or at least hang onto what you've got.

Not Your Usual Building Stone

City College of New York, Convent Avenue between 138th and 141st Streets

The stone you see on the walls of City College is not a stone usually associated with building facades, although it might look familiar. Anyone who has walked through Central Park has probably seen outcroppings of it.

The stone is the rock upon which most of Manhattan's skyscrapers stand north of Greenwich Village, and it officially bears the name of the island—it is Manhattan schist, an igneous stone with flakes of mica in it. Like Manhattan itself, it has a twinkle.

Despite its twinkle, Manhattan schist is rarely employed as a facing for buildings. At its worst, it is described as coarse, although the mica does relieve it. A few buildings, such as Broadway Presbyterian Church on Broadway and 114th Street, are faced with it, and the stone on the church might have been quarried locally, even on the site itself. Across the street from the church, on the south side of 114th Street just west of Broadway, is a remarkable sight, an undeveloped lot containing a slab of unbulldozed-away Manhattan schist.

City College, or the College of the City of New York or City College of New York, was originally called the Free Academy. It was sponsored by the city, and the city provided the college degrees at no tuition. It was the democratic idea of providing an education regardless of income and status that was the precipitating force. By the turn of the 20th century, with 50 percent of the city's population of foreign birth or the children of foreign parents, education was regarded as an "Americanizing" force. The all-male school was so successful that it became known as "The Poor Man's Harvard," to become "The Poor Man's Harvard *and Woman's Radcliffe*" when it went fully co-ed in 1951.

The Free Academy had opened in a building on Lexington Avenue and 23rd Street in 1847, but by the 1890s, the college had spread out and was occupying space in various outlying buildings. Just as Columbia and New York Universities decided to move north in the 1890s, so City College decided to move uptown, to Hamilton Heights.

The campus is perched on a cliff overlooking Harlem to the east, and therein lies one theory why Manhattan schist was used for the facades. City College's main building, today's Shepard Hall, which overlooks the cliff, was clad in the same stone as the cliff, creating the illusion that Shepard Hall is a continuation of it, that it is all one and the same. A letter writer to the *Times* believed that the desired illusion of one uninterrupted wall had been the precipitating factor in the choice of the facing stone.

The more likely guiding factor was finances. The city is notoriously strapped for money, and at the turn of the 20th century it was already paying an annual $350,000 to support the college. Between the six blocks of land along Convent Avenue and the estimated cost of construction, the bill came to almost $3 million.

The virtue of Manhattan schist is that it is cheap, so cheap in fact, that in the case of City College the schist was either the product of digging for the foundations, or it was stone that had been dug up for the construction of the subway, or a combination of the two. If the former, the stone cost nothing; if the latter, the cost was the bill for cartage. It was cheaper and less cumbersome for excavators to give the stone away than pay to have it hauled away.

This would be the first genuine campus for the college, and the architect was George B. Post, who had designed the New York Stock Exchange. Unlike Charles Follen McKim's "Municipal Classic" design for Columbia, which was designed to be an integrated part of the city, Post determined that collegiate Gothic, a style more Oxbridge than early 20th-century New York, would set the campus apart.

To serve as a foil to the dour stone, Post enriched the buildings with more than 600 terra-cotta figures, providing "just the vigorous impulse in architectural sculpture that we need," said the *Tribune*. The sculptural themes were appropriate to the buildings, so on the gymnasium you see athletes, and on Shepard Hall, which originally housed general classrooms, you find different areas of study, such as math and language.

The sculptors were the little-known Loester & Co., in association with the better-known Bruno Louis Zimm, the sculptor of the touching relief sculpture on the Slocum Memorial Fountain in Tompkins Square Park, and the relief sculpture on the Women's Health Protective Association Fountain on Riverside Drive. A native New Yorker, Zimm had studied at the Art Students League and under Augustus St. Gaudens and Karl Bitter. Here at City College, Zimm added more twinkle to the Manhattan schist.

Our Lady of Architectural Salvage

Our Lady of Lourdes Church, north side of West 142nd Street,
between Convent and Amsterdam Avenues

ast your mind back to the 1890s. On 23rd Street and Fourth Avenue, today's Park Avenue South, you would have seen the National Academy of Design on the northwest corner. On the northwest corner of 34th and Fifth stood the mansion of A. T. Stewart. And on the west side of Madison Avenue between 50th and 51st Streets was the original east wall of St. Patrick's Cathedral. What you find in Our Lady of Lourdes Church are elements salvaged from all three of those buildings.

The congregation of Our Lady of Lourdes was created in 1901, and its first pastor was the Rev. Joseph McMahon, who had served as a curate at St. Patrick's Cathedral. There was not a lot of money, and McMahon wanted his new congregation housed in its new home quickly, and he was a master scavenger.

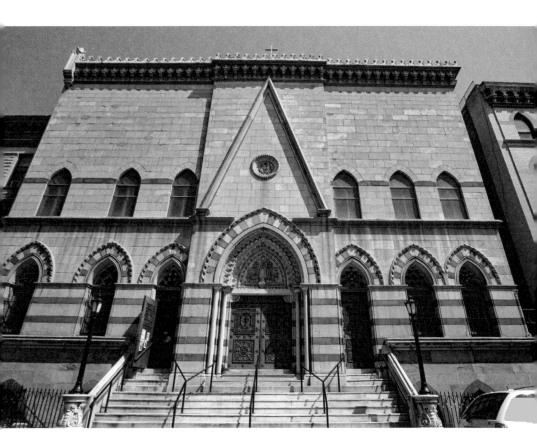

His first bit of scavenging was from the National Academy of Design. The academy had decided to move to the southeast corner of Columbus Avenue and 110th Street at the turn of the 20th century, and down came their Venetian Gothic–styled building that had been built in 1863. After the fact, McMahon acquired the stones at bargain rates. The mid-section of the facade of Our Lady of Lourdes—the arcade of windows—are the stones from the National Academy.

Then there was the former mansion of A. T. Stewart, the department store impresario, which was occupied by the Manhattan Club in the 1890s. The club couldn't afford the upkeep and maintenance on their mansion-turned-clubhouse, so down came the Stewart mansion, and McMahon picked up some of the pieces, again at bargain prices. The newel posts flanking the entrance and the marble above the facade are from the Stewart mansion.

And McMahon well knew that plans were afoot to replace the existing Renwick-designed wall at the east end of St. Patrick's for the addition of the Our Lady Chapel, and he made arrangements with Bishop Corrigan to salvage some of the wall. The gable arch above the entrance is from St. Patrick's, with the Renwick-designed gothic arches in the north end of the church (one main major arch flanked by minor arches behind the altar, and two more arches in the east and west walls), all of which are out of sight from the street. The bishop made a gift of it all to the congregation.

Having acquired the stones from the National Academy presented an unanticipated problem. The stones were in a jumble, with no key to their re-assembly. To solve the problem, the architect-builder and his crew carted the stones to an empty lot and pieced them together as if they were solving a gigantic jigsaw puzzle. When the facade was reassembled on the ground, the stones were numbered, whereupon they could be put back together in place with minor variations. The proportions are slightly different because the site is slightly narrower, and the door is slightly larger, but overall the Venetian Gothic arcade on Our Lady of Lourdes looks pretty much as it had on the National Academy.

The stones from St. Patrick's presented two different kinds of problems, but this time McMahon could react proactively to the first, and his architect-builder had the time to solve the second.

The lower stones in the wall could be numbered in place and cataloged before the wall was taken down. The solution to numbering the stones on high was to have a man in a boatswain's chair swinging along, with the "bo'sun" marking each stone, keeping a record as he went. When the stones were transported to the construction site, the architect-builder could "design by number," but here is where the second problem came in.

St. Patrick's was about 100 feet wide at the east end, and the wall was set on a slight arc. The building site for Our Lady of Lourdes was 75 feet wide, straight-sided and right-angled. After some chipping away, the arches were set in on a straight line.

The salvaged marble from the Stewart mansion posed the fewest problems. The stone was recut and installed above the midsection of the building, replacing the diamond-shaped brickwork of the Academy, and nothing had to be done to the newel posts that flank the entrance. They were simply put in position, performing the same role that they had played on 34th Street.

The architect-builder who assembled the building from all its disparate parts and who succeeded in bringing the job to a harmonious conclusion is the little heralded Cornelius O'Reilly. Born in County Cavan, Ireland, in 1835, O'Reilly had been a builder since the 1860s, and he started practicing architecture by the 1870s. He joined forces with his brother, and the O'Reilly Brothers became one of the city's leading contractors for architects and real-estate developers.

Cornelius O'Reilly was no doubt known to the Rev. McMahon, since O'Reilly was a trustee of St. Patrick's Cathedral. Although barely remembered in the 21st century, O'Reilly was at the top of the building and construction business in the late 19th century. He chaired the building committee for Grant's Tomb, for instance, perhaps the nation's most famous construction job of the 1890s. And to think that when he arrived as an Irish emigrant, there were probably still "Help Wanted" signs that included "NINA," or "No Irish Need Apply."

The Secret Garden

479 West 152nd Street–402 West 153rd Street, between
St. Nicholas and Amsterdam Avenues

This is hardly your usual community garden scratched together on an empty lot. This garden spans most of the back lots—that is, backyards—of the houses on the block from 152nd to 153rd Streets between Amsterdam and St. Nicholas Avenues.

In the late 1970s, a local resident started the garden, and her little metaphorical acorn has grown into this mighty oak tree of a garden, with bricks defining the pathway, and occasional benches, tables, and chairs flanking the path, and lush foliage and plantings everywhere filling the scene.

What is peculiar about the plot is its angle, and it was the angle of the facade of 479 West 152nd Street that attracted this writer in the first place. It is odd to find an apartment house whose side veers off obliquely in this rectilinear city, and it is all explained by something that today is generally out of sight and out of mind, until you turn a faucet and no water comes out—the Croton Reservoir.

The city's water sources were so polluted by the early 19th century that the city was suffering a health crisis. With the coming of the Croton Reservoir system, with its fresh, potable water from the dammed Croton River 40-plus miles north in

Westchester County, all that changed in 1842. We have been wallowing in Croton water ever since.

The Croton aqueduct spanned the Harlem River on a line with 174th Street, passing close to the Morris-Jumel mansion. The streets in this neighborhood had not yet been cut through, so using the street commissioners' map as their only guide, the Croton engineers placed the aqueduct under the future streets, and their platting skills were exemplary.

Following the southwesterly flow of water from St. Nicholas Avenue, you first encounter the Croton right of way in the triangular garden on the northwest corner of 153rd Street. The pipes crossed under 153rd Street and entered the block just west of St. Nicholas Avenue, angling through today's backyards to exit on 152nd Street just east of Amsterdam Avenue, and continuing southwesterly to the playground on the southeast corner. The pipes ran south under Amsterdam Avenue until they reached the Upper West Side, where the aqueduct angled southeasterly at about 106th Street. (You can see the line of the aqueduct at the rear of 145 West 105th Street.) The aqueduct thereupon flowed into the Yorkville Reservoir in the future Central Park, and down Fifth Avenue to the distributing reservoir at 42nd Street.

The Renaissance-inspired apartment house at 479 West 152nd Street bears an escutcheon with the date 1897, which makes it a very early manifestation of apartment house development in this neighborhood. In the 1890s, developers were primarily putting up row houses on the side streets, and John P. Leo, the developer and architect of this apartment house, was a leading practitioner.

Under headlines such as "Leo's List of Low-Priced, High Class Dwellings," he would offer buildings for sale that he had designed and built, including a 25-foot-wide brick and stone house on West 185th Street, a 20-foot-wide brownstone on West 146th Street, or a 19-foot-wide limestone-front house on West 149th. In 1896, Leo designed and built eight houses at 634 to 648 West 158th Street, and two years later he designed four more for a developer on the same block, 626 to 632.

Leo, a graduate of Cooper Union, class of 1877 (he won the Gold Medal for Mechanical Drawing), had a rocky beginning to his architectural career. He was a captain in the National Guard's 22nd Regiment, and when the architect George B. Post opted out of designing the regiment's armory on the east side of Broadway between 67th and 68th Streets in 1889, Leo took over. He not only pulled off some shady deals, he produced some shoddy work.

Leo allegedly ordered fixtures and furnishings that the contractors said they could have purchased for half the price, because, said the contractors, Leo wanted the commissions for himself. It's a variation on the Tammany way of doing things, but even Tammany architects such as Horgan & Slattery did work that usually withstood the test of at least a little time. Just six months after construction had begun on the armory, and the roof was already leaking. Leo was soon having troubled relationships within the regiment itself, and he resigned both commissions. He also withdrew his name from consideration for the job of superintendent of buildings in 1895 when his former comrades protested his candidacy.

But Leo was the Teflon developer, and none of this unpleasantness stuck to him. His office in the 1890s was at 2 East 125th Street, and he was a booster of Harlem and the Heights. Along with the likes of Oscar Hammerstein, Leo wanted a Harlem Board of Trade to do what was "wisest and best for the general welfare of the neighborhood," including receiving a fair allocation of city funds.

He became the president of the Builders League, whose interests he would represent at hearings on housing issues, and for whom he would design a clubhouse on West 126th Street. He would go on to chair the Board of Standards and Appeals, and serve as the street cleaning commissioner in 1921.

With all this work under his belt, few people have ever heard of John P. Leo.

You Could Lead Your Horse to Water

In the gore created by St. Nicholas Place, 155th Street, and Edgecombe Avenue

This fountain was a gift from John Hooper in 1889, who left $10,000 in his will for a fountain in Manhattan and another in Brooklyn. By the time the fountains were built in the mid-1890s, the City Beautiful movement had started, and Evangeline Blashfield addressed the Brooklyn Civitas Club on "Art and City Improvement." She said that Athens, Florence, and Venice were younger than our Eastern Seaboard cities when they began to "clothe themselves with beauty as with a garment," yet our cities had hardly begun. The installation of a beautiful fountain was seen as a step toward the realization of a beautiful city.

The most distinguishing feature of the Hooper Fountain is the 28-foot-high Ionic column topped by an ornamental, globe-shaped lantern and weather vane. The horse trough, a circular basin that was carved from a solid block of pink granite nine feet, six inches across and over a foot deep, was believed to have been the largest drinking basin in the country made from a single piece of stone. There was also a drinking fountain for people, and down at ground level were water-filled bowls for man's best friends. The water did not come out of ordinary spigots, but from the mouths of lions' heads that were cast in bronze.

The architect was the little-known George Martin Huss, who might not have designed many buildings or won many architectural competitions, but not for a lack of trying. Huss entered the competitions for the American Surety Building, and City College, and the Custom House, all of which he lost. In partnership with John H. Buck, Huss's design for the Cathedral Church of St. John the Divine made it to the top four of the 60 entries submitted in the preliminary competition, but no further. With this fountain, Huss designed a winner, and its site proved particularly auspicious.

The Harlem River Speedway, which started being constructed in 1894, the year the fountain was completed, would stretch from 155th Street to Dyckman Street

along the shore of the Harlem River, and it was designed exclusively for horse-drawn carriages and horseback riders. (It was later incorporated into the Harlem River Drive.) The Speedway cost as much as about 30 new public schools at a time when the city was in dire need of more classrooms, but this was the gilded age. The wealthy and their horses and lap dogs would make good use of this propitiously placed fountain.

By the early 1900s, troubles began for horse troughs in general. Glanders, a contagious and fatal malady among horses, was being spread by horses drinking from a common trough. Horses that were diagnosed with glanders were shot and their stables were quarantined until sanitized,

Ten polo ponies at West Point contracted the disease and were shot in 1903. In 1905, all of "Buffalo Bill" Cody's 250 horses in his *Wild West Show,* some worth more than $1,000 each, were shot because of glanders, and the saddles, bridles, and other articles were burned. None of the horses in the New York City's Street Cleaning Department were permitted to drink from public troughs, and the New York City Board of Health started closing down horse troughs except for the few operated by the ASPCA. You could lead your horse to the average trough but you couldn't let it drink. Instead, you could fill a bucket with water from a spigot and give that to your horse.

This fountain became derelict, and by the 1980s the column had toppled. In 2001, the fountain was revitalized and re-installed, although the city administration does not recommend its use. Evangeline Blashfield had been onto something though. Water or no water, it clothes our city in beauty.

A Greek Temple on the Hudson

On the northbound Henry Hudson Parkway, on a line with 190th Street

Tell a northbound motorist on the Henry Hudson Parkway as he is approaching the Cloisters that he has just passed a Greek temple on his left, and he'll no doubt say you are hallucinating. But there it stands, a perfect reproduction of a Doric peristyle, evoking Ancient Greece and the solidity of Doric architecture while evoking a pre-air-conditioned 1925, when it was built.

Designed because toilet facilities were required at Inspiration Point, a favorite spot for gazing out on the Hudson River and the Palisades beyond, the ethos of the day demanded something a little grander than an outhouse, so comfort was metamorphosed into amenity. The temple-like pavilion was built on the edge of a sharp drop 140 feet above the Hudson shoreline, with the pavilion at street level and the comfort station hugging the cliffs below. The pavilion is a peristyle, or colonnade, of fluted Doric columns supporting a roof, the result of the civilized notion that you could step into the shade of the overlook and take advantage of the view. The comfort station, which was reached by steps flanking the pavilion, was subtly out of sight of the average passerby but easily found by those in search of it.

The pavilion-cum-comfort station was built to the designs of the architect Theodore S. Videto, who had earlier designed a similar structure opposite Grant's Tomb on the west side of Riverside Drive at 122nd Street, built specifically because Grant's Tomb lacked adequate toilet facilities.

Because the pavilion at 190th Street is today on the Henry Hudson Parkway, many people assume that the pavilion was a Robert Moses project that was built in the mid-1930s in conjunction with the creation of the parkway, but it wasn't. In the mid-1920s, this stretch of today's parkway was an extension of Riverside Drive, which Moses simply appropriated for his northbound roadway. Moses' predilection was to level everything in his path, but this was just slightly off his path, and he knew a good thing when he saw the pavilion. He incorporated it.

The idea for a lookout at Inspiration Point had first been proposed by Frederick Law Olmsted, Jr., and Arnold W. Brunner in 1913. The old roadway was only about 20 feet wide, and Olmsted and Brunner said it should be widened and extended to Dyckman Street. To preserve the open views across the Hudson River, they proposed extending Riverside Park at the same time. It was the view that made Riverside Drive one of the great show places of the city.

The city started buying up land, and in 1924 Riverside Drive was closed to traffic for nine months from 165th Street north to Dyckman Street, during which time the Drive would be converted to an 80-foot-wide boulevard with more gradual curves and easier grades, and with a broad foot path bordering the Drive on the west.

Brunner's idea for a pavilion was picked up by the city, but the design that he had conceived had the pavilion on the east side of the Drive, where the view would be marred by traffic. The final design had it more logically on the west side of the Drive, and the design was not his, but Videto's.

As accustomed as New Yorkers had become to fiscal restraints and budget cutbacks by the 1980s, it should come as no surprise that the entrances to the toilets had been boarded up, that the original railings had collapsed to be replaced by concrete slabs, that the roof was completely down in some places and threatening to collapse everywhere else, and that weeds and man-made detritus were contributing to the sense of decline.

The vandals might have breached the gates in the form of bureaucratic inertia, but help was on the way. Although the comfort station remains closed, the whole place has been spruced up, with the pavilion given a paint job and a new trellis roof, and the views are still, in a word, spectacular. Tell your motorist friends to slow down, pull over, and enjoy it.

Acknowledgments

am indebted to so many people and institutions, including Claire McCarthy, Roxana Robinson, NYU's Mosette Broderick and her husband Herb, Sarah Henry of the Museum of the City of New York, Matt Bauer of the Madison Avenue BID, former Parks Department commissioner Adrian Benepe, the Parks Department's director of arts and antiquities Jonathan Kuhn, and to Clara Aich, who actually lives in the former studio of Rochette & Parzini; to Carol Salomon at Cooper Union's Library, Thomas Tarnowsky of Friends of the Old Croton Aqueduct, Lori Harris, Cynthia Worley, Richard Guy Wilson, Carol Schneider, Isidora Wilkenseld at the Cathedral of St. John the Divine, Michelle Ianello at Vornado, Kimberley Brown at the Public Hotel, Theresa Nocerino and Michael Ullman at the Sherry-Netherland, Senih Geray at the St. Regis, the Very Rev. Walter Wagner of the Church of St. Vincent Ferrer, Monsignor Robert Richie of St. Patrick's Cathedral, Matthew Spady, the expert on the Audubon neighborhood; to NYU's John H. Beckman, Columbia's Elliot Sclar, Columbia's Professor Emeritus David Rosand, Columbia's Professor Arnold Aronson, and Jean W. Ashton at the New-York Historical Society; to the reference librarians Rosa Li and Matthew Boylan at the Main Branch of the New York Public Library, to the Main Branch itself and NYPL's lending libraries, to Columbia's Avery Library, NYU's Archives and Bobst Library, and to the library in West Cornwall, CT, which, like the branch library system in New York, will arrange for an inter-library loan if it doesn't have the subject at hand.

I am naturally indebted to friends and colleagues who have led the way, to Andrew Alpern, Ellen Stern, Tony Robins, Peter Derrick, Rebecca Read Shanor, James Trager, Andrew Dolkart, Joyce Mendelsohn, and Peter Salwen, and to the reportage of the late Christopher Gray. Also, of course, my thanks to David W. Dunlap, James Barron, Sam Roberts, Charles V. Bagli, Paul Goldberger, Carter B. Horsley, and the late Dennis Duggan and Meyer Berger, all of *The New York Times*, past and present.

My thanks to the photographer Kathy Gerhardt, who, against all odds, came up with the wonderful photographs in this book and who provided two of the subjects—three if you include the source of the gargoyles in the Haas mural; to my unflagging agent, Rita Rosenkranz, and; to Amy Lyons, Katie O'Dell, and Ellen Urban and all their colleagues at Globe Pequot.

Of course, my thanks to my friends and family who have understood my long absences, especially my wife, Jane Bevans, whom I especially thank for putting up with my neglect of so many things that ought to have been cared for. This book is also dedicated to her.

Bibliography

A t the top of my list of favorite New York books is John A. Kouwenhoven's *Columbia Historical Portrait of New York*, which my father allowed me to buy as a high schooler despite the fact that it cost a small fortune, even on the sale table at Salter's Bookshop. Curiously, I don't believe that I made direct reference to Kouwenhoven in this book, but it looms large in the background.

A note on *Statues of New York* by J. Sanford Saltus and Walter Tisné. Saltus led the charge in the creation of the statue of Joan of Arc. How much he honestly had to do with the book is moot, but one fact stands out. Writers before Saltus and Tisné had included New York statues in their works, but their book just might have been the first to deal exclusively with statues in New York. (Saltus died a mysterious death in London in 1922, and the book, with Saltus given top billing, was published posthumously.)

The newspaper that I have leaned on the most heavily is *The New York Times*, but the old *New York Tribune*, with writers such as Royal Cortissoz, could give it a run for its money. Following, in alphabetical order, are many other sources, some used many times, others perhaps only once, but all invaluable to the story.

American Architect & Building News, American Architect and Architecture, American Art News, Architect and Builders Magazine, Architectural Record, The Art Amateur, The Atlanta Constitution, The Biloxi Daily Herald, The Boston Globe, The Charlotte Daily Observer, The Chicago Daily Tribune, The Christian Science Monitor, The Churchman, The Detroit Free Press, The Hartford Courant, The Jewish Messenger, Literary Digest, The Living Church, The Los Angeles Times, The New York Daily News, New York Newsday, The New York Observer, The New Yorker, The Omaha World Herald, Outlook, The Philadelphia Inquirer, Philadelphia Weekly, The San Francisco Chronicle, The Sphere (London), *Town & Country, The Wall Street Journal, The Washington Post, The Yale Daily News.*

For entry-by-entry references, including the occasional website referred to and personal footnotes, please contact me at www.johntauranac.com.

Adams, Michael Henry, *Harlem: Lost and Found*, Monacelli, 2002.
Aikman, Lonnelle, *We, the People: The Story of the U.S. Capitol*, Capitol Historical & National Geographic Societies, 1967.
Alexander, James W., *A History of the University Club, 1865–1915*, Scribner, 1915.
Allen, Frederick Lewis, *The Great Pierpont Morgan*, Harper, 1949.
Allen, Irving Lewis, *The City in Slang: New York Life and Popular Speech*, Oxford, 1993.

Alpern, Andrew, *Luxury Apartments of Manhattan*, Dover, 1992.

Alpern, Andrew, *The Dakota*, Princeton, 2015.

Amory, Cleveland, *Who Killed Society?*, Harper, 1960.

Andrews, Jack, "Samuel Yellin, Metalworker," *Anvil's Ring*, Yellin Foundation, Summer, 1982.

Andrews, Wayne, *Architecture, Ambition and Americans*, Macmillan, 1964.

Appelbaum, Stanley, *The New York World's Fair 1939/1940*, Dover, 1977.

Appleton, D. & Co., *Appleton's Annual Cyclopaedia and Register of Important Events in the Year 1876*, Appleton, 1877.

Appleton, D. & Co., *The Seward Memorial: The Ceremonies at the Unveiling of the Statue of William H. Seward*, Appleton, 1876.

Architect of the Capitol, *Art in the United States Capitol*, U.S. Printing Office, 1976.

Baldwin, Charles C., *Stanford White*, Dodd, Mead, 1931; DaCapo, 1976.

Balfour, Alan, *Rockefeller Center: Architecture as Theater*, McGraw-Hill, 1978.

Ballon, Hillary, and Kenneth T. Jackson, eds., *Robert Moses and the Modern City*, Norton, 2007.

Ballon, Hillary, ed., *The Greatest Grid*, Museum of the City of New York and Columbia, 2012.

Baral, Robert, *Turn West on 23rd: New York's Old Chelsea*, Fleet, 1965.

Barringer, Paul Brandon, James Mercer Barnett, and Rosewell Page, eds., *University of Virginia: Its History, Influence, Equipment and Characteristics*, Lewis, 1904.

Bartlett, John, *Familiar Quotations*, Little, Brown, 1968.

Batterberry, Michael and Ariane, *On the Town in New York: A History of Eating, Drinking and Entertainments*, Scribner, 1973.

Belle, John, and Maxinne R. Leighton, *Grand Central: Gateway to a Million Lives*, Norton, New York, 2000.

Benton, Charlotte & Tim Benton, Ghislaine Wood, eds., *Art Deco: 1910–1930*, V&A, 2003.

Berger, Meyer, *Meyer Berger's New York*, Random House, 1960.

Berger, Meyer, *The Story of The New York Times: 1851–1951*, Simon & Schuster, 1951.

Bergman, Edward F., *The Spiritual Traveler: New York City*, Hidden Spring, 2001.

Biedermann, Han, *Dictionary of Symbolism*, Meridian, 1992.

Birmingham, Stephen, *Life at The Dakota*, Random House, 1979.

Blashfield, Edwin Howland, Excerpts from *Memoir About Evangeline* in the New-York Historical Society, *The Evangeline Blashfield Fountain*, Municipal Art Society, 2003.

Blashfield, Evangeline Wilbour, and William Howard Blashfield, eds., *Vasari's Lives of Seventy of the Most Eminent Painters, Sculptors and Architects*, Scribner, 1896.

Bletter, Rosemarie Hogg, *Skyscraper Style: Art Deco New York*, Oxford, 1975.

Bloom, Ken, *Broadway*, Routledge, 2004.

Bogart, Michele H., *Public Sculpture and the Civic Ideal in New York City*, Chicago, 1989.

Botkin, B. A., *New York City Folklore*, Random House, 1956.

Bradbury, Ray, *Fahrenheit 451*, Simon & Schuster, 1953, 1993.

Brinnin, John Malcolm, *The Sway of the Grand Saloon*, Delacorte, 1971.

Broderick, Mosette, *Triumvirate: McKim, Mead & White*, Knopf, 2010.

Bromley, George W. and Walter S., *Atlas of the City of New York: Manhattan Island*, Bromley & Co., 1894.

Brooklyn Museum, *The American Renaissance: 1876–1917*, Pantheon, 1979.

Brown, Henry Collins, ed., *Valentine's Manual of Old New York*, Valentine's Manual, Inc., 1923, 1926.

Brown, Henry Collins, *In the Golden Nineties*, Valentine's Manual, 1928.

Burchard, John, and Albert Bush-Brown, *The Architecture of America: A Social and Cultural History*, Little Brown, 1961.

Burrows, Edwin C., and Mike Wallace, *Gotham: A History of New York City to 1898*, Oxford, 1999.

Caffin, Charles H., *American Masters of Sculpture*, Doubleday Page, 1913.

Carnegie Hill Neighbors, *Carnegie Hill: Architectural Guide*, Carnegie Hill Neighbors, 2008.

Carter, Randolph, and Robert Reed Cole, *Joseph Urban: Architecture, Theatre, Opera, Film*, Abbeville, 1992.

Case, Frank, *Tales of a Wayward Inn*, Frederick A. Stokes, 1938.

Chernow, Ron, *The House of Morgan*, Atlantic Monthly, 1990.

Chestel, Andre, *The Genius of Leonardo da Vinci*, Orion, 1961.

Churchill, Allen, *The Improper Bohemians*, Dutton, 1959.

Cirlot, J. E., *A Dictionary of Symbols*, Philosophical Library, 1971.

Collins, F. A., *The Romance of Park Avenue*, The Park Avenue Association, 1930.

Columbian Exposition, *The Historical World's Columbian Exposition,* Ward, 1892.

Condit, Carl W., *The Port of New York: A History of the Rail and Terminal System from the Beginnings to Pennsylvania Station*, Chicago, 1980.

Condit, Carl W., *The Port of New York: A History of the Rail and Terminal System from the Grand Central Electrification to the Present*, Chicago, 1981.

Cook, Clarence C., *A Description of the New York Central Park*, Huntington, 1869; Benjamin Blom, 1972.

Cook, Doris E., *Woman Sculptor: Anna Hyatt Huntington*, Privately Printed, 1976.

Cook, Leland, *St. Patrick's Cathedral: A Centennial History*, Quick Fox, 1979.

Copp, H. D., *Copp's Guide to New York City*, Visitors Guide Books, 1957.

Coppola/Copp, Philip Ashforth, *Silver Connections: A Fresh Perspective on the New York Area Subway Systems*, Vols. 1 and 2, Four Oceans, 1984.

Cott, Nancy F., ed., *No Small Courage: A History of Women in the United States*, Oxford, 2000.

Cram, Ralph Adams, *My Life in Architecture*, Little Brown, 1936.

Crawford, F. M., "The Veronese Inquisition," *Introduction to Contemporary Civilization in the West*, Vol 1, Second Edition, Richard M. Morse, ed., Columbia, 1954.

Cudahy, Brian J., *Under the Sidewalks of New York*, Stephen Greene, 1979.

Cunningham, John T., *University in the Forest: Drew University*, Afton, 1972.

D'Alton, Martina, *The New York Obelisk*, Metropolitan Museum of Art & Abrams, 1993.

Daley, Robert, *The World Beneath the City*, Lippincott, 1959.

Dalzell, Lee Baldwin and Robert F., Jr., *The House That the Rockefellers Built*, Henry Holt, 2007.

Davidson, Marshall B., and Elizabeth Stillinger, *The American Wing at the Metropolitan Museum of Art*, MMA and Knopf, 1985.

DeMille, George E., *Saint Thomas Church in the City and County of New York, 1823–1954*, Church Historical Society, 1958.

Dennis, James M., *Karl Bitter: Architectural Sculptor*, Wisconsin, 1967.

Derrick, Peter, *Tunneling to the Future*, NYU, 2001.

Didion, Joan, "Goodbye to All That," *Writing New York*, Phillip Lopate, ed.

Diehl, Lorraine B., *Subways: The Tracks That Built New York City*, Clarkson Potter, 2004.

Dolkart, Andrew S., and Gretchen S. Sorin, *Touring Historic Harlem*, N.Y. Landmarks Conservancy, 1997.

Dolkart, Andrew S., and Matthew A. Postal, New York City Landmarks, Wiley, 2004.

Dolkart, Andrew S., *Morningside Heights: A History of Its Architecture & Development*, Columbia, 1998.

Downey, Fairfax, *Portrait of an Era as Drawn by C. D. Gibson*, Scribner, 1933.

Downey, Fairfax, *Richard Harding Davis: His Day*, Scribner, 1936.

Drepperd, Carl W., *A Dictionary of American Antiques*, Branford, 1952.

Duffy, John, *A History of Public Health in New York City, 1625–1866*, Russell Sage, 1968.

Dunlap, David W., *From Abyssinian to Zion: A Guide to Manhattan's Houses of Worship*, Columbia, 2004.

Dunlap, David W., *On Broadway: A Journey Uptown Over Time*, Rizzoli, 1990.

Edwards, Richard, *New York's Great Industries*, Historical Publishing, 1884.

Ehrlich, Blake, *London on the Thames*, Little, Brown, 1966.

Evans, Cerinda W., *Anna Hyatt Huntington*, Mariners Museum, 1965.

Federal Writers Project, *New York Panorama*, Random House, 1938.

Federal Writers Project, *The WPA Guide to New York City*, Random House, 1939.

Feirstein, Sanna, *Naming New York*, NYU, 2001.

Fifth Avenue Association, *Fifty Years on Fifth*, The Association, 1957.

Fischler, Stan, *Uptown, Downtown*, H & M, 1977.

Fishman, Robert, "Revolt of the Urbs," *Robert Moses and the Modern City*, Hillary Ballon and Kenneth T. Jackson, eds.

Fitch, James Marston, *American Building: The Historical Forces That Shaped It*, Houghton Mifflin, 1966.

Fletcher, Sir Banister, *A History of Architecture on the Comparative Method*, Athlone, 1961.

Folpe, Emily Kies, *It Happened on Washington Square*, Johns Hopkins, 2002.

Foster & Reynolds, publishers, *New York: The Metropolis of the Western World*, 1917.

Fowler, Gene, *Skyline: A Reporter's Reminiscence of the 1920s*, Viking, 1961.

Francis, Dennis Steadman, *Architects in Practice in New York City, 1840–1900*, Committee for Preservation of Architectural Records, 1979.

Friar, Stephen, and John Ferguson, *Basic Heraldry*, A. & C. Black, 1993.

Garmey, Stephen, *Gramercy Park: An Illustrated History of a New York Neighborhood*, Balsam Press, 1984.

Gayle, Margot, and Carol Gayle, *Cast-Iron Architecture in America*, Norton, 1998.

Gayle, Margot, and Michele Cohen, *Guide to Manhattan's Outdoor Sculpture*, The Art Commission and Municipal Art Society, Prentice Hall, 1988.

Gayle, Margot, *Cast-Iron Architecture in New York*, Dover, 1974.

Gibbon, Guy, *The Sioux: The Dakota and Lakota Nations*, Blackwell (Wiley), 2003.

Gibson, David, "St. Brigid's Parish," see Golway's *Catholics in New York*.

Gilbert, Cass, *Notes Dictated by Gilbert*, August–November, 1918, in the collection of New York Historical Society.

Gilfoyle, Timothy J., *City of Eros*, Norton, 1992.

Gill, Jonathan, *Harlem: The Four Hundred Year History*, Grove, 2011.

Gilmartin, Gregory F., *Shaping the City*, Clarkson Potter, 1995.

Goldberger, Paul, *The City Observed: New York*, Vintage, 1979.

Goldstone, Harmon H. and Martha Dalrymple, *History Preserved*, Simon & Schuster, 1974.

Golway, Terry, ed., *Catholics in New York: Society, Culture, and Politics, 1808–1946*, Fordham and Museum of the City of New York, 2008.

Goodwin, Doris Kearns, *Team of Rivals: The Political Genius of Abraham Lincoln*, Simon & Schuster, 2005.

Gordon, Robert J., *The Rise and Fall of American Growth*, Princeton, 2016.

Gowans, Alan, *Images of American Living*, Lippincott, 1964.

Greene, Jeff, "The Legacy of Edwin Howland Blashfield," see Weiner's *Blashfield*.

Griffith, Richard, and Arthur Mayer, *The Movies*, Simon and Schuster, 1957.

Guiles, Fred Lawrence, *Marion Davies*, McGraw-Hill, 1972.

Hall, Edward Hagaman, *A Guide to the Cathedral Church of Saint John the Divine*, The Cathedral Church, 1965.

Harris, Bill, *One Thousand New York Buildings*, Black Dog & Leventhal, 2002.

Harris, Cyril, *Historic Architecture Sourcebook*, McGraw Hill, 1977.

Harris, Luther S., *Around Washington Square: An Illustrated History of Greenwich Village*, Johns Hopkins, 2003.

Harriss, Joseph, *The Tallest Tower: Eiffel and the Belle Epoque*, Houghton, Mifflin, 1975.

Hart, Harold H., *Hart's Guide to New York City*, Hart, 1964.

Haswell, Chas. H, *Reminiscences of an Octogenarian*, Harper, 1896.

Hawes, Elizabeth, *New York, New York: How the Apartment House Transformed the Life of the City*, Henry Holt, 1993.

Headley, Gwyn, and Wim Meulenkamp, *Follies: A National Trust Guide*, Jonathan Cape, 1986.

Heckscher, Morrison H., "Building the Empire City," see Voorsanger & Howat's *Art and the Empire City.*

Heilbrun, Margaret, ed., *Inventing the Skyline: The Architecture of Cass Gilbert*, Columbia, 2000.

Hemstreet, Charles, *Nooks & Corners of Old New York*, Scribner, 1899.

Henderson, Helen W., *A Loiterer in New York*, Doran, 1917.

Henderson, Mary C., *The City & the Theatre*, James T. White, 1973.

Higonnet, Anne, *Goddess, Heroine, Beast: Anna Hyatt Huntington*, Columbia, 2014.

Hitchcock, Henry-Russell, *Architecture: Nineteenth & Twentieth Centuries*, Penguin, 1958.

Holloway, Marguerite, *The Measure of Manhattan*, Norton, 2013.

Homberger, Eric, *Mrs. Astor's New York*, Yale, 2002.

Hone, Philip, *The Diary of Philip Hone, 1828–1851*, Allan Nevins, ed., Dodd, Mead, 1927.

Howard, Kathleen, *The Metropolitan Museum of Art Guide*, MMA, 1983.

Hughes, Robert, *American Visions*, Alfred Knopf, 1997.

Huxtable, Ada Louise, *Classic New York*, Anchor, 1964.

Interborough Rapid Transit, *Interborough Rapid Transit: The New York Subway*, I.R.T., 1904; reprinted, Arno Press, 1971.

Irish, Sharon, *Cass Gilbert, Architect*, Monacelli, New York, 1999.

Irish, Sharon, "Cass Gilbert in Practice, 1882–1934," see Heilbrun's *Inventing the Skyline*.

Jackson, Kenneth T., ed., *The Encyclopedia of New York City*, Second Edition, Yale & New-York Historical Society, 2010.

Jackson, Stanley, *J. P. Morgan*, Heinemann, 1984.

Janson, H. W., *History of Art*, rev., Anthony F. Janson, Abrams, 1986.

Janvier, Thomas, *In Old New York*, Harper, 1894; reprinted, St. Martin's, 2000.

Jefferson, Joseph, *The Autobiography of Joseph Jefferson*, Century, 1890.

Jones, Pamela, *Under the City Streets*, Holt, Rinehart & Winston, 1978.

Jones, Robert A., *Cass Gilbert: Midwestern Architect*, Arno, 1982.

Jonnes, Jill, *Conquering Gotham: Building Penn Station*, Viking, 2007.

Jordy, William H., *American Buildings and Their Architects*, Anchor, 1976.

Kahn, David, *General Grant National Memorial Historical Resource Study*, January, 1980.

Kahr, Joan, *Edgar Brandt: Master of Art Deco Ironwork*, Abrams, 1999.

Kanfer, Stefan, *Stardust Lost*, Knopf, 2006.

Katherens, Michael C., *Great Houses of New York: 1880–1930*, Acanthus, 2005.

Kavaler, Lucy, *The Astors*, Dodd Mead, 1966.

Keller, Lisa, "Armories," see Jackson's *Encyclopedia of New York City*.

Kessner, Thomas, *Fiorello La Guardia and the Making of Modern New York*, McGraw-Hill, 1989.

Kilham, Walter H., Jr., *Raymond Hood, Architect*, Architectural Book Publishing, 1973.

King, Moses, *King's Handbook of New York City, 1893*, Moses King, 1893; Reprinted, Benjamin Blom, 1972.

Kluger, Richard, *The Paper: The Life and Death of The New York Herald Tribune*, Knopf, 1986.

Koeppel, Gerrard T., *Water for Gotham*, Princeton, 2000.

Koffler, Jerry and Eleanor, *Freeing the Angel from the Stone*, Calandra Italian American Institute, 2008.

Kowsky, Francis R., *The Architecture of Frederick Clarke Withers*, Wesleyan, 1980.

Krinsky, Carol Herselle, *Rockefeller Center*, Oxford, 1978.

Kuntz, Tom, ed., *The Titanic Disaster Hearings*, Pocket Books, 1998.

Lamb, Mary, *History of the City of New York*, Barnes, 1880.

Landau, Sarah Bradford and Carl Condict, *Rise of the New York Skyscraper*, Yale, 1996.

Landau, Sarah Bradford, *George B. Post, Architect*, Monacelli, 1998.

Landmarks Preservation Commission (LPC), "Bayard-Condict Building," Nov 25, 1975.

LPC, "Brill Building," Mar 23, 2010.

LPC, "Daily News Building," July 28, 1981.

LPC, "George S. Bowdoin Stable," June 17, 1997.

LPC, "Hearst Magazine Building," Feb 16, 1988.

LPC, "Hecla Iron Works Building," June 8, 2004.

LPC, "Mount Morris Park Historic District Designation," Nov 3, 1971.

LPC, "New York and Long Island Coignet Stone Company Building," June 27, 2006.

LPC, "Claremont Theater Building," June 6, 2006.

LPC, "Madison Belmont Building," Sep 20, 2011.

LPC, "Our Lady of Lourdes Roman Catholic Church," July 22, 1975.

LPC, "Panhellenic Tower," February 3, 1998.

LPC, "Rogers, Peet & Company Building," December 14, 2010.

LPC, "Standard Oil Building Designation Report," Sep 19, 1995.

LPC, "Upper West Side/Central Park West Historic Designation Report," Vol. 1: Essays/Architects, Apr 24, 1990.

Langford, Gerald, *The Murder of Stanford White*, Bobbs-Merrill, 1962.

Leapman, Michael, *The Companion Guide to New York*, Prentice Hall, 1983.

Lederer, Joseph, *All Around the Town*, Scribner, 1975.

Legrand, Francois, Souvenirs de Paris, Parigramme, 2013.

Leonard, John W., *Who's Who In New York City and State*, Hamersly, 1909.

Limpus, Lowell M., *History of the New York Fire Department*, Dutton, 1940.

Lipton, James, *An Exaltation of Larks*, Grossman, 1968.

Lockwood, Charles, *Bricks & Brownstones: The New York Row House*, McGraw-Hill, 1972.

Lopate, Phillip, ed., *Writing New York: A Literary Anthology*, Library of America, 2008.

Loth, Calder, and Julius Trousdale Sadler, Jr., *The Only Proper Style: Gothic Architecture in America*, New York Graphic Society, 1975.

Lubow, Arthur, *The Reporter Who Would Be King: Richard Harding Davis*, Scribner, 1992.

Luckhurst, Kenneth W., *The Story of Exhibitions*, Studio Publications, 1951.

Lynch, Don, *Titanic: An Illustrated History*, Hyperion, 1992.

Magaziner, Henry Jonas, *The Golden Age of Ironwork*, Skipjack Press, 2000.

Marcuse, Maxwell F., *This Was New York!*, Carlton Press, 1959.

Marshall, David, *Grand Central*, Whittlesey House, McGraw-Hill, 1946.

Mason, Randall, *The Once and Future New York*, Minnesota, 2009.

Mayer, Grace M., *Once Upon a City*, Macmillan, 1958.

McAlester, Virginia & Lee, *A Field Guide to American Houses*, Knopf-Borzoi, 1984.

McFadden, Elizabeth, *The Glitter and The Gold*, Dial, 1971.

McKay, Richard C., *South Street: A Maritime History of New York*, 1934, reprinted, 7 C's Press, 1969.

McKim, Mead & White, *A Monograph on the Works of McKim, Mead & White*, first published, 1915; reissued, Benjamin Blom, 1973.

McNally, Rand, *Rand McNally's Handy Guide to New York City*, Rand McNally, 1895.

McNamara, John, *History in Asphalt*, The Bronx County Historical Society, Third Edition, 1991.

McShane, Clay, and Joel A. Tarr, *The Horse in the City*, Johns Hopkins, 2007.

Mehta, Ved, *Remembering Mr. Shawn's New Yorker*, Overlook Press, 1998.

Meikle, Jeffrey L., "New Materials and Technologies," see Benton's ART DECO.

Mendelsohn, Joyce, *The Lower East Side*, Lower East Side Press, 2001.

Mendelsohn, Joyce, *Touring the Flatiron*, Landmarks Conservancy, 1998.

Miller, Donald L., *Supreme City: How Jazz Age Manhattan Gave Birth to Modern America*, Simon & Schuster, 2014.

Miller, Sara Cedar, *Central Park, An American Masterpiece*, Abrams, 2003.

Miller, Terry, *Greenwich Village and How It Got That Way*, Crown, 1990.

Mitchell, Mary and Albert Goodrich, *The Remarkable Huntingtons, Archer and Anna*, Budd Drive Press, 2004.

Mohr, Wm. F., ed., *Who's Who in New York, 1914*, Who's Who in New York City and State, Inc., 1914.

Mooney, Michael Macdonald, *Evelyn Nesbit and Stanford White*, Morrow, 1976.

Moore, Charles, *Daniel Burnham*, Houghton Mifflin, 1921; Da Capo, 1968.

Morley, Christopher, "West End Avenue," see Phillip Lopate, ed., *Writing New York*.

Morris, James, *The World of Venice*, Pantheon, 1960.

Morris, Lloyd, *Incredible New York*, Random House, 1951.

Morrison, David D., *The Cast-Iron Eagles of Grand Central Station*, Cannonball, 1998.

Mott, Hopper Striker, *The New York of Yesterday, Bloomingdale*, Putnam, 1908.

Mullett, Alfred B., *Annual Report of Supervising Architect to The Secretary of the Treasury for the Year 1873*, Government Printing Office, 1873.

Newhouse, Alana, *A Living Lens: Photographs of Jewish Life from the Pages of the Forward*, Norton, 2007.

Norton, Thomas E., and Jerry E. Patterson, *Living It Up: A Guide to the Named Apartment Houses of New York*, Atheneum, 1984.

O'Connor, Harvey, *The Astors*, Knopf, 1941.

Okrent, Daniel, *Great Fortune: The Epic of Rockefeller Center*, Viking, 2003.

Oppel, Frank, ed., *Tales of Gaslight New York*, Castle, 1985.

Oshinsky, David, *Bellevue: Three Centuries of Medicine and Mayhem at America's Most Storied Hospital*, Doubleday, 2016.

Osofsky, Gilbert, *Harlem: The Making of a Ghetto*, Harper & Row, 1966.

Panzer, Mary, *In My Studio: Rudolf Eickemeyer, Jr., and the Art of the Camera, 1885–1930*, Catalogue, Hudson River Museum, 1986.

Patterson, Jerry E., *Fifth Avenue: The Best Address*, Rizzoli, 1998.

Pennoyer, Peter, and Anne Walker, *The Architecture of Grosvenor Atterbury*, Norton, 2009.

Pennoyer, Peter, and Anne Walker, *New York Transformed: The Architecture of Cross & Cross*, Monacelli, 2014.

Pennoyer, Peter, and Anne Walker, *The Architecture of Warren & Wetmore*, Norton, 2006.

Petronella, Mary Melvin, ed., *Victorian Boston Today: Twelve Walking Tours*, New England Chapter, Victorian Society, 2004.

Pevsner, Nikolaus, et al, *A Dictionary of Architecture*, Overlook, 1976.

Port, M. H., ed., *The Houses of Parliament*, Yale, 1976.

Rankin, Rebecca B., *New York Advancing: World's Fair Edition*, Municipal Reference Library, 1939.

Ray, Dr. J. H. Randolph, *My Little Church Around the Corner*, Simon & Schuster, 1957.

Real Estate Record and Guide Association, *A History of Real Estate, Building, and Architecture in New York City*, Real Estate Record, 1898.

Reed, Henry Hope and Francis Morrone, *The New York Public Library: The Architecture and Decoration of the Stephen A. Schwarzman Building*, Norton, 1986.

Reed, Henry Hope, *Central Park: A Photographic Guide*, Dover, 1979.

Reeves, Prof. F. Blair, *Mar-A-Lago: Photographs, Written Historical and Descriptive Data*, Historic American Buildings Survey, Office of Archaeology and Historic Preservation, National Park Service, Spring, 1967.

Reps, John W., *The Making of Urban America: A History of City Planning in the United States*, Princeton University Press, 1965.

Reynolds, D. M., *Monuments and Masterpieces: Histories and Views of Public Sculptures in New York City*, Macmillan, 1988; Thames & Hudson, 1997.

Richman, Michael, *Daniel Chester French: An American Sculptor*, Metropolitan Museum of Art & National Trust for Historic Preservation, 1976.

Rider, Fremont, *Rider's New York City: A Guide Book for Travelers*, Macmillan, 1924.

Riis, Jacob A., *How the Other Half Lives*, Scribner, 1890, revised, 1901; Dover, 1971.

Robins, Anthony W., and New York City Transit Museum, *Grand Central Terminal: 100 Years of a New York Landmark*, Stewart, Tabori & Chang, New York, 2013.

Robins, Anthony W., and New York City Transit Museum, *Subway Style: 100 Years of Architecture & Design in the New York City Subway*, Stewart, Tabori & Chang, 2003.

Robins, Anthony W., *New York Art Deco*, SUNY, 2017.

Roper, Laura Wood, *FLO: A Biography of Frederick Law Olmsted*, Johns Hopkins, 1973.

Rosenblatt, Roger, *The Boy Detective: A New York Childhood*, Harper Collins, 2013.

Ross, Ishbel, *Taste in America: An Illustrated History*, Crowell, 1967.

Rosten, Leo, *The Education of Hyman Kaplan*, first published, 1937.

Rosten, Leo, *The Joys of Yiddish*, McGraw-Hill, 1968.

Roth, Leland M., *A Concise History of American Architecture*, Harper & Row, 1979.

Rozas, Diane and Anita Bourne Gottehrer, *American Venus*, Balcony Press, 1999.

Sackville-West, V. (Vita/Victoria), *Saint Joan of Arc*, Doubleday, Doran, 1931.

Salinger, J. D., *The Catcher in the Rye*, Little, Brown and Company, 1951.

Saltus, J. Sanford, and Walter Tisné, *Statues of New York*, J. P. Putnam, 1922/23.

Salwen, Peter, *Upper West Side Story: A History and Guide*, Abbeville, 1989.

Samuel, Ann E., "Mural Painting for America: The Artistic Production of Edwin Howland Blashfield," see Weiner's *Blashfield*.

Sante, Luc, *Low Life: Lures and Snares of Old New York*, Farrar, Straus, Giroux, 1991.

Schlichting, Kurt C., *Grand Central's Engineer: William J. Wilgus*, Johns Hopkins, 2012.

Schoener, R. Reinhold, "St. Peter's," see Singleton's *Rome*.

Schwartz, Samuel I., *Street Smart: The Rise of Cities and the Fall of Cars*, Public Affairs, 2015.

Shackleton, Robert, *The Book of New York*, Penn Publishing, 1917.

Shanor, Rebecca Read, *The City That Never Was*, Viking, 1988.

Sharp, Lewis I., *John Quincy Adams Ward: Dean of American Sculpture*, Delaware, 1985.

Shaw, Charles G, *New York—Oddly Enough*, Farrar & Rinehart, 1938.

Sides, Hampton, *In the Kingdom of Ice*, Knopf, 2014.

Sigerman, Harriet, "Laborers for Liberty, 1865–1890," see Cott's *No Small Courage*.

Silver, Nathan, *Lost New York*, Houghton Mifflin, 1967.

Sinclair, David, *Dynasty: The Astors and Their Times*, Beaufort, 1984.

Singleton, Esther, *Rome: Described by Great Writers*, Dodd, Mead, 1906.

Southworth, Susan and Michael, *A.I.A. Guide to Boston*, Globe Pequot, 1984.

Stahr, Walter, *Seward: Lincoln's Indispensable Man*, Simon & Schuster, 2010.

Stern, Ellen, *Gracie Mansion: A Celebration of New York City's Mayoral Residence*, Rizzoli, 2005.

Stern, Robert A. M., Thomas Mellins, and David Fishman, *New York 1880: Architecture and Urbanism in the Gilded Age*, Monacelli, 1999.

Stern, Robert A. M., Gregory Gilmartin, and John Massengale, *New York 1900: Metropolitan Architecture and Urbanism*, 1890–1915, Rizzoli, 1983.

Stern, Robert A. M., Gregory Gilmartin, and Thomas Mellis, *New York 1930: Architecture and Urbanism Between the Two World Wars*, Rizzoli, 1987.

Stern, Robert A. M., Thomas Mellins, and David Fishman, *New York 1960: Architecture and Urbanism Between the Second World War and the Bicentennial*, Monacelli, 1997.

Stevenson, Elisabeth, *Park Maker: A Life of Frederick Law Olmsted*, Macmillan, 1977.

Stewart, William Rhinelander, *Grace Church and Old New York*, Dutton, 1924.

Still, Bayrd, *Mirror for Gotham: New York As Seen by Contemporaries from Dutch Days to the Present*, NYU, 1956.

Stokes, I. N. Phelps, *New York Past and Present, Its History and Landmarks*, New-York Historical Society and New York World's Fair, Stokes, 1939.

Stokes, I. N. Phelps, *The Iconography of Manhattan Island*, Robert H. Dodd, Robert H. Dodd, 1927; Arno Press, 1967.

Stookey, Lee, *Subway Ceramics: A History and Iconography*, Stookey, 1992.

Strong, George Templeton, *The Diary*, Allan Nevins, ed., MacMillan, 1952.

Strouse, Jean, *Morgan: American Financier*, Random House, 1999.

Stuart, Amanda Mackenzie, *Consuelo and Ava Vanderbilt: The Story of a Daughter and Mother in the Gilded Age*, HarperCollins, 2006.

Sullivan, Louis H., *The Autobiography of an Idea*, AIA, 1924; Dover, 1956.

Swanberg, W. A., *Citizen Hearst*, Scribner, 1961.

Swett, Richard N., *Leadership by Design: Creating an Architecture of Trust*, Greenway, 2005.

Talese, Gay, *The Kingdom and the Power*, World, 1969.

Tauranac, John, *Elegant New York*, Abbeville, 1985.

Tauranac, John, *Essential New York*, Holt, Rinehart & Winston, 1979.

Tauranac, John, *The Empire State Building*, Scribner, 1995; Cornell, 2014.

Thomas, Lately, *Delmonico's: A Century of Splendor*, Houghton Mifflin, 1967.

Thorndike, Joseph J., Jr., ed., *Three Centuries of Notable American Architects*, American Heritage and Scribner, 1981.

Tifft, Susan E., and Alex S. Jones, *The Trust: The Private and Powerful Family Behind The New York Times*, Little Brown, 1999.

Todd, Nancy L., *New York's Historic Armories: An Illustrated History*, SUNY, 2006.

Tomkins, Calvin, *Merchants and Masterpieces: The Story of the Metropolitan Museum of Art*, Dutton, 1970.

Trachtenberg, Marvin, and Isabelle Hyman, *Architecture from Pre-History to Post-Modernism*, Abrams, 1986.

Trager, James, *The New York Chronology*, HarperResource, 2003.

Trager, James, *West of Fifth: The Rise and Fall and Rise of Manhattan's West Side*, Atheneum, 1987.

Trevelyan, G. M., *English Social History*, Longmans, Green & Co., 1942.

Tuckerman, James H., "Park Driving," see Oppel's *Tales of Gaslight New York*.

Van Dyke, John C., *The New New York*, Macmillan, 1909.

Van Pelt, John V., *The Essentials of Composition as Applied to Art*, Macmillan, 1913.

Van Wyck, Frederick, *Recollections of an Old New Yorker*, Liveright, 1932.

Von Drehle, David, *Triangle: The Fire That Changed America*, Grove, 2003.

Voorsanger, Catherine Hoover and John K. Howat, eds., *Art and the Empire City: New York, 1825–1861*, Metropolitan Museum of Art, and Yale, 2000.

Ware, Caroline F., *Greenwich Village, 1920–1930*, Houghton Mifflin, 1935.

Wattenmaker, Richard J., *Samuel Yellin in Context*, Flint Institute of Arts, 1985.

Weiner, Mina Rieur, ed., *Edwin Howland Blashfield: Master American Muralist*, Norton, 2009.

Wheeler, George, *Pierpont Morgan & Friends: The Anatomy of a Myth*, Prentice Hall, 1973.

Whiffen, Marcus, and Frederick Koeper, *American Architecture, 1860–1976*, MIT, 1984.

White, Norval, Eliot Willensky with Fran Leadon, *AIA Guide To New York City*, Oxford, 2010.

Wilkinson, Burke, *Uncommon Clay: The Life and Works of Augustus Saint Gaudens*, Harcourt Brace, 1985.

Williams, Marilyn Thornton, *Washing the Great Unwashed: Public Baths in Urban America, 1840–1920*, Ohio State, 1991.

Williamson, Jefferson, *The American Hotel: An Anecdotal History*, Knopf, 1930.

Williamson, Roxanne Kuter, *American Architects and the Mechanics of Fame*, Texas,1991.

Wilson, Richard Guy, *McKim, Mead & White, Architects*, Rizzoli, 1983.

Wilson, Richard Guy, and Andrew J. Berner, *The University Club: An Architectural Celebration*, University Club, 1998.

Wilson, Rufus Rockwell, *New York: Old & New*, Lippincott, 1902.

Winkler, John K., *Morgan the Magnificent*, Garden City, 1930.

Woolworth Building, *The Cathedral of Commerce*, Broadway-Park Place Co., 1917 and 1920.

Wright, J. Robert, *Saint Thomas Church Fifth Avenue*, Eerdmans & St. Thomas, 2001.

Young, Thomas G., *A New World Rising: The Story of St. Patrick's Cathedral*, Something More, 2006.

Index

About the Author

John Tauranac writes on New York City's social and architectural history, he teaches the subject at NYU's School of Professional Studies, he gives lectures and tours, and he designs maps.

His books include *The Empire State Building: The Making of a Landmark* and the three editions of *New York from the Air*, which he does with the great aerial photographer Yann Arthus-Bertrand.

His first published maps were *New York Magazine*'s "Undercover Maps," which showed how to navigate undercover passageways through and under buildings in Midtown and Lower Manhattan. Maintaining his mole's eye perspective, he was the creative director of the 1979 MTA subway map, and he's still designing maps, including *Manhattan Block By Block: A Street Atlas*, which the *Times* said "offers just about all the critical information a site-seeker might need—and then some."

Tauranac was awarded a commendation for design excellence by the National Endowment for the Arts and the U. S. Department of Transportation for his contribution to the official subway map in 1981; he was named a Centennial Historian of the City of New York by the Mayor's Office for his work in history in 1998; and the School of Professional Studies presented him with the Great Teachers Award in 2010.

He lives on Manhattan's Upper West Side with his wife, Jane Bevans, an artist and lawyer.